Business Law in Africa

OHADA and the Harmonization Process

Published with the support of:

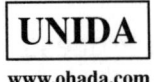 Association for a Unified System
of Business Laws

 UK Department for International
Development

 French Ministry of Foreign Affairs

 European Investment Bank

 Bank Belgolaise

Business Law in Africa

OHADA and the Harmonization Process

EVERSHEDS

Boris Martor, Nanette Pilkington,

David S. Sellers and Sébastien Thouvenot

KOGAN
PAGE

First published in 2002

Kogan Page Ltd
120 Pentonville Road
London N1 9JN
www.kogan-page.co.uk

© Eversheds 2002

British Library Cataloguing in Publication Data

A CIP record for this book is available from the British Library

ISBN 0 7494 3909 2

Typeset by JS Typesetting Ltd, Wellingborough, Northants
Printed and bound in Great Britain by Creative Print and Design (Wales), Ebbw Vale

Contents

Preface

On assuming office on 7th January 2001, President John Agyekum Kufuor identified the eradication of mass poverty in Ghana and, by implication, the rest of Africa, as the greatest challenge facing this generation of Ghanaians and Africans. The challenge with which our continent is confronted as a result of its history – a continent fragmented into many small and barely viable political and economic units – is immense. The direct result of our history has been the poverty, exploitation and marginalization of Africa within the global economy.

It is now obvious that our evolution and growth will be a function of how we manage to attract domestic and international investment into the region. An important aspect of such evolution would be a uniform and harmonized system of business laws, clearly formulated and transparently applied all over the region. With such a system in place, investors who wish to embark on regional projects would not have to contend with a multiplicity of laws, which serve to confuse, not assist, the potential investor.

A credible and transparent regional legal system will go a long way in meeting the strict criteria that investors apply in determining where to invest. Project as well as country risks can be considerably reduced by clear and uniform rules for the conduct of business within the region. An enhanced dispute resolution mechanism and harmonized business standards will reduce the risk of executing regional projects.

This book seeks to introduce and popularize the OHADA system to anglophone Africa and potential investors in the rest of the English-speaking world. It highlights the advantages that the system presents in creating a modern system of law and enhanced legal security, which should encourage investment and promote development.

The book could not have come at a more auspicious moment in the history of Africa's efforts to achieve economic growth and prosperity. The clarion call of President Kufuor's government in Ghana has been 'the Golden Age of Business'; a call for the creation of an enabling environment to stimulate the growth of the Ghanaian economy on the basis of initiative and enterprise.

Having practised corporate law for many years in my youth in France and some francophone West African states, I have always been keenly aware of the potential of a uniform business law regime to transform the climate for doing business in the region, and, based on that conviction, I chaired a regional conference on OHADA in Accra, in October 2001. It became apparent at the end of this conference that there was a strong consensus amongst a broad range of participants that OHADA could be a useful tool for facilitating the economic integration of the region. It was time for Ghana, which had always been at the forefront of the thrust for regional integration, to have a more in-depth look at the possibilities of joining this initiative. Consequently, earlier this year, I established the Ghana National Committee on OHADA, composed of several prominent jurists, to do just that. I await their recommendations.

I have no doubt in my mind that this book, which deals in a very comprehensive manner and in clear terms with the OHADA system and the process of harmonization, will in no small measure contribute to the provision of the sort of environment needed to create an appetite for ECOWAS and West and Central Africa, and, indeed, Africa, among international investors.

A great number of texts and works on OHADA have already been published in the French language, which are available to lawyers and entrepreneurs who operate in this medium, but there is no definitive work on this subject in English. This book, therefore, will supply this need and, hopefully, serve to convince policy makers in the English-speaking parts of the region of the enormous potential of OHADA. I believe it will be a valuable tool for all who wish to understand this initiative.

This book is a compulsory read for all members of the partnership for the development of Africa, and I wish to congratulate the authors and sponsors of this illuminating work. It is an important contribution to the fight for growth and prosperity in Africa.

Nana Addo Dankwa Akufo-Addo, MP
Attorney General and Minister for Justice
Accra, Ghana, 31st July 2002

Foreword

The publication of a book in English dealing with OHADA is a very important event.

The idea of harmonizing the law was first proposed by the Ministers of Finance of the Franc Zone at a meeting in Ouagadougou, where they voiced their awareness that the situation as it existed at that time was one of legal and judicial uncertainty that was hardly conducive to investment. As a result, they decided in 1991 to appoint a high-level working group to try to find a solution to the problem.

After many months of research and of contacts with the African authorities, the working group became convinced, as a result of its lengthy investigations, that it was necessary to proceed with the harmonization of business law within the framework of the establishment of a state of law. In its view, if such a project could be brought into being, this would have beneficial consequences, in particular with regard to the possibility for each State to have at its disposal modern legislation even in the absence of the necessary human resources, to benefit from cross-border exchanges, delocalization and competition, to enjoy legal and judicial security and, in a word, to benefit from the return and enhancement of investment as a result of the restored confidence of economic operators.

This harmonization was all the more necessary given that examples taken in particular from company law and from the system of collective insolvency proceedings clearly showed that the legislative activity that had been undertaken by the States of French-speaking Africa after their independence had led to disparities that were prejudicial to the establishment and growth of businesses.

Since the 1980s, certain States had undertaken and achieved the modernization of their legislation, whereas others had remained with the *Code Napoléon*, dating from 1807, together with a law on *sociétés anonymes* and a law on *sociétés à responsabilité limitée* dating from 1867 and 1925, respectively.

There can be no doubt that this situation was counter-productive within the context of economies whose ambition was to achieve integration.

But in addition to the disparities, there was also uncertainty as to the exact contours of the body of law from one country to another, and even within single countries. Other subjects of concern were the inadequate training in business law that had been received by judges and other legal officers, the difficulties in exploiting cross-border resources, and the need to find a solution to the problems of landlocked countries.

On the basis of these findings, the working group considered that it was necessary to establish an authority to issue the new law, a court to apply it, a centre for the training and further specialization of judges at a high level, and a streamlined administrative body to coordinate the operations of the various institutions. In a word, a new organization had to be created.

The ideas put forward by the working group were submitted to four Heads of State, seven Prime Ministers, some 40 Ministers, Presidents of National Assemblies and of Economic Councils, Presidents of Supreme Courts and other high-level judges, presidents of bar associations and of chambers of commerce, persons in charge of international organizations, and businessmen of all nationalities. On all sides, the ideas were welcomed favourably and even enthusiastically.

The same ideas were then discussed at meetings of Ministers of Justice and during seminars and round tables organized with the assistance of specialists in business law.

The OHADA institutions are the following:

- the Council of Ministers;
- the Common Court of Justice and Arbitration (CCJA);
- the Permanent Secretariat; and
- the Regional Training Centre for Legal Officers (ERSUMA).

In fact, OHADA is a legal tool for economic integration and development: economic integration because there can be no economic integration without legal integration.

Legal integration is what OHADA is achieving. The simplification and harmonization of the applicable law, both on the legislative plane and in court decisions, and the certainty that it engenders, are considered as factors that will stimulate growth by encouraging economic operators to invest in Africa.

Until now, both national and foreign economic operators were halted by the legal and judicial insecurity that was prevalent in the Franc Zone countries. It is to be hoped that the unification of laws and the unification of court decisions will have the expected effects.

Although OHADA was conceived in a French-speaking area, African leaders have quickly come to understand that this priceless tool of economic integration should be extended to other countries. Guinea-Bissau and Equatorial Guinea soon became members, and now, with the advent of NEPAD, OHADA's extension to English-speaking African countries is inevitable.

The friends of OHADA who believe in its success have founded an association for the unification of law in Africa, called UNIDA. Any individuals or companies who are of the same opinion are invited to join UNIDA.

UNIDA has set itself the aims of supporting OHADA in its activities and in particular of spreading knowledge of its harmonized law through-out Africa and elsewhere.

It is true that OHADA was conceived by the financial authorities of the French-speaking area. But ever since its creation in Libreville in 1992, OHADA has been open to all African countries without any linguistic discrimination.

The publication at this time of a book in English on this important institution for legal integration, which was originally designed for French-speaking Africa and which is without any doubt the prelude to economic integration, is clearly a major event in the life of OHADA; and on behalf of UNIDA I can only applaud it with enthusiasm.

This is why, as the former President of the Steering Committee that was responsible for drawing up the first OHADA legal texts, and as the President of UNIDA, I wholeheartedly support the welcome initiative that has been taken of publishing this new book, which should be of great assistance both as a research tool and as a means of spreading knowledge and understanding of OHADA law, the future law of the United Africa that has so recently been created by the Heads of State.

Judge Kéba Mbaye
President of UNIDA (Association for a Unified System of Business Laws)
Honorary Vice-President of the International Court of Justice
Former President of the Steering Committee
responsible for the implementation of the OHADA Project

Foreword

Today, we have ample demonstration of the fundamental role played by law in the sustainable development of societies. Similarly, it has clearly become essential to encourage, alongside development assistance which remains indispensable, economic activities and private investment, both conducive to growth and progress. Finally, in a globalized world, where borders have already opened up, there is a need for regional measures embracing many States so as to facilitate, with due regard for democratic principles, freedom of movement for people, the sharing of experiences and harmonization of rules and procedures.

Consequently, by combining these three ideas, OHADA is providing Africa with the means to create a secure legal framework for all businesses, thereby promoting economic integration. This is an ambitious project and, while realizing how much still needs to be done, I wish to salute what has already been achieved: a corpus of texts laying down a modernized and harmonized business law applicable in the continent's 16 OHADA member countries.

The publication of the first English-language manual setting out this new business law and describing OHADA's institutions is thus an important step forward, which the French government is pleased to support. Our contribution to this publication testifies to our determination to consolidate the efforts of African businesses, which are the main architects of the continent's development.

This project of modernizing and harmonizing business law in Africa falls quite naturally within the framework of the objectives of the New Partnership for Africa's Development (NEPAD), endorsed in June 2002 at the G8 Kananaskis summit.

Bruno DELAYE
Director General for International Cooperation and Development
French Ministry of Foreign Affairs

Foreword

The European Investment Bank welcomes the publication of *Business Law in Africa: OHADA and the Harmonization Process*. This English language book builds on the work being carried out to bridge differences between legal systems and customs of 16 principally French speaking OHADA Member States, while at the same time opening up this co-operation to more and more English speaking African countries. I congratulate OHADA on its work to date and also the *Association pour l'Unification du Droit des Affaires en Afrique* (UNIDA), a non-profit organization supported by the business and legal communities, dedicated to greater integration of the legal systems in Africa. The European Investment Bank is very pleased to have been invited to associate itself with this publication of substance, and I am certain it will also profit from its use.

Initially, when the European Investment Bank was created in 1958 under the Treaty of Rome, its core purpose was to finance investment projects within the European Union. However, almost from its inception, the Bank's owners, the EU Member States, entrusted it with specific mandates for implementing the Union's external policies, notably in sub-Saharan Africa. In fact, some of the oldest of EIB external mandates relate to the ACP – the African, Caribbean and Pacific countries that have a special long-standing historical relationships with the Union and its Member States. After two Yaoundé Conventions and a 25-year cycle of successive Lomé Conventions, we are now entering into a new era, that of the Cotonou Partnership Agreement. This completes a 40-year cycle of EIB activities on the African continent. These conventions and partnerships are almost unique, having been concluded through negotiations between two groups of States, the ACPs and the EU Members as equal partners.

The roots of the special EU-ACP relationship go back, of course, much further historically. However, this relationship was given a new dimension and impetus when the Bank's founding members formed the European Economic Community, now known as the 'EU'. The EU is no island and the Member States' wish was to maintain and to deepen their ties with other States with whom they had long-standing historic, cultural and economic ties, notably in Africa. Today the relationship has further evolved and EU Member States' co-operation policy continues to give a special focus on contributing to sustainable development and the reduction of poverty. Under the Cotonou Agreement, which was signed in June 2000, the emphasis is increasingly on 'bankable' investment projects, e.g. in public infrastructure, which is more and more managed and developed by private companies, and in directly productive sectors such as industry and services.

Within the EU-ACP relationship, the approach to supporting development has evolved over the years and as a consequence the EIB's mandates have mirrored the change. The objective of poverty reduction still remains at the fore, but the pivotal role of the private sector for achieving this is increasingly recognized. In the Bank's contribution to the economic development of the ACP countries, we are therefore giving a new emphasis on the development of the private sector, as a necessary condition for economic growth. To promote development we need to show that ACP countries can offer the necessary conditions for encouraging investors' confidence. This has to be based on a stable political, institutional and legal framework, without which the private sector cannot be expected to flourish.

The EIB's role is focused on providing support for investors by making a contribution to the long term financing of viable projects. In doing so, the EIB also brings its technical, economic and financial expert knowledge, which it obtained in almost 45 years of experience in the Union and in more than 120 countries, including those on the African continent.

Over those years, the EIB has worked in many jurisdictions and legal systems and has experienced development of legal thought and practice, mostly on a bilateral EIB-client and/or guarantor basis. The Bank, of course, also verifies legal aspects of the projects it funds.

History has left the sub-Saharan African countries not only with different languages in which the business is conducted, but of course also with two broadly different legal systems. Fourteen French-speaking African nations came together 10 years ago to create a unified legal system at the initiative of the Heads of State, and have since been joined by two other nations which are Portuguese and Spanish-speaking, respectively. This has allowed Mr Kéba Mbaye, Honorary Vice President of the International Court of Justice in The Hague, to work as a motor behind the publication of a series of uniform acts for the members of OHADA. The English-speaking African nations are now expressing serious interest in joining this excellent initiative which will help build stronger bridges between legal traditions and cultures on the continent.

Working increasingly in the private sector, the EIB has a great interest in promoting widely applicable legal codifications and a uniform register of acts and laws in ACP countries. Poverty reduction through developing the private sector as an engine of sustainable growth and social progress goes hand in hand with promoting stable political and governance conditions. A reliable set of rules and laws and uniform procedures and judicial process will help to encourage the investors' confidence, to stimulate economic growth and to push forward the integration of the ACP countries in the World economy.

Through the support of this book, the EIB hopes to make a contribution towards the establishment of the necessary institutional and legal framework for doing business in Africa.

Philippe Maystadt
President of the European Investment Bank

The Authors

Eversheds is an international law firm of over 2,100 lawyers with offices across the UK and in continental Europe and Asia. Its Paris office, under the name Eversheds Frere Cholmeley, was established over 30 years ago. It is well known for its business law practice, both in France and abroad, as well as for international arbitration and public international law. As regards Africa, the Paris office of Eversheds has advised both investors and governments on major infrastructure projects and the settlement of disputes in a wide variety of countries and with particular emphasis on the OHADA Member States. Four members of the Africa team have contributed to this book:

- Boris Martor, *Avocat à la Cour de Paris*
- Nanette Pilkington, *Avocat à la Cour de Paris*
- David S. Sellers, Solicitor, England & Wales, *Avocat à la Cour de Paris*
- Sébastien Thouvenot, *Docteur en Droit, Elève-avocat*

This book has been written in close collaboration with two African legal experts:

- Adesegun A. Akin-Olugbade, General Counsel of the African Development Bank
- Dr Martha Simo Tumnde née Njikam, Barrister and Solicitor of the Supreme Court of Cameroon, and Head of Department of Law and Vice-Dean in charge of Programmes and Academic Affairs in the Faculty of Social and Management Sciences, University of Buea, Cameroon

Acknowledgements

The authors owe a debt of gratitude to the UK Department for International Development (DFID), the French Ministry of Foreign Affairs, the Association for a Unified System of Business Laws (UNIDA), the African Development Bank, Banque Belgolaise and the European Investment Bank, without whose financial and moral support this book could not have been published. In this context, special thanks go to Alison Kennedy and Andrew Jordan of DFID; Jean-Marc Chataigner and Béatrice Birot of the French Ministry of Foreign Affairs; and Paul Bayzelon, André-Franck Ahoyo and Dany Houngbedji Rauch of UNIDA.

We are also particularly grateful to the following, for having spared us considerable amounts of their time during our visit to Cameroon and Côte d'Ivoire in May 2002, providing us with invaluable insights into the workings of the OHADA system:

H.E. Mr Seydou Ba (President of the CCJA)
H.E. Dr Kwawo Lucien Johnson (Permanent Secretary of OHADA)
H.E. Mr Pascal Edouard Nganga (Chief Registrar of the CCJA)

At the African Development Bank, Mr Chanel Boucher (Vice-President), Mr Franck Perrault (Deputy Member of the Board), and members of the Legal Department, in particular Ms Françoise Medegan and Messrs Souley Amadou, Titus Edjua and Aboubacar Fall.

Mr Pierre Laloye (*Attaché de Coopération*, French Ministry of Foreign Affairs, Yaoundé)

Maître Karim Fadika (*Avocat à la Cour d'Abidjan*)

Maître Virgile Ngassam Njike (*Avocat au Barreau du Cameroun*)

Maître Bassalifou Sylla (*Avocat au Barreau de Bamako*)

Finally, we have been helped in many ways by a number of members of the staff of Eversheds Frere Cholmeley in Paris. Our thanks in particular go to Ivréa Degeaive, Sophie Ghazal, Séverine Hatchuel-Benne, Emily Kanzari, Alexis Katchourine (for tax questions) and Sylvaine Walter.

Introduction

Africa, with its large population, abundant natural resources and pressing needs for modern infrastructures, is recognized as a continent with vast potential for development. Major efforts are now underway to promote this development. Recently, a number of African countries launched a new initiative, the New Partnership for Africa's Development (NEPAD) to attract investors and associate them with the development of the continent. It is expected that NEPAD will be at the forefront in developing public/private partnerships and privatization programmes in order to improve Africa's infrastructures.

There is no doubt that continued investment and development cannot be achieved without, on the one hand, a secure legal and commercial environment that will protect private property and, on the other hand, a strong and independent judicial system that can ensure the proper application of the law and the efficient settlement of disputes. Until recently, however, most African countries suffered from outdated or incomplete legal systems, which varied from one country to another. This gave rise to uncertainty which in turn discouraged investment in Africa. In these circumstances, a number of African States have grown increasingly aware of the advantages that arise from the creation of a modern, harmonized and easily accessible system of business law.

OHADA – the Organization for the Harmonization of Business Law in Africa – is a major step forward in this direction, as it is hoped this book will show. In its short existence since its creation in 1993, OHADA has already created a substantial body of uniform law which is applicable in the 16 different countries at present constituting its membership.

This is an astonishing achievement in so short a time. Like European regulations which apply directly throughout the European Union, the legislation issued by OHADA is directly applicable in all OHADA's Member States; but in the field of business law the OHADA legislation is much more comprehensive than the existing European regulations. As of now, the greater part of business law in the 16 Member States has been unified in areas as diverse as company law, arbitration and securities. For example, an investor wishing to establish companies in Cameroon, the Central African Republic and Senegal will be subject to the same rules in each of these countries. Moreover, the 16 Member States have established a single court with supreme jurisdiction over any disputes relating to OHADA law, in whichever of the 16 countries such disputes might arise.

The achievements of OHADA are patently a result of the strong political will of the Member States to create an up-to-date and truly African system of law and, as had been hoped, this initiative has been welcomed by the financial and business communities. On a practical level, it is expected that this will encourage the development of the private sector in Africa and that it will facilitate infrastructure projects involving several OHADA Member States.

A number of public institutions also recognize the advantages that OHADA represents, and are giving it strong support. These include the United Nations Development Programme (UNDP) and the European Union, as well as the international development agencies of various countries in the developed world, including the Department for International Development in the UK and the international development division of the French Ministry of Foreign Affairs, both of which, in addition to their other actions in support of OHADA, have kindly sponsored publication of this book.

Partly inspired by the example of OHADA, an African Law Institute has been established recently, with the support of the African Development Bank. The stated aims of this Institute are, *inter alia*, to promote law reform and the harmonization of law in African countries regardless of their legal tradition, and to strive for an improved justice system.

There is thus clearly a dynamic trend towards harmonization, and OHADA is at the forefront. Yet OHADA still remains a mystery to many in the English-speaking world, who until now have been inconvenienced by the fact that most of the voluminous material that has been published on the subject is in French.

The main objective of this book is to make the OHADA system accessible to the English-speaking community. The intention is that it should essentially be a practical guide to the uniform legislation that has been issued by OHADA to date, and also to the general business environment in the OHADA Member States. It is hoped that the book will be a useful tool for English-speaking investors, legal practitioners, scholars and students.

Our wish is that by reaching out to this wide community, the book will familiarize English-speakers with the OHADA system of law and make them more aware of its advantages and that, as a result, it may make some modest contribution towards encouraging investment in Africa and fostering economic and social development for the long term in a secure environment.

1

What is OHADA?

OHADA is an international organization created by a Treaty signed in Port-Louis (Mauritius) on 17 October 1993 by fourteen African States. The acronym stands for *'Organisation pour l'Harmonisation du Droit des Affaires en Afrique'* (Organization for the Harmonization of Business Law in Africa, occasionally referred to in English as 'OHBLA').

The idea behind the creation of OHADA sprang from a political will to strengthen the African legal system by enacting a secure legal framework for the conduct of business in Africa, which is viewed as indispensable for the development of the continent[1].

The project took shape over the course of several summit meetings of Heads of State and Government from French-speaking Africa. At a summit held in April 1991 in Ouagadougou (Burkina Faso), the Finance

---

[1] This need, and OHADA's effectiveness in helping to meet the need, is recognized by institutions such as the African Development Bank: *"Economic co-operation and regional integration offer tremendous opportunities for economic growth, enabling regional member countries to overcome the constraints of small national markets, increasing intra-Africa trade and providing opportunities for integrating African economies into the global economy. The effective implementation of economic co-operation and regional integration are founded on enabling environments that promote accountability and transparency. Also a strong institutional framework at the regional and national levels is fundamental to streamline regional agreements into national policy. At the same time the harmonization of national policies and establishment of effective transnational implementation tools, offer opportunities to push reforms conducive to good governance at regional level. For example the adoption of a regional legal framework and the establishment of a related judicial institution (OHADA) is proving an effective instrument to improve the regional environment for private sector promotion."* (*African Development Bank Group Policy on Good Governance*, 2000, paragraph 6.34).

Ministers of the Franc Zone[2] entrusted a group of jurists, led by H.E. Mr Kéba Mbaye[3], with the task of assessing the political and technical feasibility of the project. This group prepared a report which was approved in October 1992 at a summit in Libreville (Gabon). At the same summit, a steering committee of three jurists was charged with drafting an international treaty and identifying areas of law to be harmonized. One year later, the Treaty was presented for signature. It entered into force on 18 September 1995 after the requisite number of ratifications had been obtained.

At present, OHADA has sixteen members: Benin, Burkina Faso, Cameroon, the Central African Republic, Chad, the Federal Islamic Republic of the Comoros, Congo, Côte d'Ivoire, Equatorial Guinea, Gabon, Guinea, Guinea-Bissau, Mali, Niger, Senegal, and Togo. A map of the Member States may be found in Appendix C. With the exception of Guinea, all the members of OHADA are also members of the Franc Zone.

Broadly speaking, the membership currently reflects a common tradition. With the exception of Equatorial Guinea and Guinea-Bissau, where Spanish and Portuguese are spoken, respectively, and the English-speaking provinces of Cameroon, all the OHADA Member States are French-speaking. In addition, all the Member States have a civil law tradition except for the English-speaking provinces of Cameroon, which has the common law legal system.

As a public international organization, OHADA is a legal entity with its own rights and obligations, distinct from those of its Member States. The Treaty provides that it can be a party to contracts and agreements, may purchase or sell movable or immovable property, and can appear before the domestic courts.

OHADA also enjoys privileges and immunities with regard to its property and employees, so that it can perform its activities freely. The inviolability of its premises is guaranteed by Cameroon, where its headquarters are located. OHADA also has privileges of jurisdiction which allow it not to be sued before the domestic courts of Cameroon. In addition, all civil servants and employees working for bodies belonging to OHADA enjoy diplomatic privileges and immunities, as do the

---

[2] The Franc Zone is discussed further in Chapter 12.

[3] Honorary First President of the Supreme Court of Senegal, former President of the Constitutional Council of Senegal, former Judge and Honorary Vice-President of the International Court of Justice.

judges who sit at the Common Court of Justice and Arbitration (*Cour Commune de Justice et d'Arbitrage*).

OHADA has its own resources, derived from annual contributions paid by the Member States and also from contributions of aid from other international organizations and foreign States. For example, it is the beneficiary of a growth fund of 12 billion CFA francs, managed by the UNDP. This fund is designed to ensure the autonomy of OHADA for approximately ten years.

The principal aims of OHADA, as identified in its founding Treaty, are to unify business law throughout the Member States and to promote arbitration as a means of settling contractual disputes.

In pursuance of its aims, OHADA issues unified legislation in the form of Uniform Acts on particular areas of the law[4]. These Acts are directly applicable in all the Member States, and supersede the previous national legislation on the same topic in each country[5]. However, they do not prevent the Member States from enacting specific legislation which does not conflict with the Uniform Acts.

The Uniform Acts provide an overall legal framework which is, in general, based on civil law and has, to a certain extent, borrowed from modern French business law. The Acts are far from being a simple transposition of French law, however, and there are a number of substantial differences. In addition, as will be seen in the following chapters, numerous aspects of this new legislation will be quite familiar to common law jurists, and in certain areas it should also be possible for contracting parties, should they so wish, to apply common law concepts within the framework laid down by the Uniform Acts.

Moreover, the present dominance of the French language and of civil law within OHADA is expected to change with time. The aim of OHADA is to reach beyond its original members and embrace other African countries which are not necessarily either French-speaking countries or countries that operate legal systems based on civil law traditions. For this reason, the OHADA Treaty provides that any of the member States

---

[4] These Uniform Acts (*Actes Uniformes* in French) are published in French in the OHADA Official Journal (*Journal Officiel*) and in the national official journals of the Member States. English translations of the Uniform Acts issued to date have also been published in the OHADA Official Journal. However, while these are of undoubted assistance to non-French-speakers, the translations have no official value, and are sometimes not quite accurate or may not be comprehensible to English-speakers who are more familiar with common law than with civil law systems.

[5] The procedure for adoption of Uniform Acts is outlined in Chapter 3.

of the Organization for African Unity (OAU)[6] – and also non-members of the OAU, if so invited unanimously by the OHADA Member States – may join OHADA by acceding to the Treaty.

Considering the rapid progress of legal harmonization that has been accomplished by OHADA in less than a decade, OHADA should be a highly effective means of achieving legal stability in Africa.

---

[6] The Organization for African Unity has been superseded, as of July 2002, by the African Union, whose members are similarly invited to join OHADA.

2

Institutions

Four institutions have been established by OHADA: the Council of Ministers (*Conseil des Ministres*), the Permanent Secretariat (*Secrétariat Permanent*), the Common Court of Justice and Arbitration (*Cour Commune de Justice et d'Arbitrage*, abbreviated to *CCJA*) and the Regional Training Centre for Legal Officers (*Ecole Régionale Supérieure de la Magistrature*, abbreviated to *ERSUMA*). As will be seen below, these institutions all play a very important role in the development, interpretation and dissemination of OHADA law.

SECTION 1: THE COUNCIL OF MINISTERS

A. Composition

The Council of Ministers is the supreme decision-making body of OHADA. Pursuant to Article 27 of the Treaty, it is composed of the Ministers of Justice and Ministers of Finance of all the Member States.

Each Member State takes turns to preside over the Council of Ministers for one year. The order in which the States hold this office is determined alphabetically in accordance with their names in French. If for some reason a Member State is unable to assume the office when it is its turn, the Council of Ministers appoints the State immediately following it in alphabetical order.

In accordance with Article 28 of the Treaty, the Council of Ministers meets at least once a year. Meetings are convened by the presiding State on its own initiative or at the request of at least one-third of the Member States.

B. Functions

The Council of Ministers has both administrative (or regulatory) and legislative functions.

1. Administrative or regulatory functions

In the context of its administrative or regulatory functions, the Council of Ministers is responsible for:

- adopting the annual budgets of the CCJA and the Permanent Secretariat;
- deciding the amount of annual contributions payable by the Member States;
- electing the members of the CCJA;
- appointing the Permanent Secretary and the Director General of ERSUMA;
- appointing auditors to certify the accounts of the OHADA institutions;
- approving the accounts;
- regulating the organization, operation, resources and services of ERSUMA;
- adopting the rules of procedure of the CCJA;
- and, in general, adopting any regulations that may be relevant for the implementation of the Treaty.

The Council of Ministers may also request advisory opinions from the CCJA on any issue pertaining to the Uniform Acts, or the interpretation or implementation of the Treaty and the regulations issued for its implementation.

Any decision of the Council of Ministers, other than in relation to the adoption of Uniform Acts, requires a majority vote by those States represented at the meeting and voting, with each State having one vote.

2. Legislative functions

As far as its legislative functions are concerned, the Council of Ministers is responsible for the approval of the annual programmes for the harmonization of business law, and for the adoption of the Uniform Acts.

SECTION 2: THE PERMANENT SECRETARIAT

As its name indicates, the Permanent Secretariat is a permanent body of OHADA. Its headquarters are at Yaoundé, Cameroon.

A. Composition

The Permanent Secretariat is headed by a Permanent Secretary, who is appointed in accordance with Article 40 of the Treaty for a four-year term which is renewable once. The Permanent Secretary appoints the other members of the Secretariat in accordance with recruitment criteria determined by the Council of Ministers. The maximum number of appointments is defined in the Permanent Secretariat's budget. At present the Permanent Secretary is assisted by three Directors. The Directors are respectively in charge of legal affairs and relations with institutions, finance and accounts, and general administration and the OHADA Official Journal.

The Permanent Secretariat is independent from the Member States, which have no official representation within it. This is intended to ensure that the Permanent Secretariat is unaffected by political pressure.

B. Functions

The Permanent Secretariat has various administrative functions and also provides assistance to the Council of Ministers. In particular, it proposes the agenda for the meetings of the Council of Ministers as well as the annual programme for the harmonization of business law[1]. In addition, it prepares the draft Uniform Acts, presents them to the Member States for consideration, and requests the opinion of the CCJA before they are adopted. Once this procedure is completed, the Permanent Secretariat finalizes the draft, and proposes that it should be included on the agenda for the meeting of the Council of Ministers[2].

Furthermore, the Permanent Secretariat is responsible for the publication of the Uniform Acts in the OHADA Official Journal. Once a Uniform Act has been published in the Official Journal, it becomes applicable and enforceable in all the Member States[3].

---

[1] Articles 11 and 29 of the Treaty.

[2] Articles 6 and 7 of the Treaty.

[3] This provision has caused some controversy in the common law provinces of Cameroon, where it is considered to be unconstitutional to provide for direct applicability and enforceability without parliamentary intervention. Article 2(1) of Cameroon's

The Permanent Secretariat also compiles an alphabetical list of candidates for election to the CCJA and, finally, it is responsible for the Regional Training Centre for Legal Officers (ERSUMA).

The Permanent Secretariat is accorded privileges and diplomatic immunities to facilitate the execution of its functions. It is, however, presently hampered by the fact that the budget for its day-to-day running is not sufficient to allow for the required level of staffing and, moreover, there is no autonomous budget for its other activities such as the organization of meetings of the Council of Ministers. Instead, each time the Permanent Secretariat intends to organize a meeting, it is obliged to seek external financial assistance.

SECTION 3: THE COMMON COURT OF JUSTICE AND ARBITRATION (CCJA)

The CCJA is a very important and innovative institution which lies at the heart of the OHADA system. Like the Permanent Secretariat, it is a permanent institution. Its functions are provided for in Chapters III and IV of the Treaty ('Disputes concerning the interpretation and application of Uniform Acts' and 'Arbitration', respectively) and are regulated by the Rules of Procedure adopted by the Council of Ministers at N'Djaména (Chad) on 18 April 1996 and by the Rules of Arbitration adopted in Ouagadougou (Burkina Faso) on 11 March 1999.

The CCJA has its headquarters at Abidjan (Côte d'Ivoire). However, pursuant to Article 19 of its Rules of Procedure, it may, if it deems necessary, meet in any Member State with the latter's prior consent and without any financial burden for the State.

A. Composition

The CCJA comprises seven judges elected by secret ballot by the Council of Ministers for a term of seven years renewable only once. Candidates for election must be either judges, professors of law or practising lawyers

---

Constitution provides that "National sovereignty shall be vested in the people of Cameroon who shall exercise same either through the President of the Republic and Members of Parliament or by way of referendum. No section of the people or any individual shall arrogate to itself or to himself the exercise thereof". Article 14 provides that legislative power shall be exercised by the Parliament which is to legislate and control Government action, and Article 26 provides that rules governing civil and commercial obligations are reserved to the legislative power.

from any Member State, with a minimum of fifteen years of professional experience. At least five of the seven seats must be filled by judges having exercised senior judicial functions in the past; only two seats, therefore, are open to professors or practising lawyers[4].

A list of candidates is prepared by the Permanent Secretary on the basis of nominations made by the Member States. No State may nominate more than two candidates, and the CCJA may not have more than one judge from a particular Member State at any one time. The judges are elected by absolute majority of votes in the Council of Ministers. The President of the CCJA and the two Vice-Presidents are elected by the judges for a term of three and a half years.

The judges' tenures cannot be revoked once they have been elected, and they enjoy diplomatic privileges and immunities for the duration of their term of office. They are not allowed to exercise any other functions, in particular political or administrative functions.

These rules are intended to give a certain amount of independence to the judges. The supranational dimension of the CCJA is also designed to ensure that each judge is impartial and does not necessarily act in the interest of his country.

The CCJA has a registry headed by a Chief Registrar who is appointed by the President of the CCJA for a period of seven years, renewable once. The registry plays an administrative and secretarial role, and in general assists the CCJA in performing its functions.

B. Functions

The OHADA Treaty provides that the CCJA has two types of functions: judicial and arbitral.

1. Judicial functions

In its judicial capacity, the CCJA is the sole supranational court. Its purpose is to avoid the risk of conflicting interpretations of the Uniform Acts by the supreme courts of the various Member States, and to achieve a uniform judicial interpretation of the Treaty, any regulations applying the Treaty, and the Uniform Acts.

The CCJA's judicial functions are both advisory and contentious. Copies of its judgments and advisory opinions are obtainable from the Chief Registrar.

---

[4] Article 31 of the Treaty.

(a) Advisory jurisdiction

The Treaty provides for three types of advisory jurisdiction:

(i). Jurisdiction to give advisory opinions on draft Uniform Acts before they are submitted to the Council of Ministers for adoption[5]. This is a fundamental part of the process of adoption of Uniform Acts, as will be seen in Chapter 3.

(ii). Jurisdiction to give advisory opinions to any Member State or the Council of Ministers on any question relating to the interpretation or application of the Treaty, the regulations issued for its application, or the Uniform Acts[6]. While certain Member States have availed themselves of this opportunity, the Council of Ministers has yet to do so[7].

(iii). Jurisdiction to give advisory opinions to any national court hearing a case relating to the application of OHADA legislation and its interpretation[8]. To date, only one national court has requested an advisory opinion[9].

The advisory opinions and interpretations given by the CCJA are purely consultative and are not binding. However, it would seem difficult, in practice, for a national court or a Member State persistently to disregard an opinion given by the CCJA, especially since judgments of national courts relating to OHADA law are subject to final appeal before the CCJA and may be quashed if they conflict with the CCJA's opinion. This ensures that OHADA law is applied correctly.

---

[5] Article 7 of the Treaty.

[6] Article 14 of the Treaty.

[7] Côte d'Ivoire, Mali and Senegal have requested advisory opinions and Benin, Cameroon and Chad have submitted observations in those advisory proceedings. See Advisory Opinions Nos. 002/99/EP of 13 October 1999, 002/2000/EP of 26 April 2000, and 001/2001/EP of 30 April 2001, all of which deal with the interpretation and application of the Treaty and certain Uniform Acts, and possible conflicts with national legislation.

[8] Article 14 of the Treaty.

[9] The Court of First Instance of Libreville (Gabon), which requested an opinion on the rules governing annulment of certain procedural acts under the Uniform Act on Simplified Recovery Procedures and Enforcement Measures. See Advisory Opinion No. 001/99/JN of 7 July 1999.

(b) Contentious jurisdiction

(i) Scope of jurisdiction

Under Article 14 of the Treaty, the CCJA has jurisdiction with regard to all matters concerning business law where OHADA legislation has been enacted[10].

This jurisdiction is, however, exercised by the CCJA only at the highest appellate level (with the exception of issues relating to the application of criminal penalties, for which the national courts retain exclusive jurisdiction). This is in order to ensure consistency in the application of the Uniform Acts. On the other hand, pursuant to Article 13 of the Treaty, any dispute regarding the implementation of the Uniform Acts is dealt with in the first instance and on appeal by the courts of the individual Member States. As a result, the CCJA has jurisdiction only to hear appeals against decisions of the courts of appeal of the Member States or against decisions of lower courts that are subject to no ordinary appeal.

This means that the jurisdiction of the national supreme courts is replaced by that of the CCJA when there is a dispute relating to OHADA law, while the national courts retain jurisdiction in the first instance and on ordinary appeal. If, therefore, a party files proceedings before a national supreme court when the subject matter falls within the jurisdiction of the CCJA, the national supreme court must decline jurisdiction over the case and must direct the parties to go to the CCJA, even in cases where the defendant raises no objections to its jurisdiction.

(ii) Procedure

A referral to the CCJA can be made in any of three different situations, as follows:

- directly by a party who wishes to appeal a decision of a national court of appeal on the merits of any matter relating to application of the Uniform Acts[11]. The appeal must be lodged with the CCJA Registry within two months of service of the decision in question[12]. If the CCJA

---

[10] The idea is also being actively discussed that the CCJA could have supreme jurisdiction to hear cases relating to other, non-OHADA, uniform legislation which is applicable in the Member States, notably regarding insurance matters and intellectual property, with the same aim of achieving a uniform interpretation and application of the legislation in these fields.

[11] Article 14 of the Treaty.

[12] Article 28 of the CCJA's Rules of Procedure.

quashes the decision of the national court, it rehears the case on its merits[13];

- directly by a party who wishes to challenge the jurisdiction of a national supreme court if it has already unsuccessfully argued before that court that the CCJA has jurisdiction[14]. The appeal must be lodged within two months of notification of the decision of the national court. If the CCJA decides that the national court lacked jurisdiction, it will declare that court's judgment null and void; and

- by a supreme court of a Member State which considers that it does not have jurisdiction to hear the case in question, because it involves issues relating to application of a Uniform Act[15]. In such an event, all proceedings before the national supreme court are automatically suspended. However, this does not interfere with the enforcement of the earlier judgment. If the CCJA finds that it has no jurisdiction to hear the case, the matter will be sent back to the national court, which will determine the case[16].

Any lawyer who is competent to appear before the national courts of a Member State can appear before the CCJA. However, if the lawyer is not resident in Abidjan, his client must indicate an official address in Abidjan for the duration of the proceedings, for service of court papers. This may be the address of another lawyer or notary, for example.

At present, all proceedings are conducted in French, even if none of the parties concerned is French-speaking. This is already a potential problem for parties from the English-speaking provinces of Cameroon, Spanish-speaking Equatorial Guinea and Portuguese-speaking Guinea-Bissau, and will clearly have to be addressed if more non-French-speaking countries become members of OHADA[17].

The CCJA's judicial case-load has been increasing steadily: a single case was filed in 1998, two in 1999, five in 2000, and 26 in 2001; and the upward trend appears to be continuing. There is therefore a risk that at

---

[13] Article 14 of the Treaty.

[14] Article 18 of the Treaty.

[15] Article 15 of the Treaty.

[16] Article 16 of the Treaty.

[17] The problem is slightly mitigated at the moment by the presence on the Court of a judge from Guinea-Bissau. There are however no native English-speakers or Spanish-speakers on the Court. Moreover, there are at present no judges with a common law background, despite the fact that considerations of common law may arise in cases involving parties from Cameroon.

some stage, there will have to be a reorganization of the CCJA which, amongst other things, might involve the appointment of assistants for the judges, who could perhaps perform functions similar to those performed by judges' clerks in the United States.

(iii) Enforcement

The decisions of the CCJA are final and binding, are subject to no further appeal[18], and are enforceable[19].

Enforcement is governed by the rules of civil procedure applicable to national judgments in the State in which enforcement is sought. An enforcement order must be given by the proper national authority without further examination of the decision other than a verification of the authenticity of the document presented for enforcement[20].

2. Arbitral functions

The CCJA also acts as an arbitration centre. This aspect of its functions is discussed in Chapter 10.

SECTION 4: THE REGIONAL TRAINING CENTRE FOR LEGAL OFFICERS (ERSUMA)

ERSUMA is attached to the Permanent Secretariat. Its headquarters are located at Porto Novo (Benin), where it enjoys diplomatic privileges and immunities. At present, ERSUMA receives substantial funding from the European Union, which has been programmed to allow it to function efficiently over a period of three years. It has a Board of Directors which is responsible for its administration[21]; an Academic Council which

---

[18] Articles 47, 48 and 49 of the CCJA's Rules of Procedure do however allow extraordinary petitions to be filed, ie objections by a third party whose interests may be affected by the judgment; requests for revision in the event of discovery of a new and decisive fact; and requests for interpretation of the judgment.

[19] Article 20 of the Treaty.

[20] Article 46 of the CCJA's Rules of Procedure.

[21] The Board of Directors comprises the Permanent Secretary of OHADA, who acts as its Chairman; the President of the CCJA or his delegated representative; three representatives of national supreme courts of the Member States; two representatives from national training centres; and two representatives of the permanent staff of ERSUMA.

ensures academic standards; and a management team headed by a Director General, who is appointed by the Council of Ministers.

The main role of ERSUMA is to improve the legal environment in the Member States, in particular by training judges and other legal officers such as lawyers, notaries, court experts, registrars and bailiffs, in OHADA law. Academics and businessmen may also receive training.

Any judge or legal officer from any Member State may be admitted to ERSUMA. In addition, any such person from any other member State of the Organization for African Unity (or African Union) may be admitted with the approval of the Board of Directors of ERSUMA. Candidates for training are put forward by their national training centres or professional organizations, and are selected on the basis of their professional responsibilities, the nature of their legal functions, and their educational and professional background. An identical number of candidates is admitted for each Member State.

The training personnel are high-level legal professionals and academics who have in-depth knowledge and experience in OHADA law. They are not permanent staff, but are hired as visiting professors.

Each year, ERSUMA organizes a number of training sessions for various categories of legal professionals and trainers. Over the three-year period from 2000 to 2002, it is anticipated that a total of more than 5000 persons will have received training.

ERSUMA may also cooperate with any establishment or institution whose aim is to train legal officers or teach law.

ERSUMA's role in training legal professionals is extremely important. Through the high-level training that ERSUMA provides, it is hoped that professionals will learn to apply OHADA law properly and efficiently (which is not always the case at present, given the large volume of new legislation that OHADA has issued in such a relatively short period), and that these professionals will disseminate knowledge of OHADA law in their respective countries.

3

General considerations on OHADA Uniform Acts

The reasons for the creation of OHADA are obvious. Many of the laws in the Member States were out-of-date, some having remained unchanged since the colonial period. Many areas of the law were subject to uncertainty, and in some areas there were no relevant published laws. This made investment in these countries complicated at best and, at worst, almost impossible.

In its short life to date, OHADA has already made, and is continuing to make, a considerable contribution to the updating of its Member States' legal systems and to the creation of a secure legal environment for investors, by issuing Uniform Acts on various aspects of the law.

Seven Uniform Acts have now entered into force. These are in the areas of general commercial law, commercial companies and economic interest groups, securities[1], simplified recovery procedures and enforcement measures[2], collective insolvency proceedings[3], arbitration[4] and accounting law[5].

---

[1] These first three Uniform Acts were adopted by the Council of Ministers on 17 April 1997 in Cotonou (Benin) and entered into force on 1 January 1998.

[2] Adopted on 10 April 1998 in Libreville (Gabon) and entered into force on 10 July 1998.

[3] Adopted on 10 April 1998 in Libreville (Gabon) and entered into force on 1 January 1999.

[4] Adopted on 11 March 1999 in Ouagadougou (Burkina Faso) and entered into force on 11 June 1999.

[5] Adopted on 23 March 2000 in Yaoundé (Cameroon). The first part of this Uniform Act, relating to companies' individual accounts, entered into force on 1 January 2001.

These Uniform Acts apply in all the Member States and will apply automatically in any State that accedes to the Treaty in the future, 60 days after accession[6].

Students and practitioners who come from a common law tradition and who are unfamiliar with civil law systems may find it surprising that the Uniform Acts aim to regulate, in such detail, so many aspects of business law. In fact, this is undoubtedly a result of the civil law tradition that has historically prevailed in the Member States.

The civil law tradition, which is essentially derived from the Civil and Commercial Codes enacted by Napoleon, is very different from the common law tradition. While common law is judge-made law, which exists and applies on the basis of binding legal precedents developed over the centuries, civil law consists predominantly of written rules of law enacted by a parliament. Unlike countries with a common law tradition, countries with a civil law tradition do not recognize or apply the rules of precedent, nor do the courts in civil law jurisdictions apply the English concept of *stare decisis*, which creates an obligation for the lower courts to comply with the decisions of the highest courts. When a statute requires interpretation, civil lawyers will, first of all, try to determine what was the intent of the legislative body which enacted the statute, whereas common lawyers will try to find an interpretation through the existing judge-made precedents and the overall meaning of the text.

As a result of the differences in the two traditions, it could be said that there is more flexibility under common law than under civil law. However, the predominantly civil law tradition of the current Member States should not be a barrier to the accession of States with a common law tradition. The aim of OHADA is to create a common set of rules to be applied on the African continent without imposing new legal traditions and court systems. The legal and historical traditions of each country should continue to be respected, and it seems possible for common law concepts to coexist with the Uniform Acts, which are designed to create clearly identified basic rules that be completed by national rules in each of the Member States[7].

The second part, relating to consolidated and combined accounts, entered into force on 1 January 2002.

[6] Article 53 of the Treaty.

[7] The recent harmonization of Canadian federal law, mostly based on common law, with the civil law applied in the province of Quebec (Federal Law – Civil Law Harmonization Act, No. 1, 2001, c. 4) could well serve as an example for future development of OHADA on the African continent. This new Canadian legislation recognizes that the harmonious

The following chapters will deal with each of the Uniform Acts that have been issued. This chapter will briefly outline the principles that are laid down by the Treaty relating to the scope and applicability of Uniform Acts. It will then discuss the procedure for the adoption of Uniform Acts, and the legal value that is attributed to their provisions.

SECTION 1: PRINCIPLES LAID DOWN BY THE TREATY

A. Scope of the Treaty

The Treaty provides for the promulgation of harmonized legislation with regard to company law, the legal status of commercial operators, the recovery of debts, securities, enforcement measures, insolvency proceedings, arbitration, employment law, accounting law, sales, transport, and any other subject that the Council of Ministers may unanimously decide to include[8].

B. Direct applicability of Uniform Acts

1. Consequences of direct applicability

Pursuant to Article 10 of the Treaty, Uniform Acts are directly applicable and binding in the Member States, notwithstanding any conflicting provision of national law, be it previous or subsequent.

This provision gives rise to certain problems of interpretation concerning the extent to which national laws are abrogated by virtue of the Uniform Acts.

A first possible interpretation is that only national laws, or individual provisions of such laws, which are actually contrary to a Uniform Act should be considered as abrogated. This approach is rather complicated because it requires an analysis of which provisions of the national law are contrary to a Uniform Act and which are not.

---

interaction of federal legislation and provincial legislation lies in an interpretation of federal legislation that is compatible with the common law or civil law traditions, as the case may be, and that the full development of these two major legal traditions gives Canadians enhanced opportunities worldwide and facilitates exchanges with the vast majority of other countries.

[8] Article 2 of the Treaty.

A second possibility is that Article 10 should be interpreted as meaning that a Uniform Act abrogates any national law having the same subject matter. In such a case, it would be unnecessary to determine whether a national law might be contrary to a Uniform Act, since the national law would automatically disappear upon the entry into force of the Uniform Act.

It might be argued that the second interpretation would be preferable in order not only to ensure efficiency and simplify the application of Uniform Acts in each Member State, but also to achieve full harmonization. However, the actual wording of Article 10 seems to require the first interpretation.

A further complication arises from the fact that the Uniform Acts contain provisions which complement or, in certain cases, contradict Article 10 of the Treaty. For example, while Article 919 of the Uniform Act on Commercial Companies states that all laws contrary to the provisions of the Uniform Act are abrogated, Article 916 of that Uniform Act provides that it does not abrogate laws applicable to companies subject to a special regime. On the other hand, Article 336 of the Uniform Act on Simplified Recovery Procedures and Enforcement Measures is clear; it specifies that the Uniform Act shall abrogate all provisions regarding the matters to which it relates in the Member States.

The doubts to which Article 10 give rise are unfortunate, given that this article is a fundamental provision of the Treaty, with consequences for the functioning of the entire OHADA legislative system. For this reason, in the year 2000, Côte d'Ivoire requested an advisory opinion from the CCJA.

2. Interpretation of Article 10 by the CCJA

In its advisory opinion of 30 April 2001, given at the request of Côte d'Ivoire, the CCJA has provided certain indications as to the proper interpretation of Article 10 of the Treaty[9].

According to the advisory opinion, the effect of Article 10 is to abrogate and to prohibit for the future any national legislative or regulatory provision which has the same purpose as the Uniform Acts and which conflicts with these. The advisory opinion adds that this also applies to any provision identical to the provisions of the Uniform Acts, and that the word 'provision' must be read as referring to a clause, a sub-clause,

---

[9] Advisory Opinion No. 001/2001/EP.

or even a single sentence. It is further stated that in cases where not all the provisions of a national law conflict with those of a Uniform Act, the non-conflicting provisions remain applicable.

As a result of this interpretation by the CCJA, it seems that national laws must be considered in detail, and that each article should be examined separately. While this interpretation seems to run counter to the need for efficiency and simplicity in the application of the Uniform Acts, it is certainly true to the actual wording of Article 10. Moreover, the merit of the advisory opinion is that it may prevent the occurrence of situations where the promulgation of a Uniform Act would otherwise create lacunae in the national law.

3. Entry into force

Article 9 of the Treaty provides that Uniform Acts enter into force 90 days after their adoption, unless the Uniform Act itself contains special provisions in that regard, as was the case with the Uniform Act on Collective Insolvency Proceedings. Following a suggestion by the CCJA, that Uniform Act entered into force almost nine months after its adoption, in order to give the legal professions time to familiarize themselves with the new system. Uniform Acts may be relied upon against any party 30 days after their publication in the OHADA Official Journal.

4. Language

Pursuant to Article 42 of the Treaty, French is the working language of OHADA. Amongst other things, this means that the Uniform Acts are drafted and issued in French.

It is true that at present the great majority of the Member States are French-speaking countries. The only exceptions are the English-speaking provinces of Cameroon, and Equatorial Guinea and Guinea-Bissau where Spanish and Portuguese are spoken, respectively.

To date, very little has been done to accommodate the needs of non-French-speakers. While English translations of the Uniform Acts have been published in the OHADA Official Journal, these translations have no official value and are, in any event, not of the highest standard. No translations into either Portuguese or Spanish have been published in the OHADA Official Journal.

In Cameroon, the language question raises a constitutional problem. The principle of bilingualism is enshrined in Cameroon's Constitution which expressly provides that English and French are the two official languages; that the two languages are of equal value; that the State shall guarantee the promotion of bilingualism throughout the country; and that laws are to be published in both English and French in the official gazette[10]. The imposition of French as the only official language of the Uniform Acts is therefore viewed as unconstitutional and has led to serious resistance to the Uniform Acts in the English-speaking provinces of Cameroon. Moreover, on a practical level, the fact that French is the only working language of OHADA certainly gives rise to difficulties of comprehension and application of the Uniform Acts in those countries where French is not spoken. There is, therefore, a need for proper translations of the Uniform Acts, and this will become ever more pressing when more English-speaking States or States with other official languages join OHADA.

SECTION 2: PROCEDURE FOR THE ADOPTION OF UNIFORM ACTS

The procedure for the adoption of Uniform Acts is set forth in Articles 6 *et seq* of the Treaty. It comprises three phases, none of which involves the national legislative authorities of the Member States[11]. Uniform Acts may be modified in accordance with the same procedure, upon the request of a Member State[12].

A. Drafting

The topics to be dealt with are chosen in accordance with the annual programme for harmonization approved by the Council of Ministers. During the drafting phase, a preliminary draft is prepared by a recognized expert in the field in question, under the auspices of the Permanent

---

[10] Articles 1(3) and 31(3) of Cameroon's Constitution.

[11] This has again led to objections in Cameroon on constitutional grounds, because of the provisions in the Constitution that laws are to be passed by the Parliament. See Chapter 2, footnote 3. However, the Constitution allows the constitutional court to be seised by one-third of the members of the National Assembly or of the Senate if they consider that a law or a treaty is unconstitutional. The fact that this has not occurred with regard to the OHADA Treaty, which pursuant to its Article 52 has been ratified by the Member States in accordance with their constitutional procedures, suggests that ratification of the Treaty has resulted in a delegation of certain sovereign powers to OHADA and that this delegation has in turn been ratified by the parliament.

[12] Article 12 of the Treaty.

Secretariat. The preliminary draft is then transmitted to the governments of the Member States.

Although not provided for by the Treaty, national commissions have been established by the Member States to examine the preliminary drafts of Uniform Acts at this stage. The Permanent Secretary recognizes that these national commissions are very useful, and he is keen to promote their recognition as official institutions within the OHADA system, and also to ensure that they are representative of all the legal professions and the business community. In February 2002, the Council of Ministers adopted a proposal to this effect, and the Permanent Secretariat has prepared a draft model for national ministerial orders providing for their creation and institutionalization. It is hoped, subject to budgetary constraints, that this draft model can be issued during the course of 2002. In addition to providing input on a technical level, it has been suggested that these national commissions may go some way to allaying the criticism that is sometimes voiced, ie that the national legislative authorities are excluded from the adoption process for Uniform Acts[13].

The national commissions must complete their examination, and the Member States must convey any observations to the Permanent Secretariat within 90 days[14]. When this is done, the Permanent Secretariat calls a plenary session of all the national commissions in order to reach a consensus on the draft. The draft is then returned to the Member States for their observations, which are communicated to the Permanent Secretariat[15].

B. Advisory opinion

The agreed draft is next transmitted to the CCJA for an advisory opinion. The CCJA has 30 days within which to give its opinion[16], which remains confidential.

The CCJA must determine, in particular, whether the draft complies with the Treaty and with the general spirit of OHADA. The CCJA views

---

[13] This is perhaps doubtful, however, given that the national commissions are not composed of elected representatives of the people. Instead, the creation of standing committees of the national parliaments might be envisaged, or a regional parliament or inter-parliamentary committee as is the case in ECOWAS, UEMOA and CEMAC (see Chapter 12).

[14] Article 7 of the Treaty.

[15] The intervention of the national commissions and this phase of the process are not envisaged by the Treaty.

[16] Article 7 of the Treaty.

its role in this regard as extremely important, in particular because it gives it the opportunity to understand the philosophy behind a Uniform Act before it comes into existence, and to ensure that its subsequent judgments on the interpretation and application of the Uniform Act are in line with that philosophy.

C. Final adoption

The final step is adoption of the Uniform Act by the Council of Ministers. This requires a unanimous vote of the Member States which are present, not taking into account any abstentions, with a quorum of two-thirds of the Member States[17]. Consequently, while abstention of a Member State on a vote or failure to attend the meeting do not in themselves constitute obstacles to the adoption of Uniform Acts, there is nevertheless a right of veto, since the unanimity rule allows a single State, if present, to block adoption by a negative vote.

SECTION 3: LEGAL VALUE OF THE PROVISIONS OF THE UNIFORM ACTS AND LIMITS ON THEIR APPLICABILITY

The Uniform Acts contain both mandatory and non-mandatory provisions.

A. Non-mandatory provisions

Certain provisions of the Uniform Acts apply only in cases where the parties to an agreement have not provided for anything to the contrary. For example, Article 517 of the Uniform Act on Commercial Companies specifies that *'except as otherwise provided in the articles of association, shareholders' meetings shall be held at the registered office of the company or at any other place on the territory of the Member State of the registered office'*. In other words, this allows the articles of association of a company to provide for the possibility of holding shareholders' meetings in a foreign country. If, on the other hand, nothing is provided to this effect in the articles of association, the Uniform Act will apply, and shareholders' meetings must be held within the Member State where the company's registered office is located.

---

[17] Article 8 of the Treaty.

In some cases, the Uniform Acts contain provisions which are applicable only in the absence of provisions in the relevant national law on the same subject. For example, liability under a surety-bond is deemed to be joint and several under Article 10 of the Uniform Act on Securities, but the same article states that this rule does not apply if the national law of the Member State in question provides otherwise.

The Uniform Acts themselves may also provide for different options in their application. For instance, the Uniform Act relating to Commercial Companies allows a choice between different types of management structure within the same type of company.

Finally, there are cases where the Uniform Act itself expressly allows Member States to complement its provisions by enacting national laws. This is the case, for example, with regard to securities on movable or immovable property[18].

Because of the existence of non-mandatory provisions and the consequent possibility for parties to make their own contractual arrangements to the extent that these do not conflict with mandatory rules in the Uniform Acts, it is likely that parties in the common law provinces of Cameroon will integrate common law concepts into their agreements. This might be the case for trusts or nominee shareholders, for example, since there seems to be nothing in the Uniform Act on Company Law to prevent the use of these devices. Moreover, there seems to be nothing to prevent the common law courts of Cameroon from ruling in equity when dealing with cases involving application of the Uniform Acts. There is, of course, a risk if a case involving common law principles reaches the CCJA, given that the Court, as presently constituted, will be unfamiliar with these principles and may not apply them properly. This is another reason, in addition to the language problem, why further consideration should be given to the composition of the CCJA, especially if other countries with different legal traditions, including those with a common law tradition, are to be encouraged to join OHADA.

B. Mandatory provisions

In addition to non-mandatory provisions, the Uniform Acts also contain two categories of mandatory provisions.

First, there are provisions according to which certain agreements or procedures may be declared null and void if particular formalities have

---

[18] Articles 106 and 132 of the Uniform Act relating to Securities.

not been complied with. For example, Article 198 of the Uniform Act on Commercial Companies states that

> *The companies involved in a merger, spin-off or partial business transfer are required to file with the court registry a statement whereby they indicate all the actions taken with a view to the conclusion of the transaction and declare that the transaction has been carried out in conformity with this Uniform Act. Failure to do so will result in the transaction being declared null and void.*

Second, there are provisions which state that certain identified rules cannot be derogated from by agreement of the parties. Any contractual provision which purports to derogate from such rules will be considered null and void. These rules are known as public policy (or *ordre public*) rules. In some cases their public policy nature is stated expressly, as in Article 102 of the Uniform Act on General Commercial Law, which lists a number of articles contained in that Uniform Act which must be considered as rules of public policy.

C. Limits on the application of Uniform Acts

Finally, there are certain limits on the application of the Uniform Acts in the Member States. In particular, while under Article 5 of the Treaty a Uniform Act may contain provisions relating to criminal liability, it is left to the individual Member States to determine and enforce the actual criminal penalties that may be imposed within their territory. Similarly, it is for the Member States to determine the types of property that are exempt from seizure[19], or what constitutes an enforceable right on their territory[20].

Moreover, the Uniform Acts do not harmonize the administrative and judicial organization of the Member States. As a result, they use generic terms to refer to various authorities, such as 'the court having jurisdiction in commercial matters' rather than 'the commercial court' since not all the Member States have specialized commercial courts.

Other Uniform Acts contain provisions which seem impossible to harmonize, because they fall within the ambit of the Member States' individual economic and social policies. This is the case for the determination

---

[19] Articles 50 and 51 of the Uniform Act on Simplified Recovery Proceedings and Enforcement Measures.

[20] Article 30 of the Uniform Act on Simplified Recovery Proceedings and Enforcement Measures.

of any national restrictions regarding commercial rent[21], or the application of a national official interest rate when a party fails to pay the price agreed for a commercial sale[22].

---

[21] Article 84 of the Uniform Act on General Commercial Law.
[22] Article 263 of the Uniform Act on General Commercial Law.

4

General Commercial Law

The Uniform Act on General Commercial Law, which came into force on 1 January 1998, contains miscellaneous sets of rules covering a number of disparate subjects which do not fall within the ambit of the other more specific Uniform Acts. These rules cover the status of commercial operators (*commerçants*), the commercial registry, the leasing of commercial premises, the operation and sale of businesses (*fonds de commerce*), commercial intermediaries and the sale of goods. They are applicable to every individual commercial operator or commercial company[1] which has its place of business or registered office in any of the Member States, including any commercial companies in which the State or a public body is a shareholder[2].

Of particular importance in the Uniform Act are the provisions relating to the commercial registry (RCCM), which institute a centralized system of registration for all commercial companies and commercial operators and also for charges over movable property. This is vital for business security but, as many investors know to their cost, African countries often have inefficient systems of registration, if such systems exist at all. If the new registry instituted by the Uniform Act is to function properly, it will need to be fully computerized on the same system throughout the Member States. At present this has not been finalized, primarily because

---

[1] Commercial companies are defined in the Uniform Act on Commercial Companies and Economic Interest Groups, discussed in Chapter 5. For a definition of commercial operators, see Section 1 of this chapter.

[2] Article 1.

of financial reasons, but it is hoped that the funding that has now been pledged will allow the registry to function as planned within the near future[3].

SECTION 1: STATUS OF COMMERCIAL OPERATORS (*COMMERÇANTS*)

OHADA law contains provisions that are specifically applicable to persons and entities who habitually engage in commercial activities and who are defined in French as *commerçants*[4]. In English there is no equivalent defined term. For the sake of convenience, *commerçants* will be referred to in this chapter and elsewhere in the book as 'commercial operators'.

Under OHADA law, commercial operators have certain rights which are not available to persons or entities who do not enjoy commercial status, but certain specific requirements and liabilities are also imposed upon them. In their transactions commercial operators are subject to rules regarding standard of proof and limitation periods which are different from the rules that are applicable to persons and entities who do not have commercial status. The definition of what constitutes a commercial operator is therefore of great importance.

A. Definition of commercial operators and commercial transactions

Article 2 of the Uniform Act provides that '*Commercial operators are those who perform commercial transactions as their usual professional activity*'. This definition is derived from the laws that were applicable in most OHADA countries prior to the entry into force of the Uniform Act.

To facilitate the determination of whether or not a person or entity is a commercial operator under this definition, Articles 3 and 4 provide that the following activities are deemed to be commercial transactions:

---

[3] The African Development Bank has recently approved a grant of c. US$180,000 from its soft window, the African Development Fund, to finance the commercial registry held by the CCJA.
[4] Articles 2 to 18.

- the purchase of movable or immovable goods for resale;
- activities in the fields of banking, capital markets, exchange, broker-age, insurance or forwarding;
- any contracts between commercial operators for the needs of their business;
- the industrial exploitation of mines, quarries and any other natural resources;
- the leasing of movable assets;
- operations involving manufacture, transportation and telecommuni-cations;
- the business of commercial intermediaries (factors, brokers and commercial agents) and any other intermediaries involved in the purchase, sale or rental of immovable property, businesses or share-holdings in commercial companies or property companies;
- transactions carried out by commercial companies; and
- the issuance of bills of exchange and promissory notes.

As a result, any persons or entities carrying out any of the above trans-actions in their normal course of business are deemed to be commercial operators. The above list of activities is not, however, exhaustive.

Moreover, Article 6 of the Uniform Act on Commercial Companies and Economic Interest Groups provides that most types of companies are deemed to be commercial operators by virtue of their form, regardless of their actual activity[5].

B. Capacity to undertake commercial transactions

Any person or entity undertaking a commercial transaction must have the legal capacity to do so[6].

The Uniform Act prohibits minors from being commercial operators and from carrying out commercial transactions[7].

In addition, commercial transactions cannot be carried out by persons falling within the following professional categories:

- civil servants and employees of public bodies and State-owned entities;

---

[5] These include the most usual forms of company, the *société anonyme* and *société à responsabilité limitée*, discussed in detail in Chapter 5.
[6] Article 6.
[7] Article 7.

- legal professionals and law officers: lawyers, bailiffs, official auction-eers (*commissaires priseurs*), stockbrokers, notaries, court clerks, administrators and liquidators;
- registered chartered and non-chartered accountants, statutory audi-tors, in-kind contributions appraisers (*commissaires aux apports*)[8], and ship brokers;
- and, more generally, persons engaged in any regulated professional activity which prohibits the concurrent exercise of a commercial activity[9].

Moreover, persons or entities in the following situations are not per-mitted to engage in a commercial activity:

- those who have been banned from exercising a commercial activity (either temporarily or permanently) by a court in one of the Member States or by a professional body;
- those who have been sentenced to any term of imprisonment for a serious criminal offence, or to more than three months' imprisonment for contravention of economic and financial regulations or offences against property[10].

A temporary ban of more than five years or a permanent ban may however be lifted by the court after a minimum period of five years or, if the ban has been imposed in the context of insolvency proceedings, without any time limit but only if certain specified conditions have been fulfilled[11].

Despite these prohibitions, any transactions by persons who are under a ban or who belong to a professional category which forbids them from undertaking commercial transactions may be relied upon against such persons by third parties acting in good faith[12]. On the other hand, the Uniform Act contains no similar provisions regarding the prohibition on minors. In order to determine the consequences of a commercial transaction by a minor, it will therefore be necessary to consult the relevant national legislation[13].

---

[8] See Chapter 5.
[9] Article 9.
[10] Article 10.
[11] Article 11.
[12] Articles 8 and 12.
[13] In most cases, this will be the Civil Code as inherited from France upon decoloniza-tion, according to which the transaction would be null and void.

C. Consequences of commercial status

As mentioned above, commercial status carries with it a number of legal consequences. Some of these will become apparent in the following chapters in connection with various specific areas of OHADA law. On a general level, there are also consequences relating in particular to registration (to be dealt with in the following section), accounting obligations, standard of proof and limitation periods.

All commercial operators must keep accounting books. These books comprise a journal, general ledger and annual accounts ledger[14]. Annual financial statements must also be prepared in a form that complies with the provisions of the Uniform Act on Accounting Law[15]. The accounting books must bear the registration number of the commercial operator and must be initialled by the President of the competent court or by another judge acting as his delegated representative. No blanks must be left in them, nor may they be altered in any way[16].

As regards standard of proof, while written evidence is generally required for non-commercial transactions, the existence and content of commercial transactions may be proven by any means, such as, for example, presumptions or evidence of witnesses[17]. In additon, a commercial operator's accounting books may be relied upon as evidence against him in respect of commercial transactions[18].

Commercial transactions are subject to shorter limitation periods than are usually applicable to non-commercial transactions. The statutory limitation period in relation to commercial obligations between commercial operators or between a commercial operator and a person or entity not having commercial status is five years, unless shorter periods are specified elsewhere[19], such as for commercial sales, which are subject to a limitation period of only two years[20].

SECTION 2: THE COMMERCIAL REGISTRY (*RCCM*)

The Uniform Act provides for a centralized system for the commercial registry (*Registre du Commerce et du Crédit Mobilier* or *RCCM*). The

---

[14] Article 13.
[15] See Chapter 6.
[16] Article 14.
[17] Article 5.
[18] Article 15.
[19] Article 18.
[20] Article 274.

principal functions of the RCCM are the registration of commercial operators, whether individuals or legal entities, and the registration of charges over movable property[21]. Until the Uniform Act came into force, most OHADA Member States applied an old French law, dating from 1919, in this regard.

The RCCM is intended to be a vital pivot in ensuring legal security in the Member States, notably by giving creditors and potential contractual partners access to information regarding the legal status and indebtedness of their contacts.

A. *Organization of the RCCM*

The Uniform Act provides for a local commercial register to be held by the registry of each civil or commercial court which has jurisdiction under the national rules of jurisdiction of the country concerned. Centralization of the data held in each local registry is organized at two levels: in a national register held in each Member State, and a regional register held by the CCJA[22].

In order properly to deliver the type of services envisaged by the Uniform Act, all the RCCM offices within the Member States will have to be fully organized and computerized on the same system. This is proving to be a long process and the old national systems are currently operational in most countries. The matter is, however, closely followed by the Permanent Secretary of OHADA, and a small working party including a judge from the CCJA has been given the task of determining criteria for the necessary software 2002.

Given its recognition of the crucial role that the RCCM is intended to play in the OHADA system and the need for investors to have access to the information that the RCCM is designed to supply, the African Development Bank has approved a grant of financial assistance for its proper establishment.

B. *Registration of commercial operators*

All commercial companies and individual commercial operators established in any Member State, as well as branches of foreign companies, must be registered with the RCCM within one month of their establish-

---

[21] Article 19.
[22] Article 20.

ment or incorporation[23]. Once a company has been registered with the RCCM, it acquires its separate legal personality[24]. The documents required for registration are listed in Articles 25 and 26 of the Uniform Act (for individuals), Articles 27 and 28 (for companies) and Article 29 (for branches).

Failure to comply with the registration requirements, or the making of a fraudulent registration, entails the application of criminal penalties as laid down by the Member State concerned[25].

All changes to the legal status of individual commercial operators and companies must also be registered, as well as any decisions taken in the course of collective or individual insolvency proceedings and decisions imposing financial penalties upon company directors.

A commercial operator or company must be removed from the register and a notice published in a legal journal when:

- the commercial activity has ceased;
- the individual dies;
- the company has been wound up and one month has passed since completion of the liquidation procedure; or
- the company has been declared null and void[26].

Examples of standard forms to be used for filing with the RCCM are contained in Appendix D at the end of this volume. When making a filing, four originals of these forms must be submitted.

C. Registration of charges over movable property

The RCCM registers charges over shares, businesses (*fonds de commerce*), stocks, professional equipment and motor vehicles. It also registers clauses providing for retention of title, etc, and details of leasing contracts as well as charges and preferential rights in favour of the tax, customs and social security authorities[27].

When registering a charge, the beneficiary is required to submit evidence of his entitlement to the charge (such as an excerpt from a court

---

[23] Articles 25, 27 and 29.
[24] Uniform Act on Commercial Companies and Economic Interest Groups, Article 98.
[25] Article 43.
[26] Articles 36 and 37.
[27] These various types of charges are dealt with in detail in Chapter 8.

decision or an original agreement) together with four copies of the filing form to the registrar of the court having jurisdiction in the place where the debtor is located[28]. After checking that these are in order, the registrar authorizes registration.

Duly registered charges are safe from challenge by third parties for the following periods[29]:

- five years for charges over shares, businesses, professional equipment, motor vehicles and leasing agreements;
- three years for preferential rights in favour of the tax, customs or social security authorities; and
- one year for pledges of stocks or for clauses providing for retention of title.

Upon expiry of the relevant period, the registration is deleted, unless renewed by the interested party[30].

Partial or total deletion of the registration of a charge may also be requested if evidence is provided of the beneficiary's agreement to deletion[31]. Failing such agreement, the person against whom a charge has been registered may at any time apply to the court to have the registration deleted or amended, if evidence can be provided that there are serious and legitimate reasons for the deletion or amendment[32].

SECTION 3: COMMERCIAL LEASES

The Uniform Act contains a series of provisions applicable to commercial leases. These are in general very protective of the lessee. According to Article 102, a number of the provisions are mandatory[33]. Others may therefore be derogated from in a commercial lease agreement.

---

[28] Articles 44 *et seq.*
[29] Article 63.
[30] Article 63.
[31] Article 66.
[32] Article 65.
[33] The mandatory provisions are Articles 69–71, 75, 78, 79, 85, 91–95, 98 and 101.

A. Scope of the Uniform Act

Article 69, from which the parties cannot derogate, provides that the rules laid down by the Uniform Act with regard to commercial leases apply to all leases for premises located in towns with more than 5,000 inhabitants and where:

- the premises are to be used for a commercial, industrial or professional activity;
- the premises are ancillary to premises used for such purposes; or
- the lease relates to unoccupied land on which premises have been built, before or after signature of the lease, for purposes of a commercial, industrial or professional activity, if such premises have been built or are being used with the owner's consent or knowledge.

Under Article 70, the rules relating to commercial leases apply not only to private companies but also to certain State-owned companies (whether they are acting as lessor or lessee).

B. Lessor's obligations

Articles 73 and 74 of the Uniform Act require the lessor to deliver the premises in good condition and to undertake at his own expense any major works that are urgent and necessary to maintain them. This provision may however be derogated from, and the lessee may therefore be required to bear the cost of such works if this is specifically provided for in the lease agreement.

If the works prevent the lessee from using the premises fully, the rent is reduced in proportion. If they are of such a nature as to make performance of the lease impossible, the lessee may seek a court-ordered termination or a suspension for the duration of the works[34].

In the event of refusal by the lessor to carry out the works, the lessee can obtain a court order authorizing it to proceed with the works on behalf of, and at the expense of, the lessor[35]. This provision is mandatory and therefore cannot be derogated from by contract. However, given that Articles 73 and 74 may be derogated from, it appears that it is only the possibility for the lessee to apply for a court order that is mandatory,

---

[34] Article 74.
[35] Article 75.

but not the bearing of the cost of the works by the lessor in cases where this has been excluded by contract.

The lessor is not allowed to change the layout of the premises or restrict their use by the lessee without the lessee's consent[36].

Finally, the lessor is liable for any inconvenience or trouble caused to the lessee's use of the premises, whether occasioned by the lessor itself or by third parties who are legally dependent upon the lessor[37].

C. Lessee's obligations

None of the provisions of the Uniform Act concerning the obligations of the lessee are mandatory, and the parties are therefore free to negotiate such obligations as they wish.

Nevertheless, if it is not otherwise stated in the contract, the lessee must pay the rent on the due dates and must look after the premises properly and use them for the activity specified in the contract[38]. The lessor may apply to the court for termination of the lease if any damage is caused to him by the lessee using the premises for an unauthorized activity, or for an additional activity that is not provided for in the initial lease agreement[39].

The lessee is responsible for carrying out maintenance and day-to-day repairs, and must indemnify the lessor for any damage or loss in the event he fails to ensure adequate maintenance[40].

D. Determination of the rent

The rent is decided freely between the parties, unless any applicable national legislation provides otherwise. It may be revised in accordance with the provisions of the lease agreement or, failing any such provisions, every three years[41].

In the event of the parties being unable to agree upon a revision of the rent, either party may make an application to the court to set the rent[42]. In such circumstances, the court takes into account the location,

---

[36] Article 76.
[37] Article 77.
[38] Article 80.
[39] Article 81.
[40] Article 82.
[41] Article 84.
[42] Article 85.

size and condition of the premises and also the rent payable under commercial leases for similar premises in the neighbourhood.

E. Duration and right of renewal

Commercial leases may be entered into for either a fixed or an indefinite period.

The provisions of the Uniform Act relating to renewal[43] are all mandatory and cannot be varied by contract. Whether the lease is for a fixed or an indefinite term, a lessee who can demonstrate that he has used the premises properly, for purposes of the activity stipulated in the contract and for a period of at least two years, is entitled to renewal[44]. In either case, the renewal is for a three-year period unless otherwise agreed by the parties[45].

If the lease is for a fixed term, the lessee must serve notice of renewal on the lessor by bailiff three months before expiry, failing which his right to renewal lapses[46].

On the other hand, if the lease is for an indefinite term, it is the lessor who must serve notice on the lessee, giving at least six months' warning of his intention to terminate the contract. In such an event, the lessee may object to termination, again by serving notice of his objection on the lessor[47].

If the lessor refuses to renew either a fixed-term or an indefinite lease, the lessee is entitled to compensation, except where he is in breach of a fundamental provision of the contract or has ceased trading, or where the lessor intends to demolish and rebuild the premises[48]. If the parties cannot agree upon the amount of compensation, the court will determine an amount, taking into account various factors such as the turnover of the business, any capital investments made by the lessee, and the location of the premises[49].

---

[43] The Uniform Act refers to 'renewal' whether the lease concerned is for a fixed or an indefinite period. For the sake of simplicity this terminology is also used here, although strictly speaking it would be more accurate to speak of a right to continuation of the lease where an indefinite lease is concerned.

[44] Article 91.

[45] Article 97.

[46] Article 92.

[47] Article 93.

[48] Articles 94 and 95.

[49] Article 94.

F. Termination

A fixed-term lease will terminate on its due date if the lessee has failed to give three months' advance notice of his intention to avail himself of his right to renewal[50].

In the case of an indefinite lease, either the lessor or the lessee may terminate the contract by giving at least six months' notice by bailiff[51]. As mentioned above, the lessee may object to termination, with compensation being payable to the lessee if the lessor nevertheless terminates.

If, however, the lessor considers that the lessee is in breach of his obligations under the lease, and if the lessee has failed to comply with those obligations within one month of service of a formal request to do so, the lessor may seek a court order terminating the lease[52].

Neither the sale of the leased premises nor the death of one of the parties can give rise to termination of the lease[53]. These again are mandatory provisions, and the lease agreement therefore cannot provide otherwise.

G. Inventory

An inventory of the premises should be taken at the start of the lease. In the absence of any inventory, the premises are deemed to have been in perfect condition at the date the lease was executed and therefore the cost of any deterioration is to be borne by the lessee[54].

H. Sub-letting

Sub-letting is prohibited unless otherwise provided for in the lease agreement, in which event any sub-lease that is entered into by the lessee must be notified to the main lessor[55]. If the rent payable under the sub-lease is higher than that payable under the main lease, the main lessor may demand a corresponding increase in the rent payable to him[56].

---

[50] Article 92.
[51] Article 93.
[52] Article 101.
[53] Articles 78 and 79.
[54] Article 73.
[55] Article 89.
[56] Article 90.

I. Assignment

The lessee may assign the lease to a purchaser of his commercial business. However, any such assignment must be notified in writing to the lessor, failing which it will have no effect as against the lessor[57]. The lessor may only object to the assignment for serious and legitimate reasons, such as failure to pay the rent[58]. If he does object, he may apply for a court order prohibiting the assignment.

SECTION 4: THE BUSINESS (*FONDS DE COMMERCE*)

The concept of a *fonds de commerce* (business) is well known in countries whose legal system is influenced by French law. However, while there is no definition of this concept in any French legal texts, Article 103 of the Uniform Act defines a business as a collection of various tangible and intangible movable assets that as a whole allow a commercial operator to attract and retain its clientele.

A. Components of the business

Any business necessarily comprises a clientele and a logo or trading name[59]. In addition, it may comprise installations, shopfittings, equipment, furniture, stock, lease agreements, licences, trademarks and patents, drawings and models and any other intellectual property rights necessary for its operation[60].

B. Management leases (location-gérance)

A business may either be directly operated by its owner or leased to another commercial operator or company under a management lease (*contrat de location-gérance*), defined as an agreement by which the owner of a business grants to a manager (*locataire-gérant*) the right to operate the business at his own risk[61].

---

[57] Article 87.
[58] Article 88.
[59] Article 104.
[60] Article 105.
[61] Article 106.

1. Requirements for a management lease

The manager must have commercial status, and is subject to all the obligations incumbent upon commercial operators, in particular as regards registration with the RCCM[62]. The owner of the business must himself have operated it for at least one year, and must have been either an individual commercial operator or the general manager or commercial or technical manager of a commercial company for at least two years[63]. These qualifying time periods may, however, be reduced or lifted by a court in cases where the owner can show that it has been impossible for him to operate the business during the required period, either personally or through intermediaries[64].

The management lease is usually made in the form of a written agreement, and an extract from the agreement, indicating its main features, must be published in a legal journal within 15 days of its signature[65].

2. Effects of the management lease

Once the management lease has been entered into, the new manager is required to state his own commercial details (name, registered office, RCCM number), together with an indication that he is the *locataire-gérant* of the business, on all invoices, orders and other financial or commercial documents[66]. Otherwise, criminal penalties may be imposed upon him in accordance with the criminal law of the relevant Member State.

After signature, the owner of the business must amend his own details held by the RCCM, indicating that the business is now operated through a management lease[67].

Within three months of publication of the management lease, any interested parties may make an application to the court to protect their interests. If the court decides that the lease may jeopardize recovery of any debts owed by the owner, it may declare those debts immediately payable[68].

---

[62] Article 107.
[63] Article 109.
[64] Article 110.
[65] Article 107.
[66] Article 108.
[67] Article 107.
[68] Article 112.

The owner of the business also remains jointly and severally liable with the manager for all debts arising in connection with the business from the time the lease is granted until publication of the agreement (ie 15 days after its signature)[69]. Certain Member States have extended this period of joint and several liability.

3. Duration and termination of the management lease

A management lease is usually entered into for a fixed term. However, the Uniform Act also envisages early termination, without specifying any particular conditions or consequences in such an event[70]. As a result, these issues would have to be dealt with either under the agreement itself or under general contractual law.

Notice of the termination must be published in a legal journal, and the owner's registration in the RCCM must be amended accordingly[71].

Upon expiry or termination of a management lease, all debts contracted by the manager for the operation of the business become payable immediately[72].

C. Pledges over the business

Because a business may have a high value, it can be pledged in favour of creditors. This type of pledge is regulated by both the Uniform Act on General Commercial Law (Articles 46 to 50) and the Uniform Act on Securities (Articles 69 to 72 and 77 to 90)[73].

The pledge must cover certain components of the business, ie the clientele, the commercial name and logo, the commercial lease and any operating permits. It may also cover all the remaining components of the business or only some of them, such as in particular the equipment or intangible rights such as patents and trademarks[74].

A pledge may be given either by notarized deed or by private contract, or may be made by court order. Whichever form is used, it must indicate certain information including details of the parties, the amount of the debt guaranteed, the components of the business covered by the pledge,

---

[69] Article 113.
[70] Article 114.
[71] Article 107.
[72] Article 114.
[73] See Chapter 8.
[74] Uniform Act on Securities, Article 69.

and the due dates for payment of capital and interest. The pledge agreement or court order is submitted to the registry of the court for filing with the RCCM, so that third parties can obtain information on the pledge[75].

When the pledge covers intellectual property rights, it must also comply with any specific intellectual property law requirements that may be applicable relating to registration or filing[76]. For example, if patents or trademarks that are registered with the African Intellectual Property Organization (OAPI) are pledged to a creditor, the pledge itself must also be registered with OAPI so that it can be relied upon as against third parties[77].

A pledge over a business is valid for five years and can then be renewed. Once published in the RCCM, it is safe from challenge by third parties[78].

D. Sale of the business

The business can be sold in accordance with the general provisions applicable to commercial sale agreements (described in section 6 of this Chapter). In addition, there are specific provisions governing the sale of a business, which are also applicable in the event of contribution of a business to a company.

1. Formal aspects

The sale of a business is made by private contract or notarized deed which must include the following information:

- names and details of the seller and purchaser: personal details for individuals and, for companies, corporate name, legal form, registered office and corporate purpose;
- RCCM registration numbers;
- if relevant, the previous owners of the business;
- preferential rights and charges taken by creditors on the business;

---

[75] Article 46.
[76] Article 48.
[77] Revised Bangui Convention, Annex 1, Articles 33-34 and Annex 3, Articles 26-27. For further details regarding OAPI, see Chapter 12.
[78] Article 63.

- turnover during the last three years of operation or since acquisition or creation if the business has not been in operation for three years;
- commercial results over the same period;
- information concerning the lease: date, duration, names and addresses of the lessor and the seller if relevant;
- agreed price;
- location;
- components of the business that are comprised in the sale;
- name and address of a bank designated as escrow agent if the sale is entered into by private contract[79].

In the event of any omission or inaccuracy in the above details, the purchaser may, within one year of signature, apply to the court to have the sale of the business declared null and void, provided that he can demonstrate that the omission or inaccuracy has materially affected the business and has caused him damage[80].

Notice of the agreement, containing the information listed above, must be published in a legal journal within 15 days of signature[81]. Certified copies of the agreement must also be filed with the RCCM, and the seller and purchaser must each amend their respective registrations with the RCCM to reflect the occurrence of the sale[82].

2. Obligations of the seller

The seller must place the business at the purchaser's disposal from the date provided in the sale agreement, or at the date of payment in full of the consideration if the agreement provides for cash terms[83].

The seller must refrain from any actions which might adversely affect the proper operation of the business sold to the purchaser, and must indemnify the purchaser against any third-party claims relating to the business[84]. The sale agreement may include a clause whereby the seller undertakes not to set up a competing business. In order to be valid, this undertaking must be limited as to its duration or its geographical scope[85].

---

[79] Article 118.
[80] Article 119.
[81] Article 121.
[82] Article 120.
[83] Article 122.
[84] Article 123.
[85] Article 123.

The Uniform Act does not however indicate what limits would be acceptable in this regard, and it will therefore be necessary to look for the answer in the relevant national law or court decisions, at least until the CCJA gives a decision on the subject.

If the purchaser finds himself in a position where third parties are entitled to rights purportedly transferred to him under the sale, or if he discovers charges on the business that were not revealed in the agreement or any hidden defects in the business, he can seek a court order cancelling the agreement. Cancellation is possible if it can be shown that the purchaser's rights are affected to such an extent that he would not have entered into the agreement if he had been aware of the true circumstances[86].

3. Payment of the purchase price

The purchaser must pay the price on the agreed terms and conditions, either to the notary who has drawn up the agreement or, in the event of a private contract, to the bank designated as escrow agent. The notary or bank must retain this payment for a period of 30 days from the date of publication of the sale[87]. This rule is designed to protect the seller's creditors, who may raise objections within this period.

(a) Right to object to payment of the price

During the 30-day period from publication of the sale, creditors of the seller may notify their claims to the seller, the notary or bank acting as escrow agent, and the RCCM, indicating their formal opposition to payment of the price to the seller[88]. The notification must state the amount and origin of the creditor's claim and contain an election of domicile within the area of jurisdiction of the court holding the relevant RCCM. If these formalities are not complied with, the objection will be deemed to be null and void[89].

When the objection is properly made, it has the effect of a provisional measure, blocking the purchase price in the hands of the notary or bank

---

[86] Article 124.
[87] Article 125. In the English-speaking provinces of Cameroon, notaries' functions are exercised by solicitors.
[88] Articles 125 and 127.
[89] Article 127.

acting as escrow agent[90]. The creditor must then file proceedings for the determination of the merits of his claim within one month[91].

In the event of an objection, the seller may seek an amicable settlement with the creditor or apply to the court for an order to lift the opposition. The seller may only obtain payment once the objection has been set aside, either amicably or by court order[92].

If no objections have been notified within the 30-day period, the notary or bank will release the purchase price to the seller[93].

(b) Bids in excess of the purchase price

During the same 30-day period from publication of the sale, any creditor who has registered a charge or preferential right or who has opposed payment of the price to the seller can make a bid for the business which exceeds the purchase price by at least one-sixth. In such a case, the creditor must deposit with the registrar of the court an amount corresponding to the new bid, after which the court will organize a resale of the business by public auction[94].

This right (which may lead to the business being resold to the creditor having made the new bid) is essentially aimed at preventing any fraud resulting from a purchase price that does not reflect the true value of the business or from any concealment of part of the purchase price.

In practice, creditors will use this procedure only if they are really willing to acquire the business, and consequently it is likely to be rather exceptional.

4. Seller's guarantees and cancellation

The seller is guaranteed by a preferential right over the business until the purchase price has been paid[95]. In order for this right to be protected, it is advisable for the seller to have it published in the RCCM.

In addition, if the purchaser fails to make payment, the seller may apply to the court for cancellation of the sale agreement[96]. If he does so,

---

[90] For further details regarding provisional measures, see Chapter 9.
[91] Article 128 and Uniform Act on Simplified Recovery Procedures and Enforcement Measures, Article 61.
[92] Article 129.
[93] Article 125.
[94] Article 131.
[95] Articles 47 and 134.
[96] Article 135.

he must notify any creditors who have registered charges over the business and must also publish notice of the proceedings in the RCCM[97].

5. Employment law consequences

The sale of a business may create an obligation for the purchaser to take on the existing employees of the business.

At present there is no OHADA Uniform Act on employment law. Therefore, before a business is purchased, it is advisable to check whether there are any national employment regulations or collective bargaining agreements that protect employees by ensuring the continuity of their employment. For example, the Labour Codes in Burkina Faso, Chad, Mali and Niger provide that, in the event of the sale of a business, the employment contracts in force as of the date of the sale will continue between the new employer and the employees of the business[98].

6. Tax consequences

The sale of a business will also have tax consequences, with a transfer tax being imposed on the price paid. The tax rates applicable in the Member States are summarized in Appendix E.

SECTION 5: COMMERCIAL INTERMEDIARIES

The Uniform Act defines three categories of commercial intermediaries, all of which serve to facilitate commercial operations. Before stating the rules peculiar to each category, the Uniform Act lays down a series of general provisions that are applicable to all three categories.

A. *General provisions*

1. Definition and scope of powers

Commercial intermediaries have the power to act in a professional capacity on behalf of one or more principals with regard to the conclusion of commercial sale contracts with third parties[99].

---

[97] Article 136.
[98] Burkina Faso Labour Code (1992), Article 39; Chad Labour Code: Law No. 038/PR/ 96, Articles 136 and 375; Mali Labour Code: Law No. 92-020 of 23 September 1992, Article L 57; Niger Labour Code: Ordinance No. 96-039 of 29 June 1996, Articles 90 and 91.
[99] Article 137.

A commercial intermediary, who may be either an individual or a company, is by definition a commercial operator and must therefore satisfy the relevant criteria laid down by the Uniform Act[100].

Article 140 provides that the rules applicable to commercial intermediaries apply (i) if the intermediary is registered in the RCCM of one of the Member States, (ii) if he is acting in the territory of a Member State, or (iii) if the rules of private international law lead to application of the Uniform Act, even if the intermediary's principal and/or the third party are established outside the OHADA region.

The general rules applicable to agency are stated to be applicable to relations between the intermediary, his principal and third parties, in addition and subject to any specific provisions of the Uniform Act[101]. In fact the rules laid down by the Uniform Act are themselves very similar to those relating to agency under civil law. Furthermore, the Uniform Act provides that customs and usages in the relevant areas of activity are binding upon all parties concerned, as are the parties' own past practices[102].

The agreement between the principal and the intermediary may be made either orally or in writing and may be proven by any means[103].

The scope of the intermediary's powers is defined by the nature of the matter involved, unless it is specifically defined in the agreement. However, a special power-of-attorney is necessary if the intermediary is to commence legal proceedings, settle disputes, enter into arbitration agreements, undertake obligations regarding negotiable instruments, sell or pledge real property or make donations[104].

2. Effects of the intermediary's acts

Acts by a commercial intermediary acting on behalf of a principal and within the limits of his powers are binding upon the principal, on condition that the third party was aware or should have been aware that the intermediary was acting in that capacity[105].

On the other hand, acts by an intermediary who either had not been given any authority whatsoever or who was acting beyond his powers are not binding upon third parties or the intermediary's principal[106].

---

[100] See Section 1 above.
[101] Article 143.
[102] Article 145.
[103] Article 144.
[104] Article 146.
[105] Article 148.
[106] Article 151.

However, if the principal's own conduct led a third party to understand that the intermediary was acting on his behalf, the principal cannot claim that the intermediary did not have the requisite authority[107].

Acts carried out by an intermediary who either had no authority or acted beyond his powers may be ratified by the principal[108]. In the absence of ratification, the third party concerned may bring a claim for damages against the intermediary. On the other hand, the intermediary will not be held liable if the third party knew or should have known that he did not have the requisite power or was acting beyond his powers[109].

The commercial intermediary is entitled to reimbursement of any advance payments he has made or costs he has incurred in the proper performance of his instructions[110].

He must report to his principal upon request at any time, and is responsible for damages caused by any breach or inadequate performance of his instructions, unless he can prove that the damage was not caused by any fault on his part[111].

3. Termination

The circumstances in which the intermediary's agency may be terminated are listed non-exhaustively by the Uniform Act in Articles 156 and 157, as follows:

- mutual agreement between the principal and the intermediary;
- full performance of the instructions;
- revocation of the instructions by the principal;
- resignation by the commercial intermediary; or
- death, incapacity or insolvency proceedings concerning either party.

In the event of an abusive revocation or resignation, compensation is payable for any damage caused to the other party[112].

---

[107] Article 151.
[108] Article 152.
[109] Article 153.
[110] Article 154.
[111] Article 155.
[112] Article 156.

B. *Factors or commission agents* (**commissionnaires**)

Factors or commission agents (*commissionnaires*) act in their own name but on behalf of a principal in matters of sale or purchase[113]. They receive commission and are entitled to request reimbursement of all necessary costs incurred[114]. They must act in the interests of their principal with loyalty, and comply strictly with any instructions contained in their contract. If such instructions are only indicative, the factor must act as if his own interests are at stake, while complying to the extent possible with the instructions. If there are no particular instructions, he must act in such a way as to serve the best interests of his principal, while complying with applicable commercial usages[115].

Factors may retain any goods held on behalf of their principal until receipt of full payment of their commission and costs[116].

1. General principles

When the goods sent to the factor for sale do not arrive in good condition, the factor must protect his principal's right to claim against the carrier and ensure that the problems are evidenced in writing. He must also use his best efforts to protect the goods, and must notify his principal of the problem without delay. If he fails to do so, he will be liable for any damage caused by his negligence[117].

If the factor sells the goods below the minimum price specified by the principal, he will be required to pay him the difference, unless he proves that by selling at this price, he has averted damage to the principal and that he was not able to obtain his principal's timely instructions. On the other hand, the factor cannot derive any benefit for his own account from selling at a price higher or purchasing at a price lower than the amounts specified by his principal[118].

Any loans or advances granted by the factor to a third party in the absence of the principal's consent are made at the factor's own risk[119].

---

[113] Article 160.
[114] Articles 164–165.
[115] Articles 161–162.
[116] Article 166.
[117] Article 167.
[118] Article 168.
[119] Article 169.

When the factor sends goods or acts as a carrying agent, he guarantees against late delivery, damage and losses, unless these have been caused by a third party or *force majeure*[120].

If a factor acts in bad faith vis-à-vis his principal, and in particular if he informs him that he has paid a higher purchase price or obtained a lower sale price than in actual fact, he loses all rights to payment of his commission[121].

If he is found to be in breach of his instructions, the factor will be liable for any damage caused by his breach[122].

2. Del credere agents (*commissionnaires ducroire*)

A factor who guarantees the payment or other obligations of those with whom he deals is known as a del credere agent (*commissionnaire ducroire*). Because of this additional responsibility, he is entitled to additional commission, referred to as *ducroire*[123].

3. Customs agents

Certain factors are registered with the customs authorities as customs agents. These factors (*commissionnaires agréés en douane*) are responsible for paying all duties, taxes or fines to the customs authorities on behalf of their principals[124]. Once a factor has done so, he is subrogated in the rights of the customs authorities against his principal. He is liable towards his principal for any error in declarations made to the customs authorities or in the application of customs tariffs, as well as for any damage arising out of late payment. He is also liable to the customs authorities and the treasury for any customs operations that he has undertaken[125].

C. *Brokers* (courtiers)

A broker (*courtier*) is defined as an intermediary who acts neither in his own name nor for his own account, but who arranges contacts between

---

[120] Article 173.
[121] Article 171.
[122] Article 168.
[123] Article 170.
[124] Article 174.
[125] Article 175.

persons in order to facilitate or conclude commercial operations or transactions between those persons[126].

Brokers are obliged to use their best efforts with a view to concluding agreements, and are to provide all information necessary to assist the parties[127]. They must remain independent of the parties to the transaction, and cannot personally intervene in the transaction unless the parties so agree[128].

The broker is remunerated by whichever party has instructed him, and receives a percentage of the value of the transaction. This is paid when the agreement which he has facilitated is entered into, unless the agreement is subject to conditions precedent, in which case he will be paid only once those conditions have been fulfilled[129].

A broker loses his right to remuneration if he acts in the interests of the other party in contravention of his duties towards his principal, or if he receives payment from the other party without the knowledge of his principal[130].

D. *Commercial agents* (agents commerciaux)

1. General considerations

Commercial agents, without being bound by an employment contract, have the standing power to enter into negotiations and to conclude contracts for sale, purchase, rental or services, in the name and on behalf of agricultural, industrial or commercial clients[131].

Contracts between commercial agents and their principals are deemed to be in the common interest of both parties, and their relations are governed by obligations of loyalty and exchange of information[132]. The commercial agent must perform his duties in a professional manner, and the principal must enable the commercial agent to perform his duties properly[133].

---

[126] Article 176.
[127] Article 178.
[128] Article 177.
[129] Article 181.
[130] Article 183.
[131] Article 184.
[132] Article 185.
[133] Article 185.

A commercial agent may represent other principals, unless otherwise agreed in writing. However, he must not agree to represent any competitors of an existing principal without that principal's prior approval[134].

2. Remuneration

The commercial agent receives a commission. If no specific provision is included in his contract, the amount of commission is determined according to the usual practices in the sector concerned or, in the absence of any such practices, by taking into account all aspects of the transactions concerned[135].

Commission is due either when the principal has performed the transaction or should have performed it according to his agreement with the third party, or when the third party has performed the transaction[136]. The commission is due in all circumstances unless it can be shown that the contract will not be performed and if failure to perform is not due to the principal[137]. In such an event, the commercial agent will be entitled only to reimbursement of any expenses he has incurred upon the instructions of the principal[138].

3. Duration and termination

Contracts with commercial agents are usually for a fixed term and terminate upon expiry of that term without further formalities[139]. If the parties continue to act in accordance with the contract after expiry of the fixed term, the contract is deemed to have been renewed and to have become a contract of indefinite duration[140]. Contracts which are of indefinite duration may be terminated by notice, the length of which is determined according to the duration of the agreement, with a maximum of three months for a contract of three years' duration or more[141]. While the parties may not agree to apply shorter notice periods, they may agree upon longer periods. In this case, whatever period may be agreed is applicable to notice given by either party[142].

---

[134] Article 186.
[135] Article 188.
[136] Article 192.
[137] Article 193.
[138] Article 194.
[139] Article 195.
[140] Article 195.
[141] Article 196.
[142] Article 196.

The commercial agent is entitled to receive an indemnity upon termination of his contract[143]. The amount of this indemnity is determined by reference to the duration of the contract, with a maximum of three months' commission for a contract of three years' duration or more, plus any additional amount that may have been agreed between the parties as applicable to cases where the contract has existed for more than three years[144]. The commercial agent is however not entitled to payment of an indemnity if he does not serve upon the principal notice of a request for payment within one year of termination of the contract[145]. In addition, no indemnity is due in the event of gross misconduct, resignation of the commercial agent that is not for reasons of ill health or other reasons beyond his control, or assignment of the contract to a third party[146].

Table 4.1 Commercial intermediaries: summary table

Factor (commissionnaire)	Broker (courtier)	Commercial agent (agent commercial)
• Acts in his own name but on behalf of a principal • Receives commission (which may be increased if he guarantees payment by the principal) • Special category can undertake customs operations	• Acts in his own name and remains independent of parties, introducing them with a view to concluding transactions • Receives a percentage of the value of the transaction	• Acts in the name and on behalf of a principal • Receives commission • Entitled to a minimum indemnity upon termination

SECTION 6: COMMERCIAL SALE AGREEMENTS

The Uniform Act regulates sale agreements between commercial operators, laying down rules relating to the conclusion of such agreements,

---

[143] Article 197.
[144] Article 199.
[145] Article 197.
[146] Article 198.

the obligations of each party, breach of contract and, more generally, the effects of the agreement.

A. Conclusion of a commercial sale agreement

A commercial sale agreement may be made either in writing or orally, since no conditions are laid down as to form. Any means of evidence may be used to prove the existence and contents of the agreement[147].

The contract is formed when an offer has been made by one party and accepted by the other, provided the offer identifies the goods concerned and, either expressly or implicitly, determines the quantity and price or gives sufficient indications allowing these to be determined[148].

B. Obligations of the parties

Unless there are provisions to the contrary in the sale agreement, the parties to a commercial sale are bound by existing customs and practice in the relevant area of business as well as by the provisions of Articles 202 onwards of the Uniform Act[149]. International commercial sales may also be regulated by the Vienna Convention on the International Sale of Goods[150]. However, while the parties to a sale agreement may exclude application of the provisions of the Vienna Convention, the provisions of the Uniform Act governing commercial sales are mandatory.

1. Obligations of the seller

The seller is required to deliver the goods in question together with any relevant documents[151]. If the agreement does not stipulate otherwise, he must either deliver them to a carrier for onward delivery to the purchaser or, if the contract does not provide for transport, must make

---

[147] Article 208.

[148] Articles 210 and 217.

[149] Article 207.

[150] The Vienna Convention applies to sales between parties established in countries which are parties to the Convention or to sales where the rules of private international law lead to the application of the law of a party to the Convention. There are at present approximately 60 parties, and the Convention covers about two-thirds of world trade. While none of the OHADA Member States is to date a party, the Convention could apply, for example, to a contract for the sale of goods between a company in the United States (which is a party) and a company in an OHADA Member State.

[151] Article 219.

them available to the purchaser either at the place where they have been manufactured or where they are being held in stock, or at the seller's principal place of business[152].

If the agreement provides for transport, the seller must take the appropriate steps for the goods to be delivered to the place agreed with the purchaser. If he is not obliged to insure the goods himself, the seller must provide the purchaser with all information necessary to obtain insurance cover for the goods during carriage[153].

The seller must deliver goods that are in conformity with the order[154]. He is liable for any non-conformity as of the date of the transfer of risk to the purchaser, including latent defects which were hidden at that time and only come to light in the future[155]. The purchaser loses his right to claim for non-conformity if he does not act within a reasonable time following the date of discovery of the non-conformity or the date by which he should have discovered the non-conformity[156]. In any event, he loses the right if he does not act within one year of the date of receipt of the goods, unless there is a specific contractual warranty period which provides otherwise[157].

The seller is required to warrant against any other defects in the goods, and must deliver them free of any third-party rights or claims[158]. The seller is liable under this warranty if there is a hidden defect of such a nature that the purchaser would not have purchased the goods or would have paid a lower price for them if he had been aware of the defect[159].

2. Obligations of the purchaser

The purchaser must pay the price and take delivery of the goods[160]. The parties may provide in the contract that the price will be payable only after inspection of the goods by the purchaser[161]. The obligation to take delivery means that the purchaser must complete any formalities needed

---

[152] Article 220.
[153] Article 221.
[154] Article 224.
[155] Article 225.
[156] Article 228.
[157] Article 229.
[158] Article 230.
[159] Article 231.
[160] Article 233.
[161] Article 238.

to allow the seller to deliver the goods, and to remove the goods once they have reached the agreed point of delivery[162].

If payment of the price and delivery are to occur simultaneously, the seller is entitled to refuse to deliver the goods if he is not paid the agreed price plus any storage costs that might have been incurred because of the purchaser's failure to make payment on the due date[163].

C. Effects of the sale agreement

Transfer of title to goods is effective upon delivery or, if so decided by the parties, upon payment in full of the price[164]. The contract may provide for retention of title by the seller until payment in full. This is effective between the parties themselves only if it is expressly mentioned in the contract, the order or the delivery documents, and is effective as regards third parties only after registration of the retention of title with the RCCM[165].

Transfer of title normally entails the simultaneous transfer of risks. Hence, a purchaser is not exempted from the requirement to pay the price when the goods are lost or destroyed after title has been transferred, even if he has not physically taken delivery of the goods, unless the loss or destruction is due to the seller[166].

Where the sale provides for the carriage of goods, the risks are transferred to the purchaser when the goods are delivered to the first carrier[167]. If the sale occurs in the course of carriage, the risks are transferred at the time the contract is made. However, loss or damage to the goods is borne by the seller if he knew or should have known about such loss or damage when entering into the contract and did not inform the purchaser of this[168].

Goods which have not been identified and separated physically from other goods are deemed to have been put at the purchaser's disposal when they have been clearly identified for purposes of the contract. The risks are transferred only after such identification[169].

---

[162] Article 240.
[163] Article 241.
[164] Articles 283 and 284.
[165] Article 284.
[166] Article 285.
[167] Article 286.
[168] Article 287.
[169] Article 288.

D. Breach of contract

If it appears, after the agreement has been entered into, that a party will not perform a material part of its contractual obligations, because of either:

- a serious inadequacy in its ability to perform;
- insolvency; or
- the way in which it is preparing to perform, or is actually performing, the agreement

the other party may apply to the court to obtain an order authorizing it to defer performance of its own obligations[170].

If it becomes certain that one party will materially breach its obligations, the other party may apply to the court for cancellation of the contract[171].

A breach is deemed to be material when it substantially deprives a party of the benefit that it is legitimately entitled to expect under the contract, unless the failure by the other party to perform is due to a third party or to *force majeure*[172].

If a party considers that there has been a material breach of the contract, it must take all appropriate measures to mitigate its damages. If it fails to do so, the other party may request a reduction in the damages payable, equivalent to the amount of damage which could have been avoided[173].

A party may be exempted from liability if it can prove that its failure to perform was due to an event beyond its control[174]. However, there is no exemption if the failure to perform has been caused by a third party appointed by the defaulting party to perform all or part of its contractual obligations[175].

1. Breach by the seller

If the seller breaches his obligations, the purchaser is entitled to claim damages[176]. In addition, if the goods delivered do not comply with the

---

[170] Article 245.
[171] Article 246.
[172] Article 248.
[173] Article 266.
[174] Article 267.
[175] Article 268.
[176] Article 249.

contractual provisions, the purchaser may require the seller either to deliver replacement goods if the non-compliance is such as to constitute a material breach, or to remedy the non-compliance[177].

A purchaser may also give the seller a reasonable extension of the time period in which to perform its obligations. In such an event, the purchaser cannot take any action against the seller during the extended period. However, he does not lose his right to claim damages for late performance[178].

Finally, the purchaser may apply to the court for cancellation of the contract if the seller is in material breach of the contract or has failed to deliver the goods during any extension of the time period that may have been granted[179].

A purchaser may not however obtain cancellation of the contract or require delivery of replacement goods if he is not in a position to return the original goods in the condition in which he received them[180]. In such an event, he does nevertheless retain all other remedies, such as the right to claim damages or a reduction in price[181].

2. Breach by the purchaser

If the purchaser fails to perform his obligations, the seller is entitled to claim damages[182]. The seller may also give the purchaser a reasonable extension of the time within which to perform his obligations. He cannot take any action against the purchaser during the extension period. However, if he does so he does not lose the right to claim damages for late performance[183].

The seller is also entitled to apply to the court for cancellation of the sale contract where the purchaser is in material breach of the contract or fails to take delivery of the goods within any extension of the time period that may have been granted[184].

In the event of a failure to pay the contract price or any other sum that may be due, the seller is entitled to claim interest on the amount

---

[177] Article 250.
[178] Article 251.
[179] Article 254.
[180] Article 271.
[181] Article 272.
[182] Article 256.
[183] Article 257.
[184] Article 259.

concerned, calculated at the legal rate for commercial matters in the relevant Member State, without prejudice to any compensation he may also claim for damage suffered[185].

E. Limitation period

All claims must be filed within two years, failing which they will lapse[186]. However, this limitation period stops running if the claimant takes action to interrupt it, for example by serving a writ or a formal demand for payment or, if arbitration has been provided for, by beginning arbitral proceedings[187]. The question of whether a particular action is sufficient to interrupt the limitation period will depend upon the applicable national law[188].

The limitation period is interrupted as regards any other person who may be jointly and severally liable with the defendant if he is informed in writing of the proceedings filed by the claimant[189]. Similarly, any proceedings commenced by a sub-purchaser against the original purchaser of the goods also interrupt the limitation period applicable to the original purchaser's claim against the seller, on condition that the original purchaser informs the seller of such proceedings in writing before expiry of that limitation period[190].

---

[185] Article 263.
[186] Article 274.
[187] Articles 277–278.
[188] Article 277.
[189] Article 280.
[190] Article 280.

5

Commercial companies and economic interest groups

The Uniform Act on Commercial Companies and Economic Interest Groups entered into force on 1 January 1998. It forms the largest part of the OHADA reform, containing over 900 articles, and has considerably reorganized company law in the Member States. All the provisions of the Uniform Act are mandatory, and can be derogated from only when this is expressly stated in the Uniform Act[1].

The Member States inherited their initial legislation from the country that had colonized them, ie in most cases from France. French company law did not evolve very much during the colonial period, and when the French colonies achieved independence in the 1960s, most of them had legislation that dated back to 1867 and 1925. With certain exceptions (notably Guinea, Mali and Senegal), very few efforts were made at modernization after decolonization, and the old legislation was in force in most Member States at the end of the 1990s. This was also the case with anglophone Cameroon.

The new OHADA legislation relating to commercial companies takes much of its inspiration from modern French company law, and is better suited to contemporary commercial practices than the old law. As a result of the unification, commercial companies having their registered office on the territory of any one of the Member States are now subject to the

---

[1] Article 2.

same law throughout the OHADA region, whether they are foreign-owned companies or local companies.

To date, there has been very little case law specifically related to the Uniform Act and, as various doctrinal commentaries point out, it is sometimes difficult to interpret some of its provisions. Since the Uniform Act is based on French law to a great extent, French case law and doctrine may be relevant, and the courts in some countries such as Côte d'Ivoire may refer to it. However, this will not necessarily be determinative in relation to the uncertainties that arise.

Despite the influence of French law, common law lawyers will find many concepts and rules in the Uniform Act which will be familiar to them. It is, however, noteworthy that the provisions of the Uniform Act are mandatory, and that there is in general less flexibility in the way in which a company can be organized and function under OHADA law than, for example, under English law. This is not necessarily a disadvantage in a situation where one of the main objectives is to achieve business security. Indeed, as regards flexibility, there are also some differences between French company law and the Uniform Act. For example, the Uniform Act makes no provision for a *société par actions simplifiée (SAS)* of the kind recently introduced in French company law which, as its name indicates, is a company subject to simplified procedures, some of the main advantages of which are freedom in drafting the articles of association, the replacement of shareholders' meetings by written consultation or modern means of telecommunication, and the absence of any requirement for the directors to give details of their remuneration in the annual reports. Some of these possibilities, such as written consultation, are already provided for under the Uniform Act in certain circumstances, but if the Uniform Act were to be amended in the future, it might be worth considering making specific provision for a simplified type of company similar to the French SAS.

Section 1 of this Chapter discusses certain general provisions of the Uniform Act which are applicable, with certain specified exceptions, to all types of companies established in the OHADA region. This is followed in Section 2 by a detailed discussion of the *société anonyme*, a type of joint-stock company which closely corresponds to a limited company (either listed or unlisted) under English law, and which is the vehicle most commonly used by foreign investors for their projects in the region. Section 3 looks at the other type of limited company, the *société à responsabilité limitée*, which is generally used for smaller investments. Sections 4 and 5 examine in much less detail companies where the shareholders' liability is unlimited, and other structures which may be created under the Uniform Act. Section 6 deals with restructuring and transformation, and Section 7 discusses companies which make public offerings. As will be seen in that section, a regional stock exchange based in Abidjan (Côte d'Ivoire) is already in existence, and another in Libreville (Gabon) is expected to begin operations in the coming months, as is the Cameroon stock exchange. The existence of the OHADA uniform legislation relating to public offerings of securities will clearly be of vital importance to the financing of African companies and the functioning of these stock exchanges.

SECTION 1: GENERAL PROVISIONS

All commercial companies whose registered office is located on the territory of one of the Member States, including companies in which the State is a shareholder, regardless of the amount of its shareholding, are subject to the provisions of the Uniform Act[2]. Consequently, all companies incorporated as from 1 January 1998, its date of entry into force, have been subject to the Uniform Act since their incorporation. Companies that were already in existence as of that date had a two-year period, until 1 January 2000, within which to amend their articles of association so that they complied with the provisions of the Uniform Act[3].

The Uniform Act defines a commercial company as a contract between two or more persons who agree to make cash or other contributions to an activity for the purpose of sharing the resulting profits or savings, and to contribute towards losses[4].

Certain types of company may also be created by a single individual or legal entity[5]. This is the case of the private limited company (*société à responsabilité limitée* or *SARL*) and the joint-stock company (*société anonyme* or *SA*).

A. Creation of a company

The Uniform Act sets out general provisions concerning the creation of a commercial company which are applicable to every kind of company.

---

[2] Article 1.
[3] Article 908.
[4] Article 4.
[5] Article 5.

These include provisions relating to shareholders, articles of association, the registered office, the duration of the company, the various types of contributions, the various types of shares, the amount of share capital, and the registration process.

1. Shareholders

In principle, any individual or corporate legal entity may be a shareholder in a commercial company[6]. However, when a State or a State-owned company is a shareholder, specific obligations or requirements may need to be complied with under the applicable national law, as is the case for example in Côte d'Ivoire[7].

Minors and other persons not enjoying full legal capacity may not be shareholders in companies where their liability for the company's debts may exceed their contribution, ie in unlimited liability companies[8]. This is the case for all shareholders in a private partnership (*société en nom collectif* or *SNC*) and the active partners in a sleeping partnership (*société en commandite simple* or *SCS*), who must have commercial status. Moreover, a husband and wife cannot together be shareholders in an unlimited liability company such as an SNC or an SCS[9]. These restrictions do not however apply to shareholdings by such persons in an SA or an SARL.

2. Articles of association

The articles of association are established in writing either by notarized deed or by private contract. In the latter case, the articles of association must nevertheless be deposited with a notary[10].

A number of provisions must be contained in the articles of association, relating to duration, registered office, name, form, corporate objects, the identity of the founding shareholders and the amount of their respective contributions, the share capital, etc[11]. It is particularly important to ensure

---

[6] Article 7.

[7] Law No. 97-519 of 4 September 1997 defining and organizing State companies and Law No. 97-520 of 4 September 1997 on companies with public financial participation contain provisions regarding, for example, the minimum level of State representation on the Board of Directors.

[8] Article 8.

[9] Article 9.

[10] Article 10.

[11] Article 13.

at the outset that the corporate purpose is not defined too narrowly, since this may lead to unwanted restrictions in the future.

If the articles of association are not established in writing, the company is not considered as null and void, but as a *de facto* partnership (*société de fait*)[12].

3. Registered office

The address of the registered office must be chosen by the shareholders and mentioned in the articles of association[13]. The registered office may be either at the principal place of the company's activity, or the place where the financial and administrative management is located[14]. The address cannot be a PO box[15], but in practice the registered office may be temporarily located in a lawyer's or notary's office for the incorporation period.

4. Duration

The duration of a company must be indicated in its articles of association. Whereas under common law, companies are established for an indefinite duration, the duration of a company under the Uniform Act may not exceed 99 years from the date of the company's registration with the RCCM[16].

Expiry of the term results in the automatic winding-up of the company[17]. This might be perceived as a disadvantage by comparison with the flexibility that common law allows. However, an extension of the term may be decided in accordance with the conditions laid down by the Uniform Act for amending the articles of association, ie, for example, by an extraordinary shareholders' meeting in an SA, and winding-up is therefore not inevitable[18].

---

[12] See Section 4.D of this chapter.
[13] Article 23.
[14] Article 24.
[15] Article 25.
[16] Article 28.
[17] Article 30.
[18] Article 33.

5. Contributions

Each shareholder contributes to the share capital and, in return, the company issues shares corresponding to the shareholders' contributions[19]. The Uniform Act provides for three types of contribution: in cash, in kind, and in services.

(a) Contributions in cash

Contributions in cash are made in full at the time of the formation of the company or, in an SA, either in full or in instalments[20]. For all companies, in the event of a delay in payment, the cash contribution owed to the company will automatically bear interest from the date on which the payment was due, at the official rate prevailing in the relevant Member State[21].

(b) Contributions in kind

A shareholder may make a contribution in kind by transferring to the company real or personal rights and making available to the company the physical assets to which such rights relate[22]. In every type of company, contributions in kind must be made in full at the time the company is created[23]. In certain cases the value of the contribution is determined by an in-kind contributions appraiser (*commissaire aux apports*)[24].

(c) Contributions in services

Contributions may also be made in services (*apport en industrie*). With this type of contribution, the shareholder undertakes to work for the company[25]. Such contributions are possible only in SAs and SARLs.

---

[19] Articles 37 and 38.
[20] Article 41.
[21] Article 43.
[22] Article 45.
[23] Article 45.
[24] Article 49.
[25] Article 40.

6. Shares and other securities

The issued shares give their holders the right to share in the company's profits and, when the company is wound up, in its net assets[26]. In principle, they also give shareholders the right to vote on any collective decisions[27].

Shares also impose upon their holders the obligation to share the burden of the company's losses[28]. In limited liability companies, this burden is limited to the amount of each shareholder's shareholding, whereas in other types of companies it is unlimited.

These rights and obligations are proportional to the amount of each shareholder's contribution, unless the articles of association provide otherwise. However, any provisions in the company's articles which might attribute all of the profits to a single shareholder or exonerate a single shareholder from all liability for losses, and any provisions which might exclude a shareholder from sharing in any profits or charge all losses to a single shareholder, are deemed to be inapplicable and of no effect, ie can be declared null and void[29].

All the shares issued by a company must have the same nominal value[30]. The nominal value of shares may be freely determined in companies where the shareholders have unlimited liability. In an SARL the nominal value must be at least 5,000 FCFA and in an SA at least 10,000 FCFA.

As an efficient way of obtaining funds from private investors, an SA may also issue bonds, which it remunerates at a predetermined rate. Conditions for the issuance of bonds and the rights of bondholders are regulated by Articles 779 *et seq* of the Uniform Act.

7. Capital

The share capital consists of the various types of contributions mentioned above, together with any capitalized profits, premiums paid on the issuance of new shares, and reserves[31].

---

[26] Article 53.

[27] In an SA, the articles of association may however require a minimum shareholding for shareholders to be entitled to attend ordinary general meetings (Article 548); and special meetings may be held for holders of different categories of shares (Article 555).

[28] Article 54.

[29] Article 54.

[30] Article 56.

[31] Article 62.

The amount of share capital may be freely determined by the shareholders in unlimited liability companies[32]. However, for an SA the Uniform Act requires there to be a minimum registered capital of 10 million FCFA and for an SARL one million FCFA[33].

The share capital may be reduced or increased in accordance with the procedure applicable to amendments of the articles of association in the type of company in question[34].

A capital increase may be made by additional contributions by shareholders to the company or by the capitalization of reserves, profits or share premiums[35].

A capital reduction may be made by reimbursements to shareholders or by imputation of the company's losses against the capital[36]. When the reduction is made by reimbursement, the shareholders may receive either cash or other assets of the company[37].

8. Registration

All companies, except joint ventures in the form of a *société en participation* (which, as will be seen, are not really companies at all), must be registered with the RCCM[38].

Pursuant to Article 27 of the Uniform Act on General Commercial Law, companies must apply for registration with the RCCM within one month of their creation. Applications are filed with the registry of the court having jurisdiction at the place of the registered office of the company. A certificate of incorporation giving details of the company, including the registration number, is given to the company upon registration, and the details of the company are then made available to third parties at the RCCM[39].

From the date of registration, the company is considered as a corporate body[40]. Prior to registration, the existence of the company cannot be relied upon vis-à-vis third parties.

---

[32] Article 65.
[33] Articles 311 and 387.
[34] Article 67.
[35] Article 68.
[36] Article 69.
[37] Article 70.
[38] Article 97.
[39] Uniform Act on General Commercial Law, Article 30.
[40] Article 98.

B. Management powers

The generic French term of *'dirigeants sociaux'* is frequently used in the Uniform Act to refer to various members of the management of a company. Depending upon the context, this term may cover all or any of the following: managing directors, chairmen of the board, persons exercising the functions of both chairman and general manager, members of the board of directors, general managers and deputy general managers (even if they are not members of the board), and managers. Other provisions of the Uniform Act refer to specific categories of managers. For the sake of simplicity, reference will be made in this chapter only to 'the management' or 'members of the management' when the generic term is used in the Uniform Act; otherwise, the specific category in question will be identified.

The management has various defined powers within the company itself and vis-à-vis third parties:

- As regards the company, the management has in principle full management powers. However, the articles of association or a general meeting of shareholders may restrict these powers[41]. For instance, it may be provided that certain types of contracts or banking operations for a value above a defined threshold require prior authorization of the shareholders or the board of directors. However, such restrictions may not be relied upon as against third parties acting in good faith[42].
- As regards third parties, the company is bound by any act of the management which does not fall within the corporate purpose as defined in the articles of association, unless it can be shown that any third party claiming the benefit of such an act either knew that the act was *ultra vires* or could not have been unaware of this in the circumstances[43].

C. Shareholders' decisions

Every shareholder has the right to vote upon collective decisions unless the Uniform Act provides otherwise. Any provisions to the contrary that may be contained in the articles of association are deemed to be of no effect, ie may be declared null and void[44]. However, specific shares with

---

[41] Article 123.
[42] Articles 121 and 123.
[43] Article 122.
[44] Article 125.

double voting rights or with limited voting rights may be issued for an SA[45]. Also, if an SA acquires its own shares, those shares carry no voting rights[46].

There are two kinds of collective decisions: ordinary and extraordinary. The procedure to be followed for these decisions is laid down in specific provisions of the Uniform Act for each type of company.

Decisions adopted at meetings of shareholders are recorded in minutes which must indicate the time and place of the meeting, the names of the shareholders present or represented, the agenda, the text of the resolutions put to the vote and the outcome of the vote[47]. The minutes are inserted in a register kept at the registered office of the company and their pages are numbered and initialled by the registrar of the court[48].

D. Accounts and auditing requirements

The financial year corresponds in principle to the calendar year, except for the first year of the company's existence, which may have a longer or shorter duration[49].

At the end of each financial year, the management must prepare the company's annual summary financial statements (*états financiers de synthèse*), and must also prepare a management report[50].

For companies with a statutory auditor, these documents must be forwarded to the auditor at least 45 days before the date of the annual general meeting which is to be held to approve the annual accounts[51]. The appointment of statutory auditors is mandatory in an SA and is optional in an SARL unless certain thresholds as to capital, turnover and personnel are exceeded, when the appointment becomes mandatory[52].

E. Early warning procedure (procédure d'alerte)

This preliminary procedure, which is designed to alert the management when it appears that the continuation of the company's activity is at risk,

---

[45] Articles 543–544 and 548.
[46] Article 542.
[47] Article 134.
[48] Article 135.
[49] Uniform Act on Accounting Law, Article 7.
[50] Article 137.
[51] Article 140.
[52] See further details in Sections 2 and 3 of this chapter.

is an innovation for most of the Member States. It can be initiated either by a statutory auditor or by a shareholder.

1. Early warning procedure initiated by a statutory auditor

If during the course of his duties a statutory auditor becomes aware of anything which may jeopardize the continuation of the company's activities, he may ask the management for explanations[53]. The management must respond within one month, with their analysis of the situation and any measures that may be envisaged to remedy the situation[54].

In an SARL, if the management fails to respond or if the response seems unsatisfactory, the auditor prepares a special report to be sent to the shareholders or presented at the next general meeting[55].

In an SA, if the management fails to respond or gives an unsatisfactory response, the auditor requests the convening of a board meeting to deliberate upon the situation[56]. If the board of directors is not convened or if in the auditor's view the company remains at risk, the auditor prepares a special report to be presented at the next shareholders' meeting or, if the situation is urgent, at a special shareholders' meeting which may be called by the auditor himself if the management fails to call it[57].

2. Early warning procedure initiated by a shareholder

Any shareholder who is not a member of the management has the right, twice a year, to send written questions to the management regarding anything which may jeopardize the continuation of the company's activities. The management must reply to such questions within one month and, if the company has an auditor, send a copy of its response to him[58].

F. Management liabilities

The Uniform Act provides for two types of management liabilities: civil and criminal[59].

---

[53] Articles 150 and 153.
[54] Articles 151 and 154.
[55] Article 152.
[56] Article 155.
[57] Article 156.
[58] Articles 157 and 158.
[59] The relevant rules are contained principally in Articles 161–172, 330–332, 740–743 and 886–905 and also in the Uniform Act on Collective Proceedings for the Clearing of Debts, Articles 180–215.

1. Civil liability

(a) General provisions

The management may be liable either to third parties or to the company itself[60]. The Uniform Act contains both general and specific provisions in this regard. The general provisions do not attempt to define any particular actions that give rise to liability, but are worded very broadly, referring simply to faults committed in the performance of management duties, or failure to comply with the law or with the articles of association.

(i) Liability to third parties

Without prejudice to any liability of the company itself, all members of the management may individually be held liable to third parties for faults committed in the performance of their duties, or for failure to comply with the law governing their particular type of company or with the articles of association[61]. The term 'third parties' here includes shareholders of the company, insofar as they may have suffered damage distinct from that which might be suffered by the company itself[62]. In cases where several members of the management are involved in the commission of the fault, they are jointly and severally liable to third parties. However, in their relations with each other, the court may determine the share of damages to be borne by each of them[63].

For this type of liability, proceedings must be brought within three years following the commission of the fault or, where the fault has been concealed, within three years following its discovery[64].

(ii) Liability to the company

Each member of the management may be held liable to the company for faults committed in the performance of his duties, or for failure to comply with the law governing the type of company in question or with the articles of association[65]. The rules relating to time limits and the ultimate

---

[60] General provisions on liability in all types of company are contained in articles 161–172. Similar provisions relating to SAs are contained in Articles 738–743, and to SARLs in Articles 330–332.

[61] Articles 161, 330 and 740.

[62] Article 162.

[63] Article 161.

[64] Article 164.

[65] Articles 165, 330 and 740.

sharing of liability proportionate to the contribution of each member of the management are the same as for a suit by a third party[66].

In principle, a corporate action is instituted by the management itself[67]. However, in the event the management fails to take such action, the shareholders themselves may do so, subject to certain conditions. In an SA, shareholders representing at least 5 per cent of the registered capital, either individually or collectively, may institute proceedings in the company's name against one or more of the directors[68]. In an SARL, shareholders representing at least one-quarter of the total number of shareholders and at least 25 per cent of the registered capital may institute proceedings against the manager[69].

Pursuant to Articles 168, 331 and 742 of the Uniform Act, any clause of the articles of association subjecting the institution of an action in the company's interest to a prior notice or to the authorization of a general meeting or of the management, or waiving the right to institute such proceedings, is null and void. Further, Articles 169, 331 and 742 of the Uniform Act prohibit any decision by the general meeting or the management purporting to terminate such proceedings. These provisions protect minority shareholders against potential abuses by the management or the majority shareholders[70].

(b) Specific provisions

The Uniform Act also contains a series of specific provisions regarding management liabilities which arise in certain defined circumstances, as follows:

(i). If a company is declared null and void, for example, in the case of an SA because the constituent general meeting has been improperly convened or the rules relating to quorum and majority at that meeting have not been complied with, thus resulting in nullity of the company, the management in office at the time of the event

---

[66] Articles 165, 170, 330, 332, 740 and 743.
[67] Article 166.
[68] Articles 167 and 741.
[69] Articles 167 and 331.
[70] Compare this with the common law rule in *Foss v. Harbottle* (1843) 2 Hare 461, according to which minority shareholders in principle have no right to bring an action in the company's name.

giving rise to the nullity may be declared jointly and severally liable for damage suffered by third parties as a result of the nullity[71].

(ii). The shareholders and directors of an SA are jointly and severally liable vis-à-vis third parties for a period of five years for the value attributed to contributions in kind and/or special benefits when this value is different from the value determined by the in-kind contributions appraiser[72]. This liability might arise, for example, if a gross overvaluation of a contribution in kind has given third parties a misleading impression of the worth of the company's assets.

(iii). The founder shareholders and the first members of the management are jointly and severally liable for damage caused by the omission of a mandatory detail from the articles of association or for the omission or improper fulfilment of a prescribed formality for the creation of the company[73]. In the event of an amendment of the articles of association, the members of the management in office at the time of the amendment incur the same liabilities[74]. The right to institute proceedings for such liability lapses after five years from either the date of registration of the company or the date of publication of the deed amending the articles of association, as the case may be[75].

(iv). As will be seen in greater detail in Section 2 of this Chapter in relation to an SA, any agreement between a company and one of its directors is subject to prior authorization of the board of directors and subsequent ratification by a general meeting of shareholders, unless it relates to an operation concluded on arm's length terms in the normal course of business. The same rule applies to agreements to which the company is a party, in which a director has an indirect interest or where he is also a director of the other party to the agreement. When such an agreement is entered into without the prior authorization of the board of directors, or when the general meeting subsequently refuses ratification, the director concerned, and possibly the other members of the board of directors, may be held liable for any harmful consequences to the company[76]. Similar rules are applicable to SARLs[77].

---

[71] Articles 256 and 413.

[72] Articles 312 and 409.

[73] Article 78.

[74] Article 79.

[75] Article 80.

[76] Articles 443–444.

[77] Articles 350 *et seq.* See also Section 3.G of this chapter.

(v).   The management has the power to bind the company vis-à-vis
third parties. As mentioned above, the company is bound even by
acts of the management that do not fall within its objects or that
are prohibited by the articles of association, when the third party
involved has acted in good faith[78]. In such an event, and if the act
has damaging consequences for the company, the company or its
shareholders may bring a corporate action against the member of
the management concerned.

(vi). Finally, management liability can be increased in the event of the
company's insolvency. This type of liability is provided for in the
Uniform Act on Collective Proceedings for the Clearing of Debts,
which provides that one or more members of the management may
be ordered to pay part or all of the company's debts, or may
themselves be declared insolvent if they are shown to have contributed to the company's situation by faults committed in the performance of their management functions[79].

2. Criminal liability

Articles 889 *et seq* of the Uniform Act define offences giving rise to
criminal liability of the management. The penalties themselves are laid
down by the local criminal law of each Member State.

Offences subject to criminal penalties include the following:

- knowingly paying fictitious dividends[80];
- publishing or presenting to the shareholders an inaccurate account of
  the year's transactions, the financial situation or the company's assets,
  with a view to concealing the true circumstances of the company[81];
- using in bad faith the company's assets or credit, in the knowledge
  that it is for purposes that are contrary to the company's interests, for
  personal ends or in favour of another corporate body in which the
  manager concerned has a direct or indirect interest[82];
- knowingly preventing shareholders from participating in a general
  meeting[83];

---

[78] Articles 121–123.
[79] See Chapter 7.
[80] Article 889.
[81] Article 890.
[82] Article 891.
[83] Article 892.

- wrongful acts in the context of an increase or reduction of capital, including the following[84]:
  - issuance of new shares before the depositary's certificate has been issued; before the requisite prior formalities have been carried out; before the previously-subscribed capital has been fully paid up; before the new shares corresponding to contributions in kind have been fully paid up; before the required portion of contributions in cash has been paid up; or, if applicable, before the full share premium has been paid at the time of subscription;
  - failure to give a preferential subscription right to shareholders in proportion to their existing shareholding, unless otherwise decided by the general meeting or the shareholders concerned; failure to allow for a minimum 20-day subscription period; or failure to allocate any remaining unsubscribed shares to existing subscribers;
  - the provision or confirmation of inaccurate information at the general meeting held to decide upon a waiver of the existing shareholders' preferential subscription rights;
  - a reduction of capital in the knowledge that the shareholders' equality has not been respected, or that the planned reduction in capital has not been communicated to the auditors 45 days before the general meeting held to vote upon the reduction.
- failure to appoint statutory auditors when this is required by law, or failure to convene them to the general meetings of shareholders[85];
- obstructing verifications or audits by the auditors or refusing to communicate to them any relevant document[86]; or
- when the value of the company's assets falls below one-half of the value of the share capital as a result of losses appearing in the summary financial statements[87]:
  - failure to convene an extraordinary general meeting of shareholders within four months of approval of the accounts showing such losses, with a view to deciding whether the company should be wound up; or
  - in the event of a decision to wind up the company, failure to inform the commercial court, register the winding-up with the commercial registry, and publish a notice in a legal journal.

---

[84] Articles 893–896.
[85] Article 897.
[86] Article 900.
[87] Article 901.

G. Winding-up

The Uniform Act provides for seven different situations in which a company may be wound up[88]:

- upon accomplishment of the company's purpose;
- upon expiry of the term for which the company was formed (currently 99 years maximum) unless the term has been renewed;
- by annulment;
- by decision of the shareholders;
- by court order at the request of a shareholder if there are legitimate reasons for the winding-up;
- by a judgment ordering liquidation in the event of insolvency;
- for any other reason provided by the articles of association.

The winding-up of a company may be relied upon as against third parties only after its publication in the RCCM[89].

In cases where the company has several shareholders, the winding-up automatically entails liquidation of the company's assets and liabilities. In cases where a single shareholder holds all the shares, the company is not put into liquidation, but there is a total transfer of the company's assets and liabilities to that shareholder[90].

H. Types of companies

The Uniform Act has created various types of companies with either limited liability or unlimited liability. There are two types of limited liability company: the *société anonyme* (or *SA*) and the *société à responsabilité limitée* (or *SARL*). In both these types of company the liability of each shareholder for the debts of the company is limited to the amount of his shareholding. These types of company will be dealt with in Sections 2 and 3, below. Section 4 will then deal with the various categories of companies where the shareholders' liability is unlimited.

---

[88] Article 200.
[89] Article 201.
[90] Article 201.

SECTION 2: *SOCIÉTÉ ANONYME* OR SA

A. Definition

The most important type of company under the Uniform Act, which is generally used for large investments, is the *société anonyme*. This is a type of joint-stock company. It may have any number of shareholders, and it may be wholly owned by a single shareholder[91]. It must have a capital of at least 10 million FCFA, or 100 million FCFA if it makes public offerings[92].

B. Method of incorporation

Several steps are involved in the incorporation of a *société anonyme*. Although there is no legal requirement to this effect, the services of a notary are usually used in practice for all steps of the incorporation process, since in any event signatures have to be authenticated as part of the process.

1. Preparation of subscription bulletins

Subscription bulletins (*bulletins de souscription*) evidence the subscription of cash contributions. They contain certain information regarding the company, the shares and the subscriber, and are issued by the founders of the company and signed by each subscriber[93]. One original copy is held by the company, while a second is provided to the notary who in turn must draw up a statement of subscription and payment.

2. Deposit of funds and notarized statement of subscription and payment

While the share capital must be fully subscribed before the articles of association are signed, it is not necessary for it to be fully paid up before that date. Instead, subscribers must pay at least one-quarter of the value of their shares, and have a period of up to three years within which to complete payment[94].

---

[91] Article 385. This is a significant difference between OHADA law and Anglo-Saxon law, which does not allow for single-shareholder companies.
[92] Articles 387 and 824.
[93] Articles 390–392.
[94] Articles 388–389.

The funds are deposited either with a notary or in a special account opened in the name of the company[95]. This account must be held by a bank in the Member State where the registered office of the company is to be located. If the funds are deposited with a bank, the bank gives the depositor a certificate of deposit confirming that the funds have been deposited.

On presentation of the subscription bulletins and, if applicable, the certificate issued by the bank, the notary draws up a deed, referred to as the notarized statement of subscription and payment (*déclaration notariée de souscription et de versement*). This deed witnesses that the amount of the subscriptions declared corresponds to the amount appearing on the subscription bulletins and that the amount paid corresponds, as the case may be, to the total sums of money deposited in his office or appearing in the bank's certificate, which must be appended to the notarized statement[96].

Where there are contributions in kind, these must be valued by an in-kind contributions appraiser (*commissaire aux apports*), chosen from the official list of auditors in the Member State concerned. A constituent general meeting must be held to approve this valuation, and title to the in-kind contributions must be transferred to the new company[97].

3. Preparation and notarization of the articles of association

As has already been mentioned, the provisions of the Uniform Act are mandatory, except where explicitly stated otherwise. This means that where a particular type of company has been chosen, the general provisions of the Uniform Act and its specific provisions relating to the chosen type of company automatically apply, unless the Uniform Act explicitly authorizes the shareholders to derogate from them by agreement or to supplement them with their own provisions.

As a result, a company's articles of association may be quite brief, because the choice of a particular type of company provided for by the Uniform Act automatically involves the application of mandatory provisions. However, for parties who are unfamiliar with the Uniform Act it may be advisable to have fairly detailed articles of association which may be used as a guide on a day-to-day basis.

---

[95] Article 393.
[96] Article 394.
[97] Articles 45 and 408.

The articles of association are established by notarized deed or by private contract. However, when established by private contract, they must nevertheless be deposited in a notary's office[98]. The articles of association may only be amended by the same notarial procedure.

The articles are signed by the subscribers or their proxies after the notarized statement of subscription and payment has been drawn up[99].

As mentioned above in Section 1, certain indications are obligatory in the articles of association, whichever type of company is chosen. In addition, when the company is an SA, the articles will normally name the first directors and auditors[100]. However, these may be appointed subsequently by the constituent general meeting, if such a meeting is held[101].

4. Constituent general meeting

A constituent general meeting must be held if the new company makes a public offering of shares[102] or if, as has been seen, any contributions to the capital of a new company are to be made in kind. It seems however that such a meeting does not need to be held when all the contributions are made in cash and there is no public offering. Although the Uniform Act is rather ambiguous on this question, Article 101 provides that a company is effectively constituted once its articles of association have been signed, and it may therefore be inferred from this that the constituent general meeting is optional except in cases where the Uniform Act requires it to be held. In practice, however, notaries charged with the creation of an SA tend to arrange for a constituent general meeting to be held, even if this is not required under the Uniform Act.

In cases where a constituent general meeting is held, in addition to approving or rejecting the report of the in-kind contributions appraiser on the valuation of contributions in kind, it ascertains that the capital has been fully subscribed and that the shares have been paid up to the required extent. It also adopts the articles of association, appoints the first directors and auditors, and ratifies acts performed by the founders on the company's behalf prior to incorporation[103].

---

[98] Article 10.

[99] Article 396.

[100] Article 397.

[101] Article 410.

[102] See Section 7 of this chapter.

[103] Article 410.

5. Registration with the RCCM

Once the articles of association have been signed and notarized, the company must be registered with the RCCM. It is only once registration has been made that the company acquires its own separate legal personality. The following supporting documents must be attached to the application for registration, failing which it will be rejected:

- two certified true copies of the articles of association;
- two original copies of the notarized statement of subscription and payment;
- two certified true copies of a list of the first directors;
- two extracts from the criminal record of the first directors;
- any other documents that may be obligatory under the local law[104].

The application itself must indicate:

- the name of the company;
- if applicable, its trading name, acronym or logo;
- its activities;
- the form of the company, ie *société anonyme*;
- the amount of the registered capital, indicating the amounts of cash and in-kind contributions;
- the address of the registered office;
- the duration of the company;
- the full name, date and place of birth, and domicile of the directors;
- the full name, date and place of birth, and domicile of the auditors[105].

Any change in the company's details or articles must be filed and registered with the relevant RCCM and published in a legal journal.

Appendix D at the end of this volume includes copies of the forms to be used for the registration of companies with the RCCM. As mentioned in Chapter 4, however, the RCCM is not yet functioning properly in all the Member States, largely due to the absence of adequate computerization. It is hoped that this situation will be remedied in the near future and that the same forms and procedures will then be used in all the Member States.

---

[104] Uniform Act on General Commercial Law, Article 28.

[105] Uniform Act on General Commercial Law, Article 27. For an SA it is not necessary to provide a list of the shareholders. This is required only in companies where the shareholders have unlimited liability for the company's debts.

6. Publication in legal journal

Within a period of 15 days following registration of the company, a notice must be inserted in a journal which is empowered to publish legal notices in the Member State where the company is registered[106]. These are the national legal journal and any newspapers which have been specifically authorized by the competent authorities to publish such notices, and national news dailies, on condition that they make effective sales, have been appearing for more than six months, and are distributed throughout the country[107].

Article 262 of the Uniform Act sets out the details regarding the company which must be contained in the notice. The notice must be signed by the notary or by the founding shareholders.

C. Management

The Uniform Act provides for two alternative methods of management for a *société anonyme*, one of which must be chosen in the articles of association[108]:

- a sole managing director (*administrateur général*) acting as chief executive officer, assisted if required by one or more deputy managing directors; or
- a board of directors (*conseil d'administration*) presided by either (i) a chairman of the board (*président du conseil d'administration*) who must be assisted by a general manager (*directeur général*) acting as chief executive officer, or (ii) a chairman of the board also acting as chief executive officer (*président-directeur général*), who may be assisted by one or more deputy general managers.

When an SA has more than three shareholders, it cannot be managed by a sole managing director, but must have a board of directors[109]. On the other hand, if an SA is wholly owned by a single shareholder, it cannot have a board of directors, but must have a managing director[110].

---

[106] Article 261.
[107] Article 257.
[108] Article 414.
[109] Article 494.
[110] Article 417.

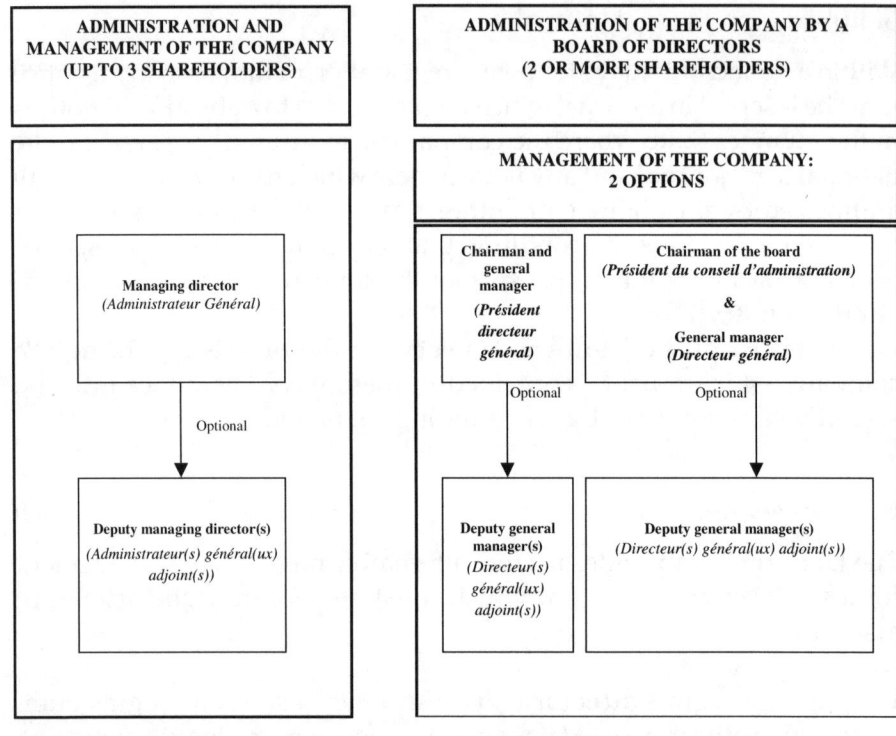

Figure 5.1 Administration and management of an SA

1. Administration and management by a managing director (*administrateur général*)

In an SA with a managing director there is no board of directors, and the managing director assumes the administration and management of the company under his own responsibility, although he may be assisted by a deputy managing director[111].

(a) Appointment and term of office

The first managing director is appointed in the articles of association or by the constituent general meeting. During the life of the company appointments are made by the ordinary general meeting[112].

---

[111] Articles 494 and 510.
[112] Article 495.

The managing director may be chosen from among the shareholders or may be a non-shareholder[113]. His term of office is freely determined in the articles of association. However, it must not exceed six years if he has been appointed during the life of the company, or two years if he has been appointed in the articles of association or by the constituent general meeting[114]. The term of office is however renewable[115].

(b) Powers

The managing director has the widest possible powers to act within the company's purpose, except for powers expressly reserved to general meetings of shareholders or as may be defined by the articles of association or by the shareholders at a general meeting[116]. He must also convene and preside over shareholders' meetings.

The managing director represents the company in its dealings with third parties. The company is bound by his acts, even when such acts do not fall within the company's objects[117].

(c) Remuneration

The managing director may have an employment contract with the company, on condition that this contract corresponds to effective employment, distinct from the managing director's functions, and subject to approval by the ordinary general meeting[118].

(d) Restrictions on number of offices held

No person may simultaneously hold more than three offices as managing director in SAs having their registered offices on the territory of the same Member State[119]. Nor may a managing director hold concurrently more than two offices as chairman and general manager or general manager of SAs having their registered office in the same Member State[120].

---

[113] Article 495.
[114] Article 496.
[115] Article 496.
[116] Article 498.
[117] Article 498.
[118] Article 513.
[119] Article 497, para 1.
[120] Article 497, para 2.

2. Board of directors

(a) General considerations relating to directors and the board of directors

(i) Composition of the board

The board of directors must have at least three and no more than twelve directors, except where the company makes public offerings, in which case it may have up to 15 directors[121]. These limits have apparently been imposed to ensure that decision-making is not too unwieldy a process.

Members of the board do not have to be shareholders of the company. However, no more than one-third of the members of the board may be non-shareholders[122]. Therefore, in an SA having three directors, two directors would have to be shareholders, and only one could be a non-shareholder. This rule may cause problems in certain companies, where shareholders may wish to bring in a number of directors from outside the company. In such a case, at least some of these directors may have to receive at least one of the company's shares in order to comply with the rule, but this will result in the original shareholders running the risk of not being able to recover that share if the director leaves the company. As directors may be changed on a regular basis, especially in groups of companies, it might be useful to explore other ways of having 'directors' qualifying shares', for example by means of a loan of shares as is the practice in France.

(ii) Appointment, term of office and revocation

The first directors must be designated in the articles of association or at the constituent general meeting[123].

During the life of the company, the directors are appointed by the ordinary general meeting[124]. Every appointment of a director must be published with the RCCM[125].

Corporate bodies may be appointed as directors. However, they must appoint a permanent representative to sit on the board during their term of office. A permanent representative does not need to be a shareholder of the company[126].

---

[121] Articles 416 and 829.
[122] Article 417.
[123] Article 419.
[124] Article 419.
[125] Article 427.
[126] Article 421.

The term of office of the directors and the method of their election may be freely determined by the articles of association. However, the term of office may not exceed six years during the life of the company, or two years in the case of appointment in the articles of association or by the constituent general meeting[127]. The term of office is however renewable unless otherwise provided by the articles of association.

Directors' tenures can be revoked at any time by decision of an ordinary general meeting of the shareholders[128]. This is referred to as *ad nutum* revocation, which means that no reasons have to be given and the director cannot claim damages for wrongful dismissal.

(iii) Powers

The board of directors has the widest possible powers to act in all circumstances in the name of the company. The board must however exercise these powers in accordance with the company's purpose and without prejudice to such powers as are expressly attributed to the shareholders[129].

In particular the board of directors has the following powers:

- to determine the company's objectives and the manner in which its business is managed;
- to supervise the general manager; and
- to draw up the company's accounts for each financial year[130].

The board of directors must also give its prior authorization if any bonds or guarantees are to be granted by the company to cover obligations of third parties[131].

The company is bound by any act of the board of directors. This includes acts which are outside the company's purpose, unless it can be shown either that any third party claiming the benefit of such an act (a) knew that the act was outside the company's purpose or (b) could not have been unaware of this in the circumstances. The company cannot rely upon publication of the articles of association as proof for this purpose[132]. On the other hand, as in certain common law jurisdictions,

---

[127] Article 420.
[128] Article 433.
[129] Article 435.
[130] Article 435.
[131] Article 449.
[132] Articles 122 and 436.

notice of the articles of association given to the third party concerned would prevent the third party from relying upon an *ultra vires* act of the board.

The board of directors may delegate to one or more of its members special powers for one or more specified purposes, but not so as to circumvent the powers granted to a general manager, unless the general manager has specifically agreed to the delegation in advance[133].

(iv) Remuneration

Like executive directors in the common law tradition, who are often senior management staff of the company, under the Uniform Act directors can be paid employees of the company[134]. Unless otherwise provided in the articles of association, all the directors are allowed to hold employment contracts with the company. In addition or in the alternative, they may receive an allowance for acting as directors[135]. Exceptional allowances may also be granted for specific assignments[136].

(v) Restrictions on number of offices held

A director may not at the same time be a member of more than five boards of directors in SAs having their registered offices in the territory of the same Member State[137]. This rule applies both to individuals acting in their own name and to permanent representatives of corporate bodies. No distinction is made as to whether the directors are shareholders of the company or non-shareholders.

The restriction only concerns boards of directors in the same country. Moreover, since it does not concern the number of director's mandates but the number of boards of directors, it therefore seems possible for an individual to be both a director in his personal capacity and have a seat as a permanent representative of a corporate body on the same board.

A director who exceeds the limit on the number of offices must resign from one of the boards within a period of three months. If he fails to do so before expiry of this deadline, he will be deemed to have resigned from his most recent directorship and must refund any remuneration that he has received on account of that directorship[138].

---

[133] Article 437.
[134] Article 426.
[135] Article 431.
[136] Article 432.
[137] Article 425.
[138] Article 425.

(vi) Co-option

If a vacancy arises on the board of directors, the board may co-opt a new director to fill the vacancy. If the number of directors falls below the minimum required by the articles of association, the board of directors must co-opt a new director or directors within three months. In either case, the co-option must be ratified by the next ordinary general meeting of shareholders[139].

If the number of directors falls below the minimum required by law, the remaining directors cannot make appointments by co-option, but must immediately call an ordinary general meeting to make up the numbers[140].

(b) Board meetings

(i) Convening

Directors must be sent notice of each board meeting by the chairman of the board in accordance with any rules that may be laid down in the articles of association[141]. The articles may specify the required notice period and the means of giving notice such as fax, registered letter, e-mail etc. If the board members have not all received proper notice, the meeting will be invalid and must be reconvened for a later date.

There is no obligation as to the number of meetings to be held each year, save for the legal requirement to approve the accounts[142]. However, directors representing at least one-third of the board may convene a meeting if no meeting has been held during the previous two months[143].

(ii) Quorum and majority

In general, all decisions are to be taken by a majority of the members of the board who are present or represented at the meeting. However, increased majority requirements may be included in the articles of association[144].

---

[139] Article 429.
[140] Article 429.
[141] Article 453.
[142] Articles 452 and 453.
[143] Article 453.
[144] Article 454.

If there is a tied vote on any issue, the chairman of the meeting has a casting vote unless otherwise provided by the articles of association[145]. If the articles of association do provide otherwise, and if there is a deadlock, the board of directors must be reconvened to meet with the same agenda at a later date.

(iii) Holding of meetings

The Uniform Act contains no specific provisions as to the place where meetings are to be held. As a result, unless the articles of association provide otherwise, meetings may be held either at the company's registered office or at any other place, which could include a location in a foreign country. On the other hand, it is not clear whether the Uniform Act allows articles of association to provide for meetings to be held by modern means of telecommunication, instead of holding physical meetings.

Meetings are chaired by the chairman of the board. If he is not present, the meeting is chaired by a director chosen from among themselves by the other directors present[146].

Unless otherwise provided by the articles of association, each director may appoint another director by letter, telex or telefax as a proxy to represent him at a board meeting. However, no director may act as proxy for more than one other person at any meeting[147].

(iv) Minutes

Resolutions passed at a board meeting must be written up in the form of minutes entered in a special register, the pages of which are numbered and initialled by a judge of the relevant court and kept at the company's registered office[148]. The intervention of the judge in this regard is intended to procure greater legal security and to ensure the authenticity of the resolutions. The minutes must indicate the date and place of the meeting and the names of the directors present or represented, or absent and not represented. They must also mention the presence or absence of any persons called to the meeting for legal reasons, and the presence of any other person who was present during all or part of the meeting.

---

[145] Article 454.
[146] Article 457.
[147] Article 456.
[148] Article 458.

The minutes must be certified as true by the chairman of the meeting and by at least one other director[149]. Copies or extracts of the minutes may be validly certified by the chairman of the board, the general manager, or by any other person duly empowered to do so[150].

The minutes are presumed to be a genuine record of the proceedings to which they relate unless the contrary is shown[151].

(c) Chairman of the board of directors/Chairman and general manager

As mentioned above, an SA with a board of directors may be managed by either one of two methods:

- by a chairman of the board of directors, appointed by the board from among its members and assisted by a general manager, who may in turn be assisted by one or more deputy general managers;
- or by a single person combining the functions of chairman and general manager (*président-directeur général*), appointed by the board of directors from among its members, who may also be assisted by one or more deputy general managers.

The Uniform Act contains a series of provisions which are applicable to the chairman of the board, whether or not he is also the general manager.

(i) Appointment, term of office and revocation

The chairman is appointed by the board of directors from among its members[152]. His term of office may not exceed the term of his directorship, but is renewable if the directorship is renewed[153]. The chairman's tenure may be revoked at any time by the board of directors (*ad nutum* revocation)[154].

(ii) Powers

The chairman presides over board meetings and the general meetings of shareholders[155].

---

[149] Article 459.
[150] Article 460.
[151] Article 461.
[152] Articles 462 and 477.
[153] Articles 463 and 478.
[154] Articles 469 and 484.
[155] Articles 465 and 480.

When he is also the general manager, he is responsible for the general management of the company[156]. He has the widest possible powers to act within the company's objects, except for powers expressly reserved for the general meetings of shareholders or those attributed to the board of directors by law or the articles of association, or within any limits defined by resolution of the board of directors or of the shareholders at a general meeting. He represents the company in its relations with third parties, and the company is bound even when his acts do not fall within the company's objects or when he has acted beyond his powers[157].

When the chairman is also the general manager he can delegate some of his powers to one or more deputy general managers, to the extent authorized by the board of directors[158].

(iii) Remuneration

The chairman may have an employment contract with the company under the same conditions as any other director, ie the contract must correspond to actual employment within the company, and it must be approved by the shareholders[159].

(iv) Restrictions on number of offices held

No-one may simultaneously hold offices as chairman in more than three SAs having their registered offices on the territory of the same Member State[160]. Likewise, it is prohibited to hold the position of chairman concurrently with offices as managing director or general manager in more than two SAs having their registered offices on the territory of the same Member State.

(d) General manager

(i) Appointment, term of office and revocation

In companies where the chairman of the board is not also the general manager, a general manager, who must be an individual, is appointed by the board of directors either from among its members or from

---

[156] Article 465.
[157] Article 465.
[158] Article 472.
[159] Articles 466 and 481.
[160] Articles 464 and 479.

outside[161]. The board of directors may freely determine the length of his term of office, which is renewable[162]. A general manager may have his appointment revoked at any time by the board of directors (*ad nutum* revocation)[163].

(ii) Powers

The general manager performs the general management of a company and represents the company in its dealings with third parties. In order to carry out his duties he has the widest possible powers to act within the company's objects, except for powers expressly reserved for general meetings of shareholders or those that are specifically attributed to the board of directors by law or the articles of association, or within any limits that may have been defined by board resolution or by a general meeting of shareholders[164]. The board may delegate some of the general manager's powers to a deputy general manager[165].

(iii) Remuneration

The general manager may enter into an employment contract with the company, the details of which are to be determined by the meeting of the board of directors which appoints him[166]. As is the case for directors, this employment contract must correspond to effective employment within the company.

(iv) Restrictions on number of offices held

There are no restrictions on the number of other offices that the general manager may hold. However, given the onerous nature of the duties of a general manager, it seems that the situation of a general manager holding a large number of such offices would not often arise in practice.

---

[161] Article 485.
[162] Article 486.
[163] Article 492.
[164] Article 487.
[165] Article 485.
[166] Articles 489–490.

D. Shareholders

1. Shareholders' rights and obligations

Any individual or corporate body may be a shareholder in a commercial company, subject to any prohibitions, incapacities or incompatibilities relating to the person of the shareholder[167]. The contributions made by each shareholder are represented by either registered or bearer shares[168].

Article 53 of the Uniform Act sets out the rights and obligations attached to shares. Such rights and obligations, which are in general proportionate to the amount of each shareholder's contribution, are the following:

- a right to a share in the company's profits whenever they are distributed;
- a right to the company's net assets when these are shared out following the winding-up of the company or when the company's share capital is reduced;
- the right to participate in and vote on the collective decisions of the shareholders taken at general meetings, subject to specific provisions of the Uniform Act relating to certain categories of shares; and
- where necessary, an obligation to share in the company's losses up to the amount of the shareholder's contribution.

In principle, the voting rights attached to shares are proportional to the percentage of the capital that they represent and each share gives entitlement to one vote. However, different classes of shares or shares with special rights may also be created[169]. It is also possible for the articles of association to limit the number of votes each shareholder may have at a general meeting, on condition that the limitation applies to all shares without distinction[170].

There is an automatic pre-emptive right to subscribe for additional shares on a capital increase[171].

In principle there is freedom of transfer of shares. However, specific provisions may be inserted in the articles of association whereby

---

[167] Article 7. See sub-section 1.A.1 of this chapter.
[168] Article 745.
[169] Articles 53, 543, 751 and 752.
[170] Article 543.
[171] See further details in sub-section (H) of this section.

transfers are made subject either to board approval or to a pre-emptive right[172].

The shareholders' powers may be defined by the articles of association. In addition, if the shareholders wish to keep certain private arrangements among themselves confidential, they may enter into a shareholders' agreement, which remains a private document unless the company makes public offerings.

2. Shareholders' meetings

The Uniform Act provides for three types of shareholders' meetings:

- ordinary general meetings[173];
- extraordinary general meetings[174];
- special meetings[175].

(a) General provisions

The board of directors or managing director, depending upon the management structure of the company, may call general meetings of shareholders. A meeting may also be called either by the statutory auditors if they have unsuccessfully requested the board of directors to call a meeting; by a court-appointed officer upon the request of any interested party or one or more shareholders who together have a shareholding representing at least one-tenth of the share capital held by the shareholders entitled to attend the meeting; or by the liquidator if the company is in liquidation[176].

Notice of a shareholders' meeting must be received by, or be brought to the attention of, the shareholders and the statutory auditors at least 15 days before the meeting in the case of a first call, and at least six days in advance if the meeting is being called with the same agenda for the second or any subsequent time[177].

Notice of the meeting must be published in a legal journal. Alternatively, if all the shares are registered shares, notice may be made to each

---

[172] Article 765.
[173] Articles 546–550.
[174] Articles 551–554.
[175] Articles 555–557.
[176] Article 516.
[177] Article 518.

shareholder personally, by letter delivered by hand against receipt or by registered mail. Whichever method is chosen, the notice must include the agenda for the meeting. The Uniform Act also lists the detailed information which must be contained in each notice as to time, date and place of the meeting, etc[178].

Each shareholder may appoint a proxy of his choice to represent him at a meeting. The appointment of the proxy is valid for one meeting only, or may be given for two meetings if these are an ordinary meeting and an extraordinary meeting held on the same day or within a period of seven days of each other. It is also valid for a meeting held on a subsequent call with the same agenda[179].

Shareholders' meetings take place at the company's registered office or at such other place in the same Member State as may be stated in the notice convening the general meeting. If the articles of association expressly so provide, they may also take place outside the Member State concerned[180].

The meeting is chaired by the chairman of the board of directors or managing director, depending upon the management structure, or, in the event he is unable to do so, by the shareholder holding or representing the greatest number of shares, or in the case of equal shareholdings, the senior director in age[181].

At each shareholders' meeting, an attendance list of those shareholders present (or their proxies) must be prepared with their identities, addresses, the number of shares they hold (or represent) and the number of voting rights attached to those shares[182].

Two tellers are appointed, whose responsibility it is to certify as true and correct the shareholders' attendance list, duly signed by the shareholders and proxies present[183].

(b) Ordinary general meetings

Ordinary general meetings are competent to take all decisions apart from those which are reserved for the extraordinary general meeting. In particular, they have the power to approve the company's financial statements;

---

[178] Article 519.
[179] Article 538.
[180] Article 518.
[181] Article 529.
[182] Article 532.
[183] Articles 530 and 533–534.

to decide upon the distribution of profits; to appoint members of the board of directors and the auditors; and to approve contracts concluded between the company and its directors[184].

An ordinary general meeting must be held at least once every year to receive and consider the company's annual accounts, not later than six months after the end of the financial year to which such annual accounts relate, subject only to an extension of this period by court order[185].

In order for an ordinary general meeting on first call validly to pass resolutions, shareholders representing at least one-quarter of the total share capital must be present or represented. On the second call of a meeting with the same agenda, no quorum is required[186].

Any resolution may be passed by simple majority of the votes validly cast at the meeting. Blank votes are not taken into account[187].

(c) Extraordinary general meetings

The extraordinary general meeting of shareholders has the power in particular to modify the articles of association[188]. This means, for example, that any increases or reductions in capital, mergers, spin-offs or partial business transfers, changes to the company's structure, moves of the company's registered office, winding-up or extension of the company's term must be authorized by the extraordinary general meeting.

No specific rules are provided for the frequency of such meetings, since by definition they are called only for extraordinary reasons which do not occur with any regularity.

In order for an extraordinary general meeting on first call validly to vote upon resolutions, shareholders holding at least one-half of the total share capital must be present or represented[189].

For a resolution to be validly voted upon on second call, the quorum is reduced to a number of shareholders holding one-quarter of the total share capital. If at the second meeting there is still no quorum, the extraordinary general meeting may be held on third call within two months of the second meeting. At the third call the quorum remains fixed

---

[184] Article 546.
[185] Article 548.
[186] Article 549.
[187] Article 550.
[188] Article 551.
[189] Article 553.

at one-quarter of the share capital[190]. The Uniform Act makes no provision for any subsequent call.

In order to be passed, any resolution must obtain at least two-thirds of the votes validly cast at the meeting[191]. However, a unanimous vote of the shareholders who are present or represented is necessary to move the company's registered office to the territory of another State[192]. Blank votes are not taken into account.

Table 5.1 Board and shareholders' meetings: quorum and majorities

	BOARD MEETING (Articles 453 *et seq* of the Uniform Act)	ORDINARY SHAREHOLDERS' MEETING (Articles 548 *et seq* of the Uniform Act)	EXTRAORDINARY AND SPECIAL SHAREHOLDERS' MEETING (Articles 552 *et seq* and 556–557 of the Uniform Act)
QUORUM	½ of all directors	**First call:** Shareholders representing ¼ of share capital **Second call:** No quorum is required	**First call:** Shareholders representing ½ of share capital **Second call:** Shareholders representing ¼ of share capital **Third call:** Within 2 months. Shareholders representing ¼ of share capital
MAJORITY	Simple majority of the votes (unless articles provide for increased majority) The chairman has a casting vote (unless specific provision to the contrary in the articles).	Simple majority of the votes validly cast at the meeting	2/3 majority of the votes validly cast at the meeting Unanimity for transfer of registered office to another State

---

[190] Article 553.
[191] Article 554.
[192] Article 554.

(d) Special meetings

The special meeting is a meeting of holders of shares of a single category[193]. Quorum and majority conditions are the same as for extraordinary general meetings[194].

E. Regulated and prohibited agreements

1. Definition

Regulated agreements are agreements between the company and a member of its management; or in which a member of the management is indirectly interested or involved; or between the company and another company or business, if a member of the management is the owner, a member of the management or a shareholder with unlimited liability of that other company or business[195]. These would include agreements relating, for example, to the provision of a company car or other advantage granted to a director by the company, and could also include agreements entered into with an affiliate company if the two companies have one or more directors in common.

Regulated agreements must, in principle, be authorized by the board of directors before they are entered into[196]. However, day-to-day operations concluded on arm's length terms are not considered as regulated agreements and do not require the board of directors' authorization[197]. The Uniform Act defines day-to-day operations as those which are habitually undertaken by a company within the framework of its activities, and arm's length terms as those which are applied under similar agreements not only by the company in question but also by other companies in the same sector[198]. Because these definitions are rather vague, it would be prudent to apply the procedure for regulated agreements if there is the slightest doubt as to whether or not a particular agreement falls within the definition.

Certain types of agreements are not merely regulated but are prohibited and are null and void if they are nevertheless entered into. Thus,

---

[193] Article 555.
[194] Articles 556–557.
[195] Article 438.
[196] Article 438.
[197] Article 439.
[198] Article 439.

members of the management or their close relatives must not be given loans by the company, be granted a current account overdraft or obtain guarantees or other undertakings for their obligations to third parties[199]. This prohibition does not however apply when the company is a financial or banking institution and when the agreement is a day-to-day operation on arm's length terms, nor does it apply to agreements between the company and a corporate entity which is a board member[200].

2. Procedure

In the event of a regulated agreement, a three-stage procedure must be followed[201]:

- As soon as he becomes aware that an agreement requires authorization, the person concerned must inform the board of directors.
- The board must vote on whether to authorize the agreement. The director concerned is not allowed to vote on the question.
- If the agreement is authorized by the board, the chairman must notify the auditors within one month of the agreement being entered into and, at the next ordinary general meeting at which the company's annual accounts are to be considered, the agreement must be submitted to the shareholders for approval. The auditors submit a special report on all regulated agreements, which must be deposited at the company's registered office at least 15 days before the holding of the ordinary general meeting. The interested party may not take part in the vote at the general meeting, and his shares are not taken into account in calculating the quorum or majority.

The auditors are responsible for ensuring that all rules relating to regulated agreements are complied with, and must report any failure to comply at the first ordinary general meeting after they become aware of the failure[202].

---

[199] Article 450.
[200] Article 450.
[201] Article 440.
[202] Article 441.

3. Liability and annulment of regulated agreements

In all cases, except where they are annulled because there has been fraud, regulated agreements are fully effective as regards the parties and third parties, even if they have not been approved by the shareholders. However, a member of the management may be held liable for any damage caused to the company resulting from any regulated agreement to which he is a party and which has not been approved by the ordinary general meeting. This liability may also be extended to the other members of the board[203].

In addition, if a regulated agreement has not been authorized by the board of directors and if it has caused damage to the company, legal proceedings to annul the agreement are allowed[204]. These may be filed by the company itself or by any shareholder, within three years of the date of the agreement or, if the agreement has been kept secret, within three years of discovery of the existence of the agreement[205].

However, an agreement which is voidable because it has not been authorized as required may subsequently be ratified by a resolution of the shareholders in a general meeting after presentation of a special report by the auditors setting out the circumstances which prevented the authorization procedure from being followed. The party to the agreement concerned may not vote on the resolution and his shares are not taken into account in calculating the quorum or majority[206].

F. *Statutory auditors* (commissaires aux comptes)

A statutory auditor and a deputy must be appointed for every SA, unless the company makes public offerings, in which case two auditors and two deputies must be appointed[207]. The auditors must be convened to all general meetings[208].

The first auditor and his deputy must be appointed in the articles of association or at the constituent general meeting[209]. The question of whether two individuals belonging to the same firm, or a firm and an

---

[203] Article 443.

[204] Article 444.

[205] Articles 445–446.

[206] Article 447.

[207] Article 702.

[208] Article 721.

[209] Article 703.

individual belonging to that firm may be appointed as statutory auditor and deputy, respectively, will depend upon the national legislation and the professional rules applicable in the Member State concerned. The initial term of office of statutory auditors and their deputies is two financial years, expiring at the end of the ordinary general meeting at which the company's annual accounts for the second financial year are submitted to the shareholders for approval[210].

After the first term of office, the auditors are appointed by the ordinary general meeting for six financial years[211]. Each such term of office expires at the end of the ordinary general meeting at which the company's annual accounts for the last of such six financial years are submitted for approval[212].

The duties of the auditor are defined in Articles 710 *et seq* of the Uniform Act. In particular, he must certify the company's summary financial statements. He must also verify the accuracy of the information given in the board's management report and in the documents on the financial situation addressed to the shareholders, and must verify the conformity of this information with the summary financial statements[213].

The auditor prepares a report in which he informs the board of directors of:

● the audits, verifications and investigations that he has conducted;
● the items in the balance-sheet and other accounting documents to which he considers amendments should be made, with any relevant remarks as to the valuation methods used in the preparation of these documents;
● any irregularities and inaccuracies which he has discovered;
● his conclusions, taking into account the above observations and amendments, as to the results of the financial year compared to those of the previous financial year[214].

The report must be made available to the chairman of the board or the managing director, as the case may be, before the meeting of the board or the decision of the managing director which adopts the annual accounts[215].

---

[210] Articles 704–705.
[211] Articles 703–704.
[212] Article 705.
[213] Articles 710 and 713.
[214] Article 715.
[215] Article 715.

In addition, as mentioned above, the auditor must prepare a special report on any regulated agreements.

Auditors can be removed from office only by court order, and only for material reasons[216]. Therefore, in the event of a change in the company's shareholding, for example, the new shareholders are not legally entitled to request the auditor's resignation.

G. Net equity position

Rules regarding the minimum net equity position have been included in the Uniform Act with a view to safeguarding the future of companies in the event that significant losses appear in their summary financial statements.

When a company's net equity falls below one-half of the company's share capital, the board of directors or managing director must convene an extraordinary general meeting, within four months following the approval of the accounts that show the losses[217].

The extraordinary general meeting then takes a decision as to whether or not the company should be wound up. In the event the meeting does not decide to wind up the company, the capital must be reduced by an amount at least equal to the amount of the losses that have not been charged to the reserves. This must occur no later than at the close of the second financial year following the year during which the losses were recorded, unless the shareholders' equity has been reconstituted in the meantime up to a value equal to at least half of the registered capital[218].

The decision of the extraordinary general meeting must be filed with the court having jurisdiction for commercial matters at the place of the registered office, and with the RCCM. It must also be published in a national legal journal[219].

If an extraordinary general meeting is not called, if there has not been a quorum on the final call of that meeting, or if the financial situation is not regularized in accordance with the decision of the extraordinary general meeting, any interested party may bring court proceedings for the winding-up of the company[220]. In such circumstances, the court may give the company a maximum period of six months within which to

---

[216] Articles 730–731.
[217] Article 664.
[218] Article 665.
[219] Article 666.
[220] Article 667.

regularize the financial situation, failing which the company will be wound up[221].

In addition, failure by the board of directors or managing director to convene an extraordinary general meeting may result in their being subject to civil and criminal penalties[222].

H. Increases and reductions of capital

The Uniform Act lays down specific rules for increases and reductions of share capital in an SA.

1. Increases of capital

(a) General conditions

The share capital of an SA may be increased either by issuing additional shares or by increasing the nominal value of existing shares[223]. The new shares are paid up either in cash, by in-kind contributions, by set-off against debts of the company that are certain, liquidated and due, or by capitalization of reserves, profits or share premiums. New shares may be issued either for their nominal value or for their nominal value plus a share premium[224].

The existing share capital of the company must be fully paid up before the issuance of new shares to be paid for in cash[225]. Non-compliance with this requirement will lead to the nullity of the operation and make the management liable to the application of criminal penalties in accordance with the national criminal law of the Member State concerned[226].

(b) Decisions to increase capital

The only body that can decide upon a share capital increase is the shareholders' extraordinary general meeting, upon presentation of reports from the board of directors or managing director and the statutory auditor[227]. The board of directors' or managing director's report

---

[221] Article 668.
[222] Article 901.
[223] Article 562.
[224] Article 563.
[225] Article 572.
[226] Articles 572 and 893.
[227] Article 564.

must include details on the reasons for the increase and the trends in the company's business since the beginning of the financial year[228].

When the increase is made by means of a capitalization of reserves, profits or share premiums, the rules as to quorum and majority are those provided for ordinary shareholders' meetings instead of the more stringent rules applicable to extraordinary meetings[229].

The shareholders may delegate their powers to the board of directors or the managing director to proceed with the capital increase in full or in instalments, to determine the detailed procedure for the increase, and to minute its final completion and accordingly modify the articles of association[230].

(c) Pre-emptive subscription rights for existing shareholders

In principle the existing shareholders have a pre-emptive subscription right with regard to the shares issued in the course of the capital increase[231]. This right is in proportion to their respective shareholdings and cannot be reduced. In other words, a shareholder who holds 10 per cent of the existing capital is entitled to subscribe for 10 per cent of the new shares and cannot be deprived of any part of this entitlement.

The only exception to this rule is if the shareholder himself waives the right or if, on certain conditions, the extraordinary general meeting decides otherwise[232]. Thus, the extraordinary meeting may decide that there will be no pre-emptive subscription right either for the whole of the amount of the increase or for one or more instalments of the increase, in favour of one or more designated beneficiaries. When such beneficiaries are already shareholders of the company, they may not take part in the vote, either on their own behalf or as proxies of other shareholders, and their shares are not taken into account for calculating the quorum and majority[233].

The shareholders may also individually waive their pre-emptive right for the benefit of one or more designated beneficiaries, or may do so without designating any beneficiary[234]. The waiver must be made in

---

[228] Article 570.
[229] Article 565.
[230] Article 568.
[231] Article 573.
[232] Article 586.
[233] Article 587.
[234] Article 593.

writing to the company before the closure of the subscription period, by letter delivered by hand against acknowledgement of receipt or by registered mail with acknowledgement of receipt[235]. When there are designated beneficiaries, the waiver must be accompanied by the acceptance of such beneficiaries[236].

During the subscription period, pre-emptive rights are freely negotiable if they are attached to shares that are themselves freely negotiable. If the shares are not freely negotiable, the pre-emptive rights may be transferred in accordance with the same conditions as the shares themselves[237].

The shareholders' meeting may decide to give an additional pre-emptive subscription right to the shareholders in the event that the share issue is not fully taken up[238]. In such cases the remaining shares are attributed to shareholders who have subscribed for a greater number of shares than their proportional entitlement, within the limits of their subscription. If there is over-subscription for the remaining shares, the shareholders will not receive the totality of the shares for which they have subscribed[239].

If after the exercise of all pre-emptive rights the whole of the share issue is not taken up, the capital may nevertheless be increased by the amount for which subscriptions have been received, on condition (i) that at least three-quarters of the issue has been taken up and (ii) that this possibility was expressly provided for by the extraordinary general meeting. Alternatively, and unless the extraordinary general meeting has decided otherwise, the remaining shares may be freely allocated; or they may be offered to the public if this has been expressly provided for by the general meeting[240].

In any event, the board of directors or managing director may decide that the share capital increase is effective if the total amount of subscriptions has reached 97 per cent of the envisaged capital increase[241].

---

[235] Article 594.
[236] Article 595.
[237] Article 574.
[238] Article 575.
[239] Article 576.
[240] Article 579.
[241] Article 580.

(d) Price of issue and reports

The price of issue for new shares or the way in which the price will be determined are decided by the extraordinary shareholders' meeting[242], upon presentation of two reports prepared respectively by:

- the board of directors or managing director, indicating the maximum amount of the increase, the reasons for it and, if applicable, the reasons for a proposal to cancel the preferential subscription right, the names of the beneficiaries of the new share issue, the number of shares allocated to each, the price of issue, and the reasons for this price[243];
- the auditors, giving their opinion on the cancellation of the preferential right (if applicable), the choices of criteria for the calculation of the price and of its amount, and the impact of the issuance on the situation of the shareholders, evaluated by reference to the equity. The auditors must verify and certify the information taken from the company's accounts on which their opinion is based[244].

When the board of directors or managing director has been delegated the power to make a share capital increase, it must prepare an additional report when it exercises this power[245]. The report must describe the details of the capital increase so that it is possible to ascertain whether the increase is made in compliance with the authorization given in advance by the shareholders. The auditors must also make a report for the same purpose. These additional reports are made available at the registered office 15 days after the board meeting or decision taken by the managing director, and are presented at the next shareholders' meeting.

(e) Subscription bulletins

Unless the preferential subscription right has been cancelled, the shareholders are given notice of the details of the capital increase at least six days in advance of the opening of the subscription period[246].

Subscription bulletins containing details of the increase, as listed by Article 603 of the Uniform Act, are prepared in two originals, one for the

---

[242] Article 588.
[243] Article 589.
[244] Article 591.
[245] Article 592.
[246] Articles 598–599.

company and the other for the notary who will prepare the notarized statement of subscription and payment[247]. A bulletin must be dated and signed by each subscriber or his authorized representative, who must also indicate the number of shares for which he has subscribed[248].

(f) Payment for shares

At least one-quarter of the nominal value of the shares must be paid upon subscription, together with the total amount of any share premium[249]. The remaining amount must be paid upon request of the board or the managing director in one or more instalments within three years as from the date of the capital increase[250]. However, shares which are issued partly against cash contributions and partly by the incorporation into the capital of reserves, profits or share premiums must be fully paid up upon subscription[251].

The management must deposit all payments within eight days of their receipt, on a bank account in the Member State where the registered office is located or with a notary[252]. If a bank is used, it must issue a certificate acknowledging receipt of the funds[253].

In the event of payment by means of a set-off against debts owed by the company, the debts must be recorded in an accounting statement prepared by the board of directors or the managing director and certified by the statutory auditors[254].

(g) Preparation of the notarized statement of subscription and payment

The management acknowledges all subscriptions and payments in a notarized statement of subscription and payment[255]. After reviewing the subscription bulletins and, if applicable, the bank's certificate of deposit of the funds, the notary certifies that the statement by the management and the amounts indicated on the bulletins correspond to the amounts

---

[247] Article 601.
[248] Article 602.
[249] Article 604.
[250] Article 605.
[251] Article 606.
[252] Article 607.
[253] Article 610.
[254] Article 611.
[255] Article 612.

received by him or indicated in the bank's certificate, which must be appended to the notarized statement[256].

When the increase is effected by means of a set-off against debts, the notary delivers his statement upon presentation of the accounting statement prepared by the management and certified by the auditors, which is then appended to the notarized statement[257].

(h) Completion of increase and withdrawal of funds

The increase must be completed within three years after the shareholders' meeting has decided or authorized it[258]. It is deemed to have been completed upon the issuance of the notarized statement of subscription and payment.

The funds may only be withdrawn once the capital increase has been completed. Withdrawal may be made against presentation, to the notary or the bank, of the notarized statement of subscription and payment[259].

Notice of the capital increase is published with the registry of the court and the RCCM in accordance with the provisions of Article 264 of the Uniform Act.

(i) Increases of capital through in-kind contributions and/or with specific advantages

In-kind contributions and/or specific advantages[260] which may be granted in connection with an increase of capital must be valued by an in-kind contributions appraiser, appointed by the court upon the request of the board or managing director[261]. The appraiser may be assisted by one or more experts whose fees are borne by the company[262].

The appraiser's report is filed with the company's registered office eight days in advance of the extraordinary general meeting which is to

---

[256] Article 613.

[257] Article 614.

[258] Article 571.

[259] Article 615.

[260] Specific advantages are specific rights conferred individually upon one or more shareholders which derogate from the usual rights conferred by law upon shareholders. As these rights may create inequality among the shareholders, the law requires the shareholders to vote upon their validity on the basis of an appraiser's report.

[261] Article 619.

[262] Article 621.

be held to vote upon the contributions or advantages[263]. Once the valuation of the contributions or advantages has been approved, the meeting formally acknowledges completion of the share capital increase[264]. If the meeting decides to reduce the value attributed to the contributions or advantages, the beneficiaries or their representatives must indicate their acceptance of the reduction, failing which the capital increase cannot take place[265].

2. Reductions of capital

(a) General conditions

The share capital may be reduced either by reducing the number of shares or by reducing the nominal value of the existing shares[266].

The reduction of capital may be authorized or decided by the extra-ordinary general meeting, which may delegate all the necessary powers to the board of directors or the managing director, as the case may be, to effect the reduction[267]. The reduction may not affect the equality among the shareholders, unless the shareholders who would be adversely affected expressly agree otherwise[268].

The minimum authorized capital for an SA is 10 million FCFA[269]. As a result, the capital cannot be reduced below this amount.

(b) Procedure

The proposal for reducing the capital must be communicated to the auditor at least 45 days before the date of the extraordinary general meeting called to vote upon it[270]. The auditor then presents a report to the extraordinary general meeting and the shareholders vote upon the reduction.

Notice of the capital reduction is published with the registry of the court and the RCCM in accordance with the provisions of Article 264.

---

[263] Article 622.
[264] Article 624.
[265] Article 625.
[266] Article 627.
[267] Article 628.
[268] Article 628.
[269] Article 387.
[270] Article 629.

In particular, the minutes of the extraordinary general meeting must be filed with the court.

(c) Objections by creditors

Creditors of the company cannot object to a capital reduction when it is due to losses[271]. Otherwise, creditors whose entitlement arose before the filing with the court of the minutes of the shareholders' meeting may object to the reduction in urgent proceedings before the court within 30 days from such filing[272].

The reduction process may not begin during that 30-day period, or before the court has decided on any objection that may have been filed within that period[273]. When the objection is granted, it interrupts the reduction process until the debts in question have been paid or until the company has provided satisfactory guarantees to ensure their payment[274].

I. Financial assistance – Purchase by the company of its own shares

The Uniform Act prohibits an SA from giving financial assistance to a third party for the purchase of its own shares. Unlike certain common law systems, the Uniform Act contains no exceptions to this rule, and does not provide for a 'whitewash procedure', which enables a company to give what would otherwise be unlawful financial assistance if that company's net assets are not thereby reduced or, to the extent that they are reduced, if the assistance is provided out of distributable profits.

1. Principle

Pursuant to Article 639, the subscription or purchase by an SA of its own shares, either directly or by an individual acting in his own name but on behalf of the company, is prohibited. The founding shareholders or, in the event of a capital increase, the directors or managing director must pay for any shares subscribed for or acquired illegally by the company in contravention of this prohibition. Any person who may have sub-

---

[271] Article 632.
[272] Articles 633–634.
[273] Article 636.
[274] Article 637.

scribed for or purchased shares in his own name but for the benefit of the company is jointly and severally liable with the board of directors or managing director for payment of these shares, and is also deemed to have subscribed for the shares for his own account.

The same article further provides that an SA cannot grant advances or loans or provide security for subscription to or purchase of its own shares by a third party.

The granting to the company of its own shares as a pledge, directly or through an individual acting in his own name but on behalf of the company, is also prohibited, unless this is done in the context of a day-to-day transaction by a banking institution[275]. Any shares pledged in contravention of this prohibition must be returned to their owner within a one-year period.

2. Exceptions

There are however a few exceptions to the principle that a company may not purchase its own shares.

First, if a reduction in capital is decided which is not due to losses, the company may buy its own shares in order to cancel them[276].

Second, an extraordinary general meeting may authorize the board or managing director to acquire a certain number of shares to be attributed to employees of the company[277]. In such an event, the acquisition is subject to the following conditions:

- the shares must be attributed to the employees within one year of their acquisition;
- the company cannot hold more than 10 per cent of the total number of its own shares, either directly or indirectly;
- the shares acquired must be transformed into registered shares and must be fully paid up at the time of acquisition;
- the company's net equity must not fall below one-half of the total amount of the company's authorized capital and non-distributable reserves as a result of the purchase of the shares;
- shares held by the company do not give any entitlement to dividends.

---

[275] Article 642.
[276] Article 639.
[277] Article 640, para 1. This enables any OHADA company to put in place incentive plans for employees, such as stock options, which may be organized in compliance with the laws applicable in the company's Member State.

Moreover, a company may also acquire its own shares to the extent they are fully paid up, when it obtains them by virtue of a transfer of another company's assets and liabilities or by virtue of a court decision[278]. This exception mainly arises in the context of mergers, spin-offs and partial business transfers. The company may keep such shares for a maximum period of two years; if it has not transferred them by the end of this period it must cancel them.

Finally, the company may redeem its shares when a potential transferee has not been approved[279].

3. Procedure

When the company decides to purchase its own shares with a view to cancelling them and thereby reducing its capital, it must first notify the shareholders of its offer to purchase shares, by publishing a notice in a legal journal containing the following information: name, form, registered office, amount of share capital, number of shares to be purchased, price offered per share, method of payment, period of offer, and address for acceptance of the offer[280]. When all the shares are registered, the shareholders may instead be informed of the offer by hand-delivered letter with acknowledgement of receipt or registered mail[281].

Where several shareholders agree to sell their shares, and where the number of shares offered for sale to the company exceeds the purchase offer, the number of shares purchased from each shareholder is reduced in proportion to his shareholding[282]. If an insufficient number of shares are offered for sale to the company, the company reduces its capital in proportion to the number of shares purchased[283].

The above procedure does not apply to purchases of the company's shares that are carried out to facilitate a share capital increase, a merger or a spin-off, when the general meeting has authorized the purchase of a maximum of one per cent of the company's total shares for cancellation, or where the company buys shares because a potential transferee has not been approved.

---

[278] Article 641.
[279] Article 647, para 2.
[280] Article 643.
[281] Article 644.
[282] Article 645.
[283] Article 646.

J. Transformation

An SA may be transformed into another type of company. Further details are given in Section 6 of this chapter.

SECTION 3: *SOCIÉTÉ À RESPONSABILITÉ LIMITÉE* OR *SARL*

An SARL is the other type of commercial company in which the shareholders are liable for the company's debts only up to the amount of their respective contributions. SARLs are dealt with in Articles 309 to 384 of the Uniform Act.

A. Shareholders

An SARL may be constituted by one or more individuals or corporate bodies[284]. It is therefore possible for it to have only a single shareholder, and there is no maximum number of shareholders.

Shareholders have rights regarding company policy and financial rights:

- the right to be informed at all times as to the affairs of the company; in particular, prior to general meetings, they have the right to receive certain information and to ask questions concerning the management of the company[285];
- the right to ask questions to be answered by the management at general meetings[286];
- the right to vote at general meetings[287]; and
- the right to receive dividends[288].

B. Share capital

The share capital of an SARL must be at least one million FCFA. It is composed of shares having an equal nominal value which may not be less than 5,000 FCFA[289].

---

[284] Article 309.
[285] Articles 344–345.
[286] Article 345.
[287] Article 334.
[288] Article 346.
[289] Article 311.

Contributions in kind must be valued by an in-kind contributions appraiser where their total amount is equal to at least five million FCFA. The report of the in-kind contributions appraiser is appended to the articles of association[290].

Funds derived from the subscription of shares must be immediately deposited by the founders of the company on a special bank account against a receipt or with a notary[291]. The deposit of funds is then recorded by a notary who draws up a notarized statement of subscription and payment together with a list of subscribers[292].

As is the case for an SA, when the net equity falls below one-half of the registered share capital, the management or the auditor must consult the shareholders within four months to decide whether to wind up the company[293].

If the shareholders decide not to wind up the company, they have an alternative between:

- either recapitalizing the company within two years; or
- reducing the share capital, in which case the capital must not fall below one million FCFA[294].

If these measures are not implemented, any interested person may apply to the competent court for an order to wind up the company[295].

C. Management

An SARL is managed by one or more managers (*gérants*). A manager must be an individual, and may be either a shareholder or a non-shareholder. He is appointed in the articles of association or, during the life of the company, by the majority of the shareholders holding more than one-half of the registered capital[296].

The manager may receive remuneration for the exercise of his functions, in accordance with the articles of association or any subsequent shareholders' decision[297].

---

[290] Article 312.
[291] Article 313.
[292] Article 314.
[293] Article 371.
[294] Article 372.
[295] Article 373.
[296] Article 323.
[297] Article 325.

1. Appointment, term of office and revocation

A manager is appointed for four years unless the articles of association provide otherwise, and his term of office is renewable[298]. His tenure may be revoked by a decision of shareholders holding more than one-half of the company's shares. If there are no legitimate reasons for the revocation, damages may be payable[299]. In other words, unlike directors of an SA, managers cannot be removed *ad nutum*. Any shareholder may also seek a court-ordered revocation if there are legitimate reasons for it. This provision allows minority shareholders to prevent abuses by majority shareholders acting in collusion with the manager.

2. Powers

Insofar as relations with the shareholders are concerned, managers may perform any acts of management in the interests of the company unless the articles of association restrict their powers. If there are several managers, an objection by one manager to the acts of another manager cannot be relied upon as against third parties, unless such third parties were aware of the objection[300].

Vis-à-vis third parties the company is bound by all acts of the manager, including those which are outside the company's purpose, unless it can be shown either that a third party claiming the benefit of such an act either knew that the act did not fall within the company's purpose or could not have been unaware of this in the circumstances. Publication of the articles of association is insufficient proof of knowledge for this purpose[301].

D. *Collective decisions*

Collective decisions are generally taken at general meetings. However, the articles of association may provide for the possibility of a written consultation of the shareholders except in the case of the annual general meeting held to approve the annual accounts[302]. This is a possibility that does not exist in an SA.

---

[298] Article 324.
[299] Article 326.
[300] Article 328.
[301] Article 329.
[302] Article 333.

1. Written consultation

When decisions are taken by means of a written consultation, the text of the proposed draft resolution and any necessary related documents are sent to each shareholder. The shareholders then have a minimum period of 15 days from receipt of the draft resolution to vote upon the resolution[303].

2. General meetings

(a) Convening of a general meeting

An ordinary general meeting must be held each year within six months from the closing date of the financial year[304].

Shareholders are convened to general meetings by the manager or by the statutory auditor. In addition, one or more shareholders holding one-half of the company's shares, or at least one-quarter of the shareholders in number holding at least one-quarter of the company's shares, may request the convening of a meeting. Moreover, any shareholder may petition the court for the appointment of a court officer to convene a meeting[305].

Shareholders must be convened to a general meeting at least 15 days before the meeting is due to be held. The notice of the meeting must indicate the agenda and be delivered either by registered mail with acknowledgement of receipt or by letter delivered by hand against receipt. If these conditions are not complied with, the general meeting may be annulled[306].

A shareholder may be represented by a proxy, who must be either his spouse or a shareholder of the company unless the articles of association provide otherwise or unless there are only two shareholders in the company[307].

(b) Chairman of meeting

The general meeting is chaired by the manager or one of the managers, unless none of the managers is a shareholder. In this case it is chaired

---

[303] Article 341.
[304] Article 348.
[305] Article 337.
[306] Article 338.
[307] Article 334.

by the shareholder holding the greatest number of shares or, in cases where there are equal shareholdings, by the senior in age[308].

3. Different types of collective decisions

Ordinary collective decisions are required for the following items:

- approval of the annual accounts;
- appointment and removal of managers;
- appointment of auditors;
- approval of regulated agreements; and
- in general, any questions which do not involve an amendment of the articles of association[309].

Extraordinary collective decisions are necessary only for amendments to the articles of association[310].

4. Quorums and majorities

(a) Ordinary collective decisions

No particular quorum is required for collective decisions in an SARL.

Resolutions are adopted on first call by one or more shareholders holding more than one-half of the share capital. Where this majority is not obtained, the shareholders must be consulted a second time. In this case resolutions are passed by simple majority vote unless the articles of association provide otherwise[311]. However, if the shareholders are called to vote upon the revocation of a manager's tenure, an absolute majority vote is required for the revocation to be passed[312].

(b) Extraordinary collective decisions

Amendments to the articles of association are adopted if shareholders representing at least three-quarters of the share capital vote in favour, unless the resolution concerns a share capital increase by means of a

---

[308] Article 341.
[309] Article 347.
[310] Article 357.
[311] Article 349.
[312] Article 349.

capitalization of profits or reserves, which requires shareholders holding at least one-half of the share capital to vote in favour[313].

Unanimity is however required if the shareholders' obligations are to be increased, if the company is to be transformed into a *société en nom collectif*, or if the registered office is to be transferred to a State other than a Member State[314].

5. Minutes

At each general meeting, minutes are prepared indicating the shareholders present or represented, with their addresses, the number of shares they own and the number of voting rights attached to their shares. The minutes must include the resolutions put to the vote and the result of the vote, and must be signed by each of the shareholders present[315].

If decisions have been taken by means of a written consultation, minutes are also prepared, to which the response of each shareholder is annexed. These minutes are signed by the manager or managers[316].

E. Transfers of shares

Unless the articles of association provide otherwise, transfers of shares between shareholders or to close relatives of shareholders are unrestricted[317].

The articles of association may lay down rules governing the transfer of shares to third parties against payment. If they do not, Article 319 of the Uniform Act makes such transfers subject to the consent of the majority of non-transferring shareholders holding at least three-quarters of the company's shares (the transferring shareholder's shares not being taken into account for this calculation).

Finally, in the event of the death of a shareholder, the articles of association may provide that the shareholder's heirs may become shareholders only with the prior approval of the other shareholders[318].

---

[313] Articles 358 and 360.

[314] Article 359. The equivalent provision regarding SAs (Article 551) requires unanimity if the registered office is to be moved to any other State. It is not clear whether the distinction in the rules applicable to SAs and SARLs is intentional, or whether it is the result of an oversight.

[315] Article 342.

[316] Article 342.

[317] Article 318.

[318] Article 321.

Where there is no consent to a transfer of shares to a third party, the shareholders are jointly and severally obliged to acquire the shares within three months, at a price to be determined either between the transferor and the company or, failing agreement between the parties, by a court-appointed expert[319].

If a share transfer does go ahead, either to another shareholder or to a third party, a transfer deed must be made in writing. The transfer may be relied upon as against the company after compliance with any one of the following formalities:

- notification of the transfer to the company by bailiff;
- acceptance of the transfer by the company in a notarized deed;
- filing of an original copy of the share transfer deed with the company's registered office, against an acknowledgement of receipt delivered by the company's manager[320].

The transfer may be relied upon as against third parties after the accomplishment of any one of the above formalities, amendment of the articles of association to reflect the change, and publication with the RCCM.

F. Auditors

At least one statutory auditor must be appointed in an SARL when one of the following three conditions is met:

- its share capital exceeds ten million FCFA;
- the annual turnover exceeds 250 million FCFA;
- the permanent staff exceeds 50 employees[321].

The latter two criteria raise certain difficulties of interpretation which are not answered in the Uniform Act. For example, it is not clear what must happen regarding the appointment of an auditor if either of these criteria is met during a single year but if the turnover or number of permanent staff then drops below the relevant threshold in subsequent years.

---

[319] Article 319.
[320] Article 317.
[321] Article 376.

When none of the above criteria is fulfilled, the appointment of a statutory auditor is optional.

The auditor is appointed for three years by resolution of one or more shareholders holding more than one-half of the share capital. However, if this majority is not attained, a simple majority vote is sufficient, regardless of the proportion of capital held[322]. In addition, shareholders representing at least one-tenth of the share capital may request the court to appoint an auditor in cases where the appointment is optional[323].

G. Regulated and prohibited agreements

1. Definition

Regulated agreements are agreements which are concluded directly or indirectly between an SARL and one of its managers or shareholders. They also include agreements concluded with another business or company in which the owner or a member of the management is also a manager or shareholder in the SARL in question[324]. However, transactions occurring in the normal course of business and on arm's length terms are not regarded as regulated agreements[325].

Prohibited agreements are agreements whereby an individual shareholder or a manager or one of their close relatives contracts a loan from the company, obtains an overdraft on a current account or otherwise receives a financial benefit from the company, or obtains from the company an endorsement or guarantee of his obligations towards third parties[326]. If such agreements are entered into despite the prohibition, they may be declared null and void.

2. Procedure

Regulated agreements must be authorized in accordance with a two-stage procedure:

- If the company has a statutory auditor, the manager informs him within one month of the conclusion of any such agreement[327]. The

---

[322] Article 379.
[323] Article 376.
[324] Article 350
[325] Article 352.
[326] Article 356.
[327] Article 351.

auditor then prepares a special report which must include the identity of the parties and the purpose and main terms of the agreement[328]. If the company does not have a statutory auditor, the manager prepares this report[329].

- The shareholders must decide whether to authorize any such agreement at the annual general meeting. The decision is taken by one or more shareholders holding more than one-half of the share capital. The interested party may not take part in this vote, and his shares will not be taken into account in calculating the majority[330].

If the general meeting refuses to authorize a regulated agreement, the agreement nevertheless remains fully effective[331]. Unlike the provisions relating to SAs in this regard, those relating to SARLs do not provide an exception to this rule in the event there has been fraud. It seems that this is however only an unfortunate oversight, but in any event it may be inferred that general principles of contract law will allow the annulment of such agreements.

A shareholder or manager may be held liable for any damage caused to the company by any regulated agreement to which he is a party and which has not obtained the required authorization[332]. Any proceedings in this regard must be filed within three years of the date of the agreement in question, unless its existence has been concealed, in which case the three-year period runs from the date of discovery of the existence of the agreement.

SECTION 4: UNLIMITED LIABILITY COMPANIES

In addition to limited liability companies, the Uniform Act also provides for a number of types of companies where the shareholders, or some of them, have unlimited liability. Since these companies are used much more rarely than limited liability companies, they will be dealt with only briefly.

---

[328] Article 353.
[329] Articles 350 and 353.
[330] Article 354.
[331] Article 355.
[332] Article 355.

A. Société en nom collectif *or* SNC

A *société en nom collectif* (*SNC*) is a kind of private partnership which is defined by Article 270 of the Uniform Act as a company where all the shareholders have commercial (*commerçant*) status and have unlimited joint and several liability for the company's debts. There is no minimum or maximum number of shareholders.

The registered capital of an SNC is represented by shares of equal nominal value, which may be transferred only with the unanimous consent of the shareholders[333].

A manager (*gérant*) may be chosen from among or outside the shareholders. Unlike the manager of an SARL, the manager of an SNC may be a corporate body. In such an event, the management of that corporate body are subject to the same obligations and liabilities as if they were personally managers of the SNC[334].

If the articles of association do not make any provision for management, all the shareholders are deemed collectively to be the managers of the SNC[335].

If the manager is a shareholder appointed in the articles of association, his tenure can be revoked only by a unanimous vote of the other shareholders. Unless the articles of association or a unanimous vote of the remaining shareholders provide otherwise, this revocation entails the winding-up of the company[336]. If, on the other hand, the manager is not designated in the articles of association, his tenure may be revoked by a vote of the shareholders representing a majority in both number and capital, without his own shareholding, if any, being taken into account for purposes of this calculation[337]. Revocation is not *ad nutum*, and may give rise to the payment of damages if it occurs without legitimate reasons[338].

Any decision which does not fall within the powers of the manager must be taken unanimously by the shareholders unless the articles of association provide otherwise[339].

---

[333] Article 273.
[334] Article 276.
[335] Article 276.
[336] Article 279.
[337] Article 280.
[338] Article 281.
[339] Article 283.

An annual shareholders' meeting must be held to approve the accounts; otherwise decisions may be taken by written consultation[340]. The quorum for the annual meeting is the majority in number of the shareholders, representing at least one-half of the share capital. The meeting is chaired by the shareholder holding and representing the highest number of shares[341].

B. Société en commandite simple *or* SCS

A *société en commandite simple* (*SCS*) is a type of sleeping partnership in which there are two categories of shareholders. Shareholders in the first category are indefinitely and jointly and severally liable for the company's debts. These shareholders are 'active partners' (*associés commandités*). The second category of shareholders is 'sleeping partners' (*associés commanditaires*) who are liable for the company's debts only up to the limit of their contribution to the capital[342]. This type of company did not exist in all the Member States before the entry into force of the Uniform Act.

The name of a sleeping partner must not be used as part of the company's name. Otherwise, that partner will be jointly and severally liable with the active partners for all the company's debts[343].

The following indications must be included in the articles of association: amount of contributions, respective shareholdings of each active and sleeping partner, and the respective shares in the profits of each sleeping partner and of the active partners collectively[344].

In principle, shares may not be transferred without the unanimous consent of all the shareholders. Nevertheless, the articles of association may provide that sleeping partners' shares are freely transferable to other shareholders; that sleeping partners' shares may be transferred to third parties with the unanimous consent of the active partners and the majority consent in number and capital of the sleeping partners; or that an active partner may transfer some of his shares to a sleeping partner or a third party on the same conditions as to consent[345].

---

[340] Articles 284 and 288.

[341] Article 288.

[342] Article 293.

[343] Article 294.

[344] Article 295.

[345] Article 296.

Unless otherwise provided by the articles of association, the active partners all manage the company[346]. On the other hand, a sleeping partner may not perform any management activities vis-à-vis third parties, even if he has a power-of-attorney to do so[347]. Otherwise, he becomes indefinitely and jointly and severally liable, like the active partners, for all debts and undertakings of the company arising out of his actions or, if his actions are particularly numerous or serious, he may be held liable for all the debts and obligations of the company[348].

Any decision which does not fall within the powers of the managers must be taken collectively by the shareholders[349].

The articles of association may organize the procedure for collective decisions, in particular in relation to the possibility of written consultation, quorums and majorities[350]. However, an annual meeting must be held to approve the accounts. For there to be a quorum, a majority of the shareholders must be present, representing at least one-half of the capital[351]. In addition, any active partner, or one or more of the sleeping partners representing one-quarter of the sleeping partners in number and capital, may request the holding of a shareholders' meeting[352]. In such an event, the rules of quorum and majority contained in the articles of association will be applicable.

The company must at all times comprise at least one active partner. Otherwise, it will be wound up if a new active partner is not found, or if the company is not transformed into another type of company within one year[353].

C. Société en participation

A *société en participation* is, strictly speaking, not a company at all. It is a type of joint venture where the partners agree that it will not be registered with the RCCM and will not have its own corporate personality[354].

This definition has several consequences. For example, a *société en participation* cannot:

---

346 Article 298.
347 Article 299.
348 Article 300.
349 Article 302.
350 Article 302.
351 Article 306.
352 Article 308.
353 Article 308.
354 Article 854.

- have a registered office, a corporate name or its own assets and liabilities;
- enter into contracts;
- be a party to court proceedings; or
- be subject to collective insolvency proceedings.

The partners are free to agree on the purpose of the joint venture, the rights of the partners, and rules for its functioning and winding-up[355]. Nevertheless, relations between partners are governed by the provisions applicable to SNCs, unless the partners have provided otherwise[356]. Furthermore, the partners must comply with the mandatory rules laid down in the general provisions of the Uniform Act relating to commercial companies, other than those which are specifically related to corporate personality[357].

As regards relations with third parties, each partner contracts in his own name and is solely liable for any obligations that are undertaken. However, if the partners expressly represent themselves as acting as partners in their relations with a third party, they are indefinitely and jointly and severally bound by each other's undertakings[358].

The *société en participation* is a very flexible instrument which may prove very useful if it is desired to form an undisclosed consortium or joint venture. However, liability issues and tax exposure for the partners should be carefully analysed when the joint venture agreement is drafted.

D. Société de fait

A *société de fait* is a *de facto* company where two or more individuals or corporate bodies act as if they were in partnership without having properly formed between themselves one of the types of company recognized by the Uniform Act[359]. This may arise when:

- a company recognized by the Uniform Act has been created but the requisite incorporation formalities have not been complied with;

---

[355] Article 855.
[356] Article 856.
[357] Article 855.
[358] Article 861.
[359] Article 864.

- a company recognized by the Uniform Act has been properly created but has not been registered with the RCCM; or
- a company of a type not recognized by the Uniform Act has been created[360].

Any interested party may ask the court to confirm the existence of a *société de fait*[361]. If the court does so, the rules applicable to the share-holders of an SNC are then applicable to the partners[362].

SECTION 5: OTHER STRUCTURES

A. *Economic Interest Groups* (Groupement d'intérêt économique *or* GIE)

The concept of the GIE, which was originally created by French company law in 1967 and has subsequently been adopted in European law, is a new concept for the majority of the Member States.

A GIE is not a company but is defined as a legal entity whose exclusive purpose is to facilitate or develop the economic activities of its members and to improve or increase the results of such activities[363].

Since its creation by the Uniform Act, the GIE has proven to be a real success in the Member States. It can enable African companies better to cooperate and share facilities or know-how in order to face international competition in the African market.

1. General provisions

A GIE can be constituted without capital and does not in itself give rise to the generation and distribution of profits[364]. The members' partner-ship rights are not freely transferable, and any provision to the contrary is considered to be null and void[365]. Because a GIE is an auxiliary structure set up to facilitate its members' own activities, the members retain their own legal identity within the GIE, and are jointly and

---

[360] Article 865.
[361] Article 866.
[362] Article 868.
[363] Article 869.
[364] Article 870.
[365] Article 871.

severally liable for its debts unless otherwise agreed with any third party with whom the GIE may contract[366]. However, the agreement establishing a GIE may determine the respective contributions of each partner towards its debts. If no provision is made in this regard, each member bears an equal part of the debts[367].

(a) Constitution

A GIE may be created by two or more individuals or legal entities and may have a commercial or a non-commercial purpose[368].

It is formed by a written contract which serves as articles of association, indicating the GIE's name; duration; corporate purpose; management organization; and details of the members[369]. The GIE must be registered with the RCCM. Upon registration it acquires its own corporate personality[370].

During its existence, the GIE may accept new members under the conditions laid down in the contract. Any amendments to the contract must be made and published in accordance with the same procedure as for the original contract[371].

(b) Activity

A GIE's activity must be connected to the economic activity of its members and be ancillary to that activity[372]. For example, a GIE might be established for the sharing of cocoa production facilities by cocoa producers, or the sharing of oil exploration equipment or storage tanks by oil companies.

If the GIE has a commercial purpose it has the legal capacity to enter into commercial transactions, to conclude commercial leases and to own a business (*fonds de commerce*). It may issue bonds if all its members are SAs[373].

---

[366] Article 872.
[367] Article 876.
[368] Article 871.
[369] Article 876.
[370] Article 872.
[371] Article 876.
[372] Article 869.
[373] Article 875.

2. Collective decisions

The general meeting of the GIE's members is competent to take any decision. The rules of quorum and majority may be determined by the contract. Failing any provision to this effect, the Uniform Act provides that all decisions must be taken unanimously by the members[374].

The contract may attribute to any member of the GIE a number of votes different from that allocated to the others. If the contract contains no provisions in this regard each member has one vote[375].

3. Management

A GIE is managed by one or more directors. If a director is a legal entity, the entity must appoint an individual as its permanent representative[376].

The partnership contract or the general meeting is free to organize the management of the GIE. It appoints the directors and defines their powers, terms of office and conditions of revocation. In its relations with third parties, a GIE is bound by any acts of a director which fall within its purpose[377].

4. Winding-up

A GIE may be wound up in the following circumstances:

- when its term expires;
- when its purpose has been achieved;
- by decision of the general meeting;
- by a court for legitimate reasons; or
- by the death of an individual member or the winding-up of a legal entity which is a member of the GIE, unless the contract provides otherwise[378].

5. Transformation

A GIE may be transformed into an SNC, without it being necessary to wind up the GIE and create a new company. In addition, any type of

---

[374] Article 877.
[375] Article 877.
[376] Article 879.
[377] Article 879.
[378] Article 883.

company whose corporate purpose corresponds to that of a GIE may be transformed into a GIE, again without any winding-up or creation of a new corporate body[379].

B. *Branches* (Succursales)

A branch is defined as a commercial, industrial or service establishment belonging to a company or individual and having a certain degree of management autonomy, without having a legal personality independent from that of its owner. The rights and obligations arising out of the activity or existence of a branch appertain to the owner of the branch[380]. A distinction must therefore be made between branches and subsidiaries. The latter are separate and autonomous companies with their own legal personality and share capital which, although they are held by a parent company, must be registered with the RCCM in their own name and have their own rights and obligations.

The Uniform Act makes a distinction between two types of branches:

- branches of companies registered in a Member State; and
- branches of foreign companies, ie companies which are not registered in one of the Member States.

Branches of companies that are already registered in one of the Member States must be registered with the RCCM in the Member State in which they are established, within one month of their establishment[381].

A branch registered by a company which is not registered in a Member State is subject to the laws of the Member State in which it is established, in the absence of any international agreement or laws to the contrary[382]. It must be registered with the RCCM within one month of its establishment.

Within two years of its establishment, any such branch must be transferred to a company registered in one of the Member States unless it is expressly exempted from this requirement by a decree issued by the minister in charge of commerce in the Member State where the branch is located[383].

---

[379] Article 882.
[380] Articles 116–117.
[381] Article 119.
[382] Article 118.
[383] Article 120.

SECTION 6: RESTRUCTURING AND TRANSFORMATION

A. Mergers, spin-offs and partial business transfers

Articles 189 to 199 of the Uniform Act contain general provisions dealing with three different types of restructuring: mergers (*fusions*), spin-offs (*scissions*) and partial business transfers (*apports partiels d'actifs*), regardless of the type of company concerned. Articles 382 and 383 deal with mergers and spin-offs exclusively concerning SARLs, and Articles 670 to 689 deal with mergers and spin-offs between SAs and, where specified by Article 382, between SARLs.

These restructuring provisions apply to restructuring operations between companies in the same Member State, and also to cross-border restructuring operations between companies in several Member States[384]. They therefore represent a significant simplification in the conduct of such operations.

The general definition given in the Uniform Act states that a merger is a '*transaction whereby two companies join to form a single company either by the creation of a new company or by the absorption of one company by the other*'[385]. Although this definition refers only to mergers between two companies, there seems to be no reason why it should not be possible to merge more than two companies at the same time.

A spin-off is defined as a '*transaction whereby a company's assets and liabilities are shared out among several existing or newly-created companies*'[386].

A partial business transfer is defined as a '*transaction whereby a company contributes an autonomous division of its activity to another existing or newly created company*'[387]. These transactions are governed by the rules applicable to spin-offs.

The Uniform Act makes the traditional distinction between the creation of new companies as a vehicle for the merger or spin-off and the use of existing companies. The use of existing companies is generally preferable as this is less likely to involve a risk of losing custom, and the system is also often more advantageous from a tax point of view.

The legal regimes applicable to all three types of restructuring are very similar and will therefore be dealt with together, with an indication,

---

[384] Article 199.
[385] Article 189.
[386] Article 190.
[387] Article 195.

where applicable, of any provisions that might be relevant to only one type. Different terminology is used in French depending upon whether assets and liabilities are transferred to an existing company or to a new company set up for the purpose, reference being made to 'absorption' only when the transfer is made to an existing company or companies. However, for the sake of simplicity in the following discussion, reference will be made to the 'absorbing company' and to the 'absorbed company' regardless of which mechanism is used, unless it is necessary in the context to make the distinction.

1. Main features

Mergers and spin-offs result in the transfer to the absorbing company or companies of all the assets and liabilities of the absorbed company or companies and the winding-up of the latter[388]. Where there is a partial business transfer, on the other hand, only the assets and liabilities relating to the transferred part of the business are transferred, and the company is not wound up[389].

(a) Transfer to the absorbing company of all assets and liabilities of the absorbed company or division

All the assets and liabilities of the absorbed company or division are transferred to the absorbing company or companies[390]. The transfer is an automatic consequence of the restructuring.

(i) Automatic transfer

Automatic transfer means that all the assets and liabilities of the absorbed company, including those which may not have been mentioned in the restructuring deed due to errors or omissions, are transferred to the absorbing company[391]. As a result, an absorbing company may be obliged to pay a debt of the absorbed company which has not been mentioned among the liabilities in the restructuring deed.

There is, however, a doubt, which has not yet been resolved, as to the automatic transfer of certain contracts in the context of a restructuring when the law prohibits their assignment.

---

[388] Articles 189–190.
[389] Article 195.
[390] Articles 189–190.
[391] Article 191.

A similar doubt arises as to any public law contracts signed between a Member State or one of its agencies and a private company. Here the issue is whether an absorbed company which for example has a business permit, a consent resulting from an investment agreement, or a concession agreement, may transfer these to the absorbing company.

The general rule that is usually applied in such cases is that an essential condition of contractual relations existing between a public entity and a private entity is the identity of the persons involved (*intuitus personae*). It is likely, therefore, that such contracts may not be transferred save with the prior consent of the public entity, and that failing such consent the public entity may consider that the contract concerned is no longer binding upon it.

The situation is perhaps simpler if the private entity which is a party to such a contract is not absorbed by a different company, but is taken over by a third party. Although the Uniform Act provides no answer to this question, according to the opinion of the French Advisory Council (*Conseil d'Etat*) given in similar circumstances, the term 'third party' refers to a legal entity which is distinct from the original party to the contract[392]. By analogy, a change in the legal structure of the company, a take-over of the company, the company becoming a subsidiary of another company, or a change in the ownership of its shares cannot be regarded as events requiring the consent of the contracting public entity, since none of these transactions leads to the creation of a new legal entity or to the assignment of the contract to a third party.

However a merger or spin-off leading to the winding-up of the contracting party and the transfer of its assets and liabilities to another company is a different situation, where it may be assumed that consent is needed. Since the Uniform Act contains no provisions in this regard, the answer to the question of whether a transfer to which consent has not been given is effective will have to be sought in the national law of the Member State concerned.

(ii) Allocation of shares

The Uniform Act provides that, as a result of a merger or spin-off, the shareholders of the absorbed company become shareholders of the absorbing company[393].

---

[392] French *Conseil d'État*, Financial Section, Advisory Opinion No. 364.803 of 8 June 2000 requested by the Ministry of Finance.
[393] Article 191.

In other words, mergers and spin-offs lead to an exchange of shares, with the shareholders of the absorbed company contributing their shares in the absorbed company in exchange for shares in the absorbing company. It is therefore necessary for an exchange ratio to be established between the shares of the absorbed company and those of the absorbing company. In restructurings involving SARLs or SAs, a merger or spin-off appraiser (*commissaire à la fusion* or *commissaire à la scission*) is appointed by the court to prepare a report on the details of the operation[394]. He plays an important part in relation to this exchange ratio, in that he certifies the valuation of each of the companies involved in the restructuring and expresses an opinion as to the fairness of the ratio.

An exception to the above principle is that no exchange of shares may take place when the absorbed company's shares are held either by the absorbing company or by the absorbed company itself.

(iii) Employment aspects

Mandatory employment law provisions which protect employees must be complied with in any restructuring. Attention must therefore be paid to the employment law applicable in each of the Member States concerned, in order to determine what provision is made for the transfer of employees in the event of a merger or spin-off. National employment laws sometimes guarantee the protection of the employees, through the automatic continuation of their employment contracts. In such an event, the absorbing company will be considered to be the new employer. For example, the Labour Codes in Burkina Faso, Cameroon, Chad, Mali and Niger provide that in the event of a merger, the employment contracts in force on the date of the change will continue between the new employer and the employees of the absorbed company[395].

(b) Winding-up of the absorbed company

The merger or spin-off leads to the automatic winding-up of the absorbed company. There is no need, however, to liquidate the company, since all its assets and liabilities are transferred to the absorbing company[396]. This

---

[394] Articles 382, 672 and 684.
[395] Burkina Faso Labour Code (1992), Article 39; Cameroon Labour Code: Law No. 92-007 of 14 August 1992, Article 42; Chad Labour Code: Law No. 038/PR/96, Articles 136 and 375; Mali Labour Code: Law No. 92-020 of 23 September 1992, Article L 57; Niger Labour Code: Ordinance No. 96-039 of 29 June 1996, Articles 90 and 91.
[396] Article 191.

rule is, of course, useful in that it facilitates the restructuring process by avoiding the delays inherent in liquidation.

2. General conditions

Restructuring may take place between companies of different types, and in principle this does not raise many difficulties. More complicated problems may arise if the nationalities of the companies are different.

(a) Restructuring involving companies of different types

Article 196 states that unless provided to the contrary elsewhere in the Uniform Act, restructurings may involve companies of different types. There appears in fact to be no provision expressly to the contrary in the Uniform Act. However, GIEs would seem to be excluded since, by definition, they are not companies. Also, it would seem difficult to include *sociétés en participation* which, although they are referred to as companies, have no corporate personality and no assets or liabilities in their own name, or *sociétés de fait*, which have not been properly incorporated. Therefore a restructuring may involve companies of any other type referred to in the Uniform Act, ie SAs, SARLs, SNCs, and SCSs.

Since commercial companies in which the State or a public entity is a shareholder are governed by the Uniform Act[397], it seems that the Uniform Act would also apply to any restructuring involving a State-owned company.

(b) Restructuring involving companies in liquidation

Companies in the process of being liquidated may be involved in a merger[398]. However, such companies may only be the absorbed company, and never the absorbing company. There is no similar provision for spin-offs and partial business transfers involving such companies. However, this may well have been an oversight in the Uniform Act since there seems to be no reason for making such a distinction.

(c) Restructuring involving companies of different nationalities

The Uniform Act should facilitate international restructuring within the OHADA region, as its cross-border nature removes the possibility of any

---

[397] Article 1.
[398] Article 189.

conflict of laws that might otherwise occur in a restructuring involving companies having their registered offices in different countries. As a result, there is a single set of rules and procedures which would apply, for example, to a restructuring between a company incorporated in Senegal and a company incorporated in the Central African Republic. Questions will, however, remain as to the law applicable to a restructuring between a company governed by the Uniform Act and a company that is incorporated in a country which is not a Member State. In such a case, although the Uniform Act contains no express provisions in this regard, it would seem possible to apply the Uniform Act to the restructuring, subject of course to any contrary mandatory provision in the laws of the third party State.

3. Restructuring procedure

For each company involved, a restructuring generally requires the drafting of a restructuring deed (a merger, spin-off or partial business transfer deed, as the case may be), and the appointment of an appraiser if an SA or an SARL is involved[399].

(a) The restructuring deed and the report on the envisaged restructuring

The details of the restructuring are presented in a restructuring deed, a draft of which is prepared by the management of each of the companies involved in the restructuring process[400].

Two publication formalities must then be completed by each of the companies involved[401]. First, the draft deed must be filed with the competent courts where the registered offices of the companies are situated. Second, a notice describing the envisaged restructuring must be inserted in a legal journal one month before the date of the first general meeting to be held to vote upon the restructuring. These formalities are a guarantee for the shareholders that no further amendments to the deed can be made, and they are also a means of informing the creditors of the companies concerned.

Specific employment regulations in each of the Member States concerned may also require the employees' representative bodies to be consulted or informed about the restructuring project.

---

[399] Save for the Simplified Restructuring Procedures, described below.
[400] Article 193 of the Uniform Act specifies the clauses to be contained in the deed.
[401] Article 194.

When SAs are involved in the restructuring, the board of directors of each of the SAs must prepare a report indicating the legal and economic reasons for the envisaged restructuring[402]. This report must be made available to the shareholders 15 days before the date of the meeting which is to be held to vote upon the restructuring[403].

(b) The role of the appraiser

One or more appraisers must be appointed whenever the restructuring is to occur between SAs or SARLs, or if it involves both SAs and SARLs[404]. The appraiser prepares a written report on the envisaged restructuring, expressing an opinion on the value of the contributions in kind and on any special benefits granted, and on the fairness of the exchange ratio for the shares. The appraiser must also verify the accuracy of the liabilities to be borne by the absorbing company. As a result, he must make detailed investigations, and the Uniform Act specifies that he may obtain any relevant document from each company involved in the restructuring process and may make any verifications that may be necessary in order to ensure the proper performance of his task[405]. When several appraisers have been appointed, they submit only one report if they have been appointed on behalf of all the companies involved.

(c) Decision

The decision as regards restructuring is generally made by each company involved in accordance with the conditions applicable to an amendment to its articles of association, using the procedure applicable in the event of an increase in capital or the winding-up of the company.

Article 674 requires that in an SA, the draft restructuring deed, the special management reports, the financial statements and other company records be made available to the shareholders at the company's registered office at least 15 days before the date of the meeting which is to be held to vote upon the restructuring. This period of time is shorter than under French law, which requires that these documents be made available at least one month before the meeting. Article 674 also obliges the company to have specific accounting statements prepared in the same

---

[402] Article 671.
[403] Article 674.
[404] Article 672.
[405] Article 672.

way as for its previous annual financial statements, if those financial statements concern a financial year ended more than six months earlier than the date of the restructuring deed. The new accounting statements must be drawn up as of a date not earlier than three months before the date of the draft restructuring deed.

When SAs are to merge, the decision may be made only by resolution of the extraordinary general meeting of each company, and the management of the company cannot be authorized to take the decision on the shareholders' behalf[406]. A majority of two-thirds of the votes cast at the general meeting is required for the resolution to be passed.

The restructuring must also be approved by a special general meeting in SAs if the restructuring is to result in the cancellation of specific rights granted to a given category of shareholders[407].

In an SARL, a general meeting must be convened for the purpose of taking an extraordinary collective decision. Pursuant to the Uniform Act the decision must be taken by shareholders holding at least three-quarters of the registered capital[408].

In SNCs the restructuring must be approved by all the shareholders unanimously[409].

In SCSs it must be approved by the active partners unanimously and by sleeping partners representing the majority of the sleeping partners' capital[410].

Article 197 specifies however that, as an exception to the rules relating to majority in SAs, SARLs and SCSs, the decision must be taken by all the shareholders unanimously if the restructuring is to lead to an increase in the commitments of the shareholders of one of the companies concerned.

(d) Simplified restructuring procedures

Article 676 of the Uniform Act allows for a simplified restructuring procedure to be applied in an SA or an SARL when the absorbing company holds the whole of the share capital of the absorbed company or companies throughout the period between the date on which the restructuring deed is filed with the court and the date on which the

---

[406] Article 671.
[407] Article 671.
[408] Articles 215 and 358.
[409] Articles 215 and 274.
[410] Articles 215 and 296.

restructuring is completed. In other words the simplified procedure is available when the absorbed company is a 100 per cent subsidiary of the absorbing company.

Under the simplified procedure, it is unnecessary to obtain the approval of the extraordinary general meeting of the absorbed company or companies. The restructuring simply has to be approved by an extraordinary general meeting of the shareholders of the absorbing company. No appraiser is needed, and there is no need for a report by the management. However it may in certain circumstances be advisable to apply for the appointment of an *ad hoc* appraiser to certify the assets and liabilities contributed by the absorbed company as listed by the management.

A simplified procedure is also applicable when the restructuring is effected by means of the creation of new companies, when no contributions are made other than the absorbed companies. In such circumstances, only the approval of the absorbed companies is required, it being understood that these also approve the articles of association of the new companies, there being no need to obtain approval from the new companies either for the restructuring itself or for the articles of association[411]. Furthermore, when there is a spin-off or a partial business transfer, and the shareholders are attributed rights in the capital of the new companies which are proportional to their rights in the old company's capital, there is no need to have a report prepared by an appraiser[412].

4. Creditors' rights

In the restructuring process, the rights of creditors vary depending on whether they are bondholders or not.

(a) Creditors who are not bondholders

In principle the creditors of an absorbed company who are not bondholders of that company become creditors of the absorbing company[413].

However, creditors of any of the companies involved in a restructuring process who are not bondholders of such companies, and whose claim has arisen prior to the publication of the draft restructuring deed, may

---

[411] Articles 677 and 685
[412] Article 685.
[413] Article 679.

object to the transaction within 30 days of the publication[414]. Such objections do not have the effect of preventing or suspending the restructuring[415], contrary to what happens when creditors object to a share capital reduction[416]. Instead, the court before which any objections are filed will either reject the objections or order payment of the debts concerned and/or the provision of satisfactory guarantees.

This right to object to the restructuring is available both to the creditors of the absorbed company, who can thus seek to avoid changing debtors, and to the creditors of the absorbing company, in order for them to seek to avoid competing with the creditors of the absorbed company.

In addition, creditors may avail themselves of any specific provisions that may be contained in their agreements with the companies involved and which provide for the immediate payment of debts in the event the company becomes involved in a merger or spin-off[417].

(b) An exception: bondholders

In accordance with Articles 678 and 686 of the Uniform Act, the draft restructuring deed must be submitted to the bondholders' meetings of the absorbed companies, unless an offer is published in a legal journal to reimburse their bonds upon request, in which case the absorbing company becomes their debtor.

This procedure is not applicable within the absorbing company. In the absorbing company the bondholders' general meeting may nevertheless authorize the bondholders' representatives to object to the restructuring. Such objections are governed by the same rules as objections made by creditors who are not bondholders.

5. Finalization of restructuring

(a) Effective date

The effective date of the restructuring is the date upon which the transfer of all the absorbed company's assets and liabilities takes place. This date depends on whether or not the restructuring involves the creation of a new company, as follows[418]:

---

[414] Article 679.
[415] Article 679.
[416] Article 637.
[417] Article 680.
[418] Article 192.

- When one or more new companies are to be set up, the restructuring is effective as of the date on which the last of these companies is registered with the RCCM;
- When the restructuring involves an absorption by an existing company or companies, it takes effect as of the date of the last general meeting approving the transaction. However, the deed may provide for another date as the effective date. This date may not be later than the end of the current financial year of an absorbing company, nor can it be before the end of a previously closed financial year of an absorbed company.

(b) Filings and penalties

In addition to the formalities described above, the Uniform Act requires that the companies involved in the restructuring register a statement with the court, summarizing all the actions undertaken for the restructuring and certifying that the transaction has been carried out in compliance with the Uniform Act[419]. The statement must be signed by the representatives of the management bodies of all the companies taking part in the restructuring. The restructuring procedure is invalid if this is not done.

The Uniform Act does not lay down any specific time-frame during which the situation may be remedied if the restructuring procedure is found to be invalid. However, Article 251 provides that the right to have the restructuring declared null and void lapses six months after the last registration with the RCCM. Until then any interested person may bring legal proceedings for the restructuring to be declared null and void, although the right will be deemed to have lapsed if the reason justifying the annulment no longer exists on the date on which the court rules on the merits of the case[420].

If, on the other hand, there are grounds for annulment, the court may allow a certain time for the situation to be remedied, and it cannot declare the restructuring null and void until two months after the proceedings have been commenced[421]. In these circumstances, it may be necessary to convene a general meeting of shareholders. When this is the case, the court allows sufficient time for the meeting to be held. If no decision has

---

[419] Article 198.
[420] Article 246.
[421] Article 247.

been taken by the time the court's deadline expires, the court will rule on the matter, upon the request of any party.

B. *Transformation of a company*

1. Definition

Transformation of a company occurs when the company changes its legal form by means of a decision of its shareholders[422]. The decision does not involve the creation of a new company and the existing company is consequently deemed to continue with the same legal personality[423]. As a result, any rights and obligations of the company existing before its transformation remain fully valid and binding[424].

Transformation is subject to the legal formalities laid down by the Uniform Act for any modification of the articles of association. However, the transformation of a company in which the shareholders have limited liability into a company in which their liability becomes unlimited is subject to the unanimous decision of the shareholders[425].

2. Effects

A decision to transform the company cannot be retroactive but is effective as of the day on which it has been decided by the shareholders[426]. Nevertheless, the decision will only be valid as against third parties once the legal formalities have been completed: ie publication in a legal journal; filing of minutes with the commercial court; and modifications of entries in the RCCM and of entries in the land registry if the company owns real estate[427].

The terms of office of the management bodies are terminated upon a decision to transform the company[428]. However, the statutory auditors remain in office if the company's new legal form requires it to have auditors[429].

---

[422] Article 181.
[423] However, the company loses its legal personality if it is transformed into a legal form that is not provided for by the Uniform Act.
[424] Article 186.
[425] Article 181.
[426] Article 182.
[427] Article 265.
[428] Article 184.
[429] Article 187.

3. Specific regulations concerning SAs and SARLs

An SA or an SARL may be transformed into another form of company if, at the time of the decision, it has existed for at least two years and has drawn up and approved its first two financial statements, and if its net equity is at least equal to its share capital[430].

The shareholders decide upon the transformation after the presentation of a report prepared by the statutory auditor or, if there is no statutory auditor, by a specially appointed auditor[431]. The report must certify that the company's net equity is at least equal to the amount of the share capital.

SECTION 7: PUBLIC OFFERINGS

Public offerings enable companies to raise money and finance their projects, notably by issuing shares or bonds which may then be acquired by either local or foreign investors. In the Member States, public offerings are regulated not only by the Uniform Act, but also by two other regional integration organizations, UEMOA and CEMAC[432]. Since each of these organizations has its own rules, different sources of supra-national law need to be consulted in order to understand the legal regime applicable to companies which want to seek private funding in the Member States.

The legal concept of public offerings is referred to in the Uniform Act. Articles 81 to 96 contain general provisions, Articles 823 to 853 contain specific provisions applicable to SAs, and Article 905 contains criminal law provisions. In addition, UEMOA and CEMAC have put into place an institutional and legal framework to promote and organize public offerings.

In the context of UEMOA, the regional financial market is organized around three major institutional bodies: the *Conseil Régional de l'Épargne Publique et des Marchés Financiers* (Regional Council for Public Savings and Financial Markets or *CREPMF*), which is a public body regulating and controlling public offerings[433]; the *Bourse Régionale des Valeurs*

---

[430] Articles 374 and 690–691.

[431] Articles 375 and 691.

[432] UEMOA, which covers the West African Member States, and CEMAC, which covers the Central African Member States, are discussed further in Chapter 12.

[433] The Regional Council was created by a convention dated 3 July 1996 adopted by the Council of Ministers of UMOA (now UEMOA). Its powers have been further defined

Mobilières (Regional Stock Exchange or *BRVM*) replacing the pre-existing Abidjan Stock Exchange in Côte d'Ivoire[434]; and the *Dépositaire Central/ Banque de Règlement* (Central Depository/Settlement Bank or *DC/BR*)[435], the latter two bodies being SAs which have been granted a concession to operate a public service. Authorized *sociétés de gestion et d'intermédiation* (management and intermediation companies or *SGI*) also exist in each UEMOA Member State[436].

Financial markets in the CEMAC region do not seem to be as efficiently organized as in the UEMOA region. Two competing stock exchanges are to be set up: a national stock exchange in Douala, called the *Bourse Camerounaise des Valeurs Mobilières* (Cameroon Stock Exchange or *BCVM*)[437], and on a regional level the *Bourse des Valeurs Mobilières d'Afrique Centrale* (Central African Stock Exchange or *BVMAC*) based in Libreville (Gabon)[438]. A Supervisory Commission for the Central African

---

by a regulation of the Council of Ministers of UMOA (*'Règlement général relatif à l'organisation, au fonctionnement et au contrôle du marché financier régional de l'UMOA'*). This Regulation provides that the Regional Council will be in charge of organizing public offerings, authorizing and monitoring the market entities and traders, and finally monitoring the legality of transactions on the stock exchange. The Regional Council must approve the creation of stock exchange institutions and the activities of management and intermediation companies. It gives its prior approval to the listing of any SA or the floating of unlisted securities in the UEMOA member States, and monitors any information that is disclosed. In this context, it checks the publications required by any laws or regulations or by the courts, such as the information document, notice and circulars whose publication is required by the Uniform Act.

[434] The BRVM has an electronic spot market and currently has 38 listed companies. It has two divisions: a first market division for shares, and a second market division for bonds.

[435] The DC/BR holds accounts for the trading of securities and the payment of all transactions. The DC/BR also has a guarantee fund which intervenes in the event an account-holder fails to make delivery or payment. This is aimed at guaranteeing market integrity.

[436] SGIs have the exclusive right to trade in listed securities. They hold and manage securities accounts.

[437] The Cameroon Stock Exchange will be a spot market and the quotation will be made by a single fixing. There will be two divisions: the first division reserved for companies with a registered capital of at least 500 million FCFA which have achieved a minimum net margin of 3 per cent p.a. over the last three financial years; and the second division for companies with a registered capital of at least 200 million FCFA.

[438] Additional Act No. 11/00-CEMAC-CCE-02 of 14 December 2000. It seems that the BVMAC will probably be organized in a way very similar to the BRVM, in that it will have a primary market and a secondary market and a supervisory body like the Regional Council will be set up. It also seems that market transactions will be made by brokers, and that a supervisory committee will ensure that transactions are made properly.

Financial Market has also been created[439]. Although numerous public announcements have been made regarding the creation of these two stock markets, the first transactions have however not taken place to date and BVMAC is not expected to start functioning until 2003.

A. Scope of public offerings

1. Definition

Companies which make public offerings are defined as those which, in order to obtain funds, seek investment from the public. The establishment and operation of such companies is governed by specific rules aimed at protecting investors.

The Uniform Act provides that there is presumed to be a public offering in any of the following three situations[440]:

- the listing of securities on the official list of a stock exchange in a Member State, ie either the BRVM, the BCVM or the BVMAC;
- the public offering of securities through credit institutions or brokers, or through canvassing and advertising; or
- the placing of securities with over 100 persons.

In other words, it is possible for a company to be subject to the rules governing public offerings even if it is not listed on a stock exchange. In particular, issuers of securities must pay particular attention to the fact that a company will be deemed to make public offerings if it has a total of at least 100 shareholders and bondholders.

2. Companies authorized to make public offerings

Only SAs are allowed to issue negotiable securities and offer them to the public[441]. The Uniform Act specifies that SAs making public offerings must have a registered capital of not less than 100 million FCFA[442] and must be administered by a board of directors[443].

---

[439] Additional Act No. 03/01-CEMAC-CE-03 of 8 December 2001.
[440] Article 81.
[441] Article 58.
[442] Article 824.
[443] Article 828.

A peculiarity of the Uniform Act lies in the fact that any company with its registered office in any one of the Member States may issue securities in any other Member States, offering them to residents in those other countries. The regime applicable to international public offerings within the OHADA region therefore does not raise any particular problems when the issuing company has its registered office in a Member State.

However, foreign companies making public offerings in OHADA countries need to comply with UEMOA or CEMAC regulations, as the case may be. For instance, Article 174 of the UEMOA Regulation provides that no person, State-owned or privately owned entity or mutual fund which is not resident in the UEMOA region may be listed on the regional stock exchange. Furthermore, for unlisted securities, Article 176 of the same Regulation provides that any offering of such securities to the public by or on behalf of a non-resident company is subject to the prior approval of the Regional Council.

3. Types of securities and public offerings

The Uniform Act provides that securities may be offered in the context either of a new issue or of a sale of existing securities ('*titres*'), without giving a definition of the word '*titre*'[444]. Although in various other provisions rules are laid down for the issuance of both shares and bonds, and also shares in non-closed mutual funds, it should be borne in mind that the definitions of securities and instruments may differ depending on whether reference is made to the Uniform Act or to the UEMOA or CEMAC regulations.

In addition, although the Uniform Act has not created a specific regime, it may be possible in practice to create hybrid securities combining both shares and bonds and/or representing a receivable against the company. Such securities may for example be bonds reimbursable in shares or convertible into shares, or shares or bonds giving a right to subscribe for shares[445]. In the context of the development of the African financial markets and/or venture capital transactions, these instruments may be very useful. However, in the absence of any specific OHADA regulations, it will be necessary to verify whether any national or other supranational regulations are applicable to such securities or may restrict the contractual freedom of shareholders and companies in this regard.

---

[444] Article 83.
[445] Whilst most commonly issued by companies making public offerings, it seems that these may also be issued by SAs which do not make public offerings.

B. Procedural guarantees and publication formalities

With a view to protecting investors the Uniform Act lays down certain procedures for public offerings and creates certain requirements as to information and publication of offers made to the public. The Uniform Act also requires increases in capital or the floating of new securities to be made according to specific terms.

1. Procedural guarantees

Companies making public offerings must fulfil three main conditions, which are required as guarantees: (i) they must obtain a performance bond from one or more credit institutions in the country where the public offering is made, if the value of the public offering, regardless of its form, exceeds 50 million FCFA; (ii) they must use the services of any such credit institution to provide financial support and make a presentation of the public offering; and (iii) when the value of the public offering exceeds 50 million FCFA, they must appoint one or more auditors in the Member State or States where the offering is made, to verify the financial statements and sign a prospectus[446].

2. Prospectus, notice and other publications

(a) The prospectus

A company making a public offering must prepare a prospectus to inform the public, if the total value of the public offering exceeds 50 million FCFA[447]. It must be prepared and distributed in every country where the public offering is to be made. The prospectus includes in particular information regarding the structure of the issuer, its financial standing, its activities and prospects for development, as well as any information relating to the securities offered to the public[448].

However, it is not necessary to prepare a prospectus in the following circumstances:

- the amount of the public offering does not exceed 50 million FCFA;
- the offering is made in consideration for contributions made on the occasion of a merger or a partial business transfer;

---

446 Article 85.
447 Article 86.
448 The contents of the document are detailed in Articles 87–89.

- it concerns shares in non-closed mutual funds;
- it is addressed to particular persons in the context of their professional activities;
- it relates to securities that are given free of charge in the event of payment of a dividend or incorporation of reserves in the share capital;
- the securities are offered as a result of the exercise of a right attached to securities which have already been the subject of a prospectus; or
- they are offered in replacement for shares in the same company and their issuance does not result in an increase of the share capital of the issuing company[449].

The prospectus must be signed by the statutory auditor and/or by auditors appointed in the Member States where the transaction is being made. It is then submitted for approval to the competent stock exchange supervisory body in the Member State in which the issuer is registered, and in each of the Member States where securities are being offered to the public (ie in the UEMOA countries to the Regional Council). If there is no such body, the draft memorandum is submitted for approval to the Ministry of Finance of the State or States concerned[450]. The supervisory body may require amendments or order further investigations from the auditors or the insertion of a warning in the document, and may require the company to provide an appropriate guarantee if the public offering is made in a State other than the State where the company has its registered office.

Approval must be granted or refused within one month of delivery of the prospectus to the supervisory body, unless further investigations are required, in which case the period may be increased to two months[451]. Failure to respond is deemed to be an approval of the document. Reasons must be given for any refusal, the usual reasons being either insufficient information given to the supervisory body or circumstances that do not sufficiently protect investors.

Once the prospectus has been approved by the relevant authorities it must be published in a legal journal and a brochure must be made

---

[449] Article 95.

[450] Article 90.

[451] Article 115 of the UEMOA Regulation provides that failure to obtain prior approval leads to the transaction being null and void with respect to both the applicant and the public to which the offer is made. Article 118 provides that the Regional Council may, by a duly reasoned decision, veto any listing of securities if it considers that such listing may lead to investors running serious risks.

available to any interested person at the registered office of the issuing company[452].

(b) The notice and circulars

A notice must be prepared when the public offering is to be made either to establish an SA, to increase the capital of a company which already makes public offerings or to make a bond issue[453]. This notice is published in legal journals in the Member States concerned. Circulars must also be prepared, which are more generally aimed at informing the public of the envisaged public offering[454].

(c) Publication obligations during the life of the company

Any listed company and, in certain circumstances, its unlisted subsidiaries, must publish its accounting and financial statements in a legal journal[455].

3. Regime applicable to the issuance of shares relating to an increase in capital

(a) Procedure

Any company which increases its capital by means of a public offering must prepare a prospectus and a notice with a specific content as well as circulars to inform the public of the transaction[456].

If the company was created without any public offering, and if the public offering is made less than two years after the creation of the company, ie within two years of signature of its articles of association, any particular benefits granted at the time the company was created must be valued by an in-kind contributions appraiser, who must also audit the assets and liabilities of the company[457].

---

[452] Article 93.
[453] Article 825. The content of this notice is defined by Articles 826, 833 and 842.
[454] Article 827.
[455] Articles 846–853.
[456] Articles 832 and 835. Details of the required contents are provided in Article 833.
[457] Article 836.

The payment of the paid-up fraction of the face value of the shares and of the whole of any share premium must occur not later than 35 days following the deadline for subscriptions[458].

(b) Pre-emptive subscription right

In principle, shareholders have a pre-emptive right to subscribe for any new issue of shares. However, the extraordinary general meeting of shareholders may decide to cancel this pre-emptive subscription right in favour of one or more identified or unidentified persons[459]. In such an event, the meeting decides upon the price at which the new shares will be issued, after hearing reports from the board of directors and the statutory auditor.

Certain conditions are laid down for such increases in capital where shares are issued to the public without the existing shareholders exercising their pre-emptive subscription right, as follows:

(i). If the new shares are to carry the same rights as the existing shares, the company must issue them within three years of the decision by the general meeting to issue them. If the company's shares are already listed, the issuing price must be calculated by reference to the average quoted price of the shares over 20 consecutive days chosen within the 40-day period preceding the issuance. If the shares are not listed, the issuing price must be equal to the equity that each share represents in the latest balance sheet, or must be determined by a court-appointed expert[460].

(ii). If the new shares do not carry the same rights as the existing shares, they must be issued within two years of the decision by the general meeting to issue them. The issuing price will be determined by the extraordinary general meeting on the basis of a report by the board of directors and a special report by the statutory auditor. If the issuance has not been completed as of the date of the annual general meeting following that extraordinary general meeting, a further extraordinary meeting must be held to decide whether to maintain or adjust the price[461].

---

[458] Article 840.
[459] Article 839.
[460] Article 837.
[461] Article 838.

C. Penalties

Any person having an interest may apply for the winding-up of a listed company if the legal requirements regarding its minimum capital have not been complied with[462].

In addition, the management of a company which makes a public offering without complying with the publication procedures and/or publishing the information required under the Uniform Act may be subject to criminal penalties[463]. In this regard the individual Member States are free to determine the applicable penalties.

---

[462] Article 824.
[463] Article 905.

6

Accounting Law

The most recently enacted Uniform Act is the Uniform Act on Accounting Law which was adopted in Yaoundé on 24 March 2000. It lays down a harmonized accounting system for companies located in the Member States, setting out comprehensive provisions for accounting organization, the obligation to present annual accounts, rules for the evaluation and determination of net income, auditing, publication of accounting information, consolidated accounts and criminal penalties.

The Uniform Act entered into force on the following dates:

- 1 January 2001 for companies' individual accounts, ie those which are not consolidated or combined with the accounts of any other company, with regard to transactions and corporate accounts for the financial year open as of that date; and
- 1 January 2002 for consolidated and combined accounts, with regard to transactions and corporate accounts for the financial year open as of that date.

SECTION 1: SCOPE OF THE UNIFORM ACT ON ACCOUNTING LAW

The Uniform Act provides that the following types of companies must keep financial accounts: companies governed by commercial law; public, para-public and semi-public companies; cooperatives; and more generally any entity manufacturing or producing marketable or non-marketable goods and services, if that entity habitually exercises an economic activity (whether for financial gain or otherwise, and whether the activity concerned is its main activity or merely accessory to its main activity)[1].

An express exception excludes from this list companies that are subject to public accounting rules applicable in the Member State concerned.

SECTION 2: GENERAL ACCOUNTING PRINCIPLES

The general accounting principles laid down by the Uniform Act will be familiar to those who have some knowledge of modern accounting systems. Their fundamental aim is to ensure the reliability, clarity and comparability of financial information both within the company itself and as supplied to the public.

In order to achieve this aim, companies are required to prepare their accounts in accordance with the terminology and guiding principles set out by the Uniform Act[2]. In particular, they must comply with the obligations of regularity, accuracy and transparency[3].

Article 6 of the Uniform Act requires further that:

- the principle of conservatism is to be complied with at all times, meaning that a realistic assessment must be made of the events and transactions to be entered into the accounts for each financial year;
- the company should comply in good faith with all applicable rules and procedures;
- the persons in charge of the accounts should establish and implement internal audit procedures, in order to be properly informed as to the reality and importance of all events, transactions and situations pertaining to the company's activity;
- the information should be presented and circulated in a clear form, without any attempt to conceal the reality of the situation.

Annual financial statements must be prepared for each financial year, which must coincide with the calendar year unless it is the first year of the company's existence or the company is in liquidation[4]. These statements comprise a balance sheet, a statement of profit and loss, a

---

[1] Articles 1 and 2.
[2] Article 4.
[3] Article 3.
[4] Article 7.

financial table showing the sources and uses of funds, and an annexure indicating any facts that are not apparent in the other financial documents and that may have a significant bearing on the assets, the financial situation or the financial results of the company[5]. In particular, further information or justification must be provided in this annexure in cases where application of an OHADA accounting rule is not sufficient or is inappropriate to give a truthful image of the situation and transactions of the company[6].

The annual financial statements are considered as an unseverable whole. They must describe properly and truthfully the events, transactions and situations pertaining to the financial year in question, in such a way as to give an accurate image of the company's assets, financial situation and results, based on an appropriate, honest, clear, accurate and comprehensive description of such events, transactions and situations[7].

In order to enable a proper comparison of financial statements for one year with those for another, the same terminology and methods for describing the events, transactions and situations should always be used[8].

Detailed provisions for complying with these general principles are set out in Chapters II–V of the Uniform Act.

SECTION 3: NEW OBLIGATIONS CREATED BY THE UNIFORM ACT

Two new sets of obligations created by the Uniform Act are noteworthy. First, the Act provides for three different tiers of accounting obligations depending on the size of the company. Second, it provides for the preparation of consolidated or combined accounts in respect of groups of companies.

A. *The three-tier system of accounting obligations*

The ordinary system for presenting financial statements and keeping accounts applies to all companies, unless the small size of a company

---

[5] Article 8.
[6] Article 10.
[7] Articles 8 and 9.
[8] Article 9.

allows a simplified system to be applied. In this context, a company's size is assessed by reference to its turnover during the financial year in question[9].

A company may thus use the simplified system instead of the ordinary system if its turnover during the financial year in question does not exceed 100 million FCFA[10].

Very small businesses may use a third system instead of either of the above two systems. This is known as the minimum cash-based system, and constitutes an exception to the general provisions laid down by the Uniform Act[11]. For a company to be allowed to use this system, the year's income must not exceed a threshold of between 10 million and 30 million FCFA, depending upon the type of activity of the company.

Financial statements are to be prepared in accordance with models set out in the appendix to the Uniform Act, except in the case of banks and other financial establishments and insurance companies, which are subject to specific accounting models[12]. The information contained in these statements is divided into several categories, which are in turn further sub-divided.

The models have been prepared for each of the three systems outlined above as follows:

- The ordinary system includes a balance sheet, a statement of profit and loss, a financial table of resources and uses of funds, a statistical annexure, and an annexure providing information additional to that given in the other financial statements[13].
- The simplified system includes a balance sheet, a statement of profit and loss, and the annexure providing additional information. All of these documents are simplified in accordance with the provisions of the Uniform Act[14].
- The minimum cash-based system consists of a statement summarizing the income and expenditure of the financial year and showing the net profit or loss of that financial year. The statement is prepared on the basis of the cash-based accounting that all companies applying this system are required to use[15].

---

[9] Article 11.
[10] Article 11.
[11] Article 13.
[12] Article 5. See Section 4 of this chapter.
[13] Article 26.
[14] Article 27.
[15] Article 28.

B. Consolidated accounts and combined accounts

The Uniform Act provides for an obligation to prepare consolidated accounts when a company having its registered office or main activity in one of the Member States controls, either alone or with others, one or more other companies or when it exerts a significant influence over them[16]. Detailed procedures are laid down for the preparation of consolidated accounts.

Two or more companies must prepare combined accounts (ie as though they were a single company) if, in one region of the OHADA area[17], they form an economic whole with a single strategic decision-making centre situated outside that region, and on condition that there is no legal domination of any of the companies by another[18]. These accounts are to be prepared in accordance with the detailed rules applicable to consolidated accounts, except where otherwise specified[19].

SECTION 4: LINKS WITH OTHER EXISTING ACCOUNTING SYSTEMS

Specific accounting requirements have also been laid down by other regional organizations. For example, UEMOA has established an accounting system referred to as SYSCOA[20]. Given the existence of SYSCOA, and also the current trend towards adopting international accounting standards, the utility of the Uniform Act might be questioned. The answer may simply lie in the fact that the Treaty, which dates from 1993 and thus pre-dates SYSCOA, specifically mentions accounting law as one of the areas of law to be harmonized by OHADA. In any event, in order to avoid any potential conflict, the UEMOA authorities and the Permanent Secretary of OHADA will need to ensure that there is full consultation and cooperation on this and other subjects that involve both organizations.

---

[16] Article 74.
[17] A 'region of the OHADA area' is defined in the Uniform Act as an institutionalized economic grouping formed by several Member States, such as CEMAC or UEMOA (which are discussed briefly in Chapter 12).
[18] Article 103.
[19] Article 104.
[20] UEMOA Regulation No. 4/96/CM of 20 December 1996, B.O. UEMOA November 1997.

Finally, specific accounting obligations may be established in relation to certain sectors such as insurance (under the auspices of CIMA[21]) and banking (under the auspices of UEMOA and CEMAC[22]).

---

[21] CIMA Insurance Code, Articles 401 *et seq*. For further details regarding CIMA, see Chapter 12.

[22] In the UEMOA region, the Accounting Model for Banks entered into force on 1 January 1996. In the CEMAC region the Central African Banking Commission (COBAC) is empowered to issue an accounting model and define accounting procedures, in accordance with Article 9 of the Convention creating COBAC, dated 16 October 1990.

7

Collective proceedings for the clearing of debts

The Uniform Act on Collective Proceedings for the Clearing of Debts entered into force on 1 January 1999, and is applicable to all such proceedings commenced after that date. As was the case for company law, there was an urgent need for a modern system to deal with insolvency and related situations. Most Member States' legislation on the subject had not been reformed since the colonial era and, moreover, the French law that was applicable in most Member States at the time of decolonization was itself in urgent need of reform. Since decolonization, only a handful of States had adopted legislation similar to the French reforms of 1967, and even fewer had kept up with more recent French reforms. As a result, until 1999, the majority of Member States applied legislation dating back to the early 19th century.

The Uniform Act is designed to remedy this situation by laying down procedures that are more suited to the modern business environment. It provides for three different types of collective proceedings for the clearing of debts for both companies and individuals, namely:

- preventive settlement (*règlement préventif*)
- administration (*redressement judiciaire*)
- liquidation (*liquidation judiciaire*)

The Uniform Act also contains certain provisions specifically relating to international collective proceedings taking place in several Member States simultaneously.

A recent example of the application of the Uniform Act, which has had considerable coverage in the press, is the decision by the Abidjan Commercial Court, on 25 April 2002, to put the African inter-State airline Air Afrique into liquidation, following its declaration of insolvency.

SECTION 1: PREVENTIVE SETTLEMENT

A. Definition

Article 2 of the Uniform Act defines preventive settlement as a procedure designed to avert insolvency or a cessation of activity, and to permit the clearing of debts by means of a composition agreement (*concordat préventif*).

B. Conditions

Preventive settlement is open to any individual pursuing a commercial activity and any corporate body pursuing a commercial or non-commercial activity, including publicly owned companies. It may not be requested more than once during the same five-year period.

Only the debtor may commence preventive settlement proceedings. It must not be insolvent at the time the proceedings are commenced. Insolvency (*cessation des paiements*) is a defined term under the Uniform Act, meaning a situation where it is impossible for a debtor to meet all its due liabilities with its available assets[1].

C. Procedure

1. Application for preventive settlement

The debtor must file an application addressed to the President of the court, listing any debts for which it wishes to obtain a suspension of enforcement by the creditor concerned[2]. The application must be accompanied by various documents including the debtor's financial statements, a detailed list of assets and liabilities, the cash-flow situation, and details of the work force and related costs[3].

---

[1] Article 25.

[2] Article 5.

[3] Article 6.

The court with which the application must be filed is the court that has jurisdiction over commercial matters at the principal place of business or registered office of the debtor, regardless of whether the debtor has a commercial or a non-commercial activity. The same court also has jurisdiction for all disputes arising in relation to the proceedings, unless these relate to administrative, criminal or employment matters that are subject to the exclusive jurisdiction of a specialized court[4].

Within 30 days of filing the application, the debtor must also file an offer of composition[5]. If the debtor fails to file this offer within the time limit, its application for preventive settlement will be declared inadmissible. The offer should specify, in particular, the means by which it is envisaged that the financial situation of the company will be remedied. These might include the granting by creditors of grace periods or reductions in debts, or the divestiture of certain assets or of a branch of the company's activities. The offer should also give details of the persons who will be responsible for ensuring compliance with the composition agreement and all undertakings made by them which are necessary for the improvement of the situation, including the way in which it is proposed that outstanding debts will be settled; and any redundancies of staff and replacements of management personnel that are envisaged.

2. Suspension of individual proceedings

The composition offer is transmitted to the President of the court immediately it is filed, so that he may issue an order for the suspension of any individual proceedings filed by creditors with a view to enforcing their claims[6].

The effect of the President's order is not only to suspend any individual proceedings, including provisional measures and enforcement measures, that may already have been begun by creditors against the debtor, but also to prohibit any new individual proceedings. The debts concerned by the suspension and prohibition are those that have arisen prior to the order, on condition that they are included on the list submitted by the debtor with its application for preventive settlement[7].

---

[4] Article 3.
[5] Article 7.
[6] Article 8.
[7] Article 9.

Despite the suspension, a creditor may, nonetheless, seek a judgment formally recognizing the existence of his right, but he may not enforce the judgment once it has been obtained[8].

The only limited exception to the suspension rule concerns the debtor's employees, who remain entitled to pursue their claims for payment of salaries or wages. Otherwise, even the claims of secured creditors or creditors with preferential rights are suspended[9].

It is important to note, however, that the suspension applies only to debts that have arisen prior to the date of the decision ordering suspension. Any debts properly arising after that date are payable normally.

As a result of the suspension, any deadlines which would otherwise have resulted in a creditor's foreclosure or other loss of a right by reason of the passing of time are suspended for a corresponding period[10]. In addition, to the extent that the creditors do not grant a waiver under the composition agreement, they also retain their right to any interest accruing on the debts, although this interest is not actually payable during the period of suspension[11].

While the primary purpose of preventive settlement is to allow a company to improve its financial situation and find its feet again, the Uniform Act also seeks to protect the creditors who are affected by the suspension, and to ensure that there is no preferential treatment of certain creditors to the detriment of others. Thus, as a general rule, the debtor is prohibited, unless otherwise authorized by a reasoned decision of the President of the court, from paying any of the debts covered by the suspension, disposing of any assets other than in the normal course of business, granting any security, or reimbursing any guarantors who may have paid on its behalf debts which had arisen prior to the suspension order[12].

It seems, however, that there is a loophole in the Uniform Act, since Article 9 provides for suspension only in relation to debts that have been listed by the debtor in its application. In other words, a debtor could favour certain creditors by not mentioning them in the application.

---

[8] Article 9.
[9] Article 9.
[10] Article 9.
[11] Article 10.
[12] Article 11.

3. Appointment of expert

At the same time as the suspension of individual proceedings is ordered, the President of the court also appoints an expert to prepare a report on the economic and financial situation of the company, the prospects for its recovery, and any measures contained in the composition offer[13].

The expert has very wide access to information. Notwithstanding any laws or regulations to the contrary, he may obtain information from the company's auditors and accountants, employees' representatives, administrative authorities, social security bodies, and banks and credit information companies[14].

The expert must inform the court of any failure by the debtor to comply with the prohibitions mentioned above regarding divestiture of assets, preferential treatment of creditors, etc.[15]

In addition, he must meet both the debtor and the creditors, and make use of his good offices in an attempt to reach an agreement between them as to the steps to be taken for the company's recovery and the clearing of its debts[16].

Within two months (or a maximum of three months if so authorized by the President of the court), the expert must file with the court a report outlining the composition agreement that has been proposed by the debtor or agreed between the debtor and creditors. Failure to file the report within the deadline may result in the expert being held liable towards the debtor or creditors[17].

4. Composition agreement (*concordat*)

Once the expert's report has been filed, the debtor is called to a hearing before the court, along with the expert and any creditor who, in the opinion of the President of the court, should be heard[18]. Neither this hearing nor the session at which the judgment is delivered is open to the public. There are three possible outcomes:

---

[13] Article 8.
[14] Article 12
[15] Article 12.
[16] Article 12.
[17] Article 13.
[18] Article 14.

(i). If the court finds that the company is insolvent, it orders it to be put into administration or liquidation[19].

(ii). The court may alternatively decide that preventive settlement proceedings are unjustified, ie that the debtor's financial situation does not warrant such treatment. In such an event, the court will reject the composition offer and cancel the order suspending individual proceedings[20].

This means that the parties will return to the status quo before the suspension order, ie the creditors can again individually pursue their claims against the debtor and are bound by no grace periods or reductions in the amount of their claims. However, there is a *de facto* grace period of a few months between the suspension order and delivery of the judgment. Because of this, and because no liabilities or penalties are provided for in the event the court finds that preventive settlement proceedings are unjustified, it is to be feared that unscrupulous debtors may commence such proceedings abusively, knowing at the outset that they are unjustified. The only deterrents contained in the Uniform Act are the fact that interest continues to run, and the rule that preventive settlement proceedings may be commenced only once in the same five-year period, which is designed to prevent a debtor from repeatedly and abusively obtaining a suspension of his creditors' claims.

(iii). Finally, if the court considers that the company's situation justifies a preventive settlement, it issues a judgment ordering such a settlement and ratifying the composition agreement, noting any grace periods and reductions that have been granted by the creditors and any measures proposed by the debtor which are aimed at securing the recovery of the company[21]. The court will only ratify the composition agreement if:
  – all conditions for its validity have been complied with;
  – there is no reason of collective interest or of public policy (*ordre public*) that might militate against its ratification;
  – there are serious prospects that its implementation will allow the company to recover and to clear its debts;
  – there are sufficient guarantees that it will be properly performed; and

---

[19] Article 15.1.
[20] Article 15.3.
[21] Article 15.2.

– any grace periods granted by the creditors do not exceed three years (or one year in the case of employees of the company).

In the event that the composition agreement contains a request by the debtor for a grace period of no more than two years, the court may impose this grace period on any creditor who has refused to grant a grace period or a reduction in the amount of the debt, unless this would endanger the creditor's own business[22]. This provision is however not applicable to employees who have a claim for outstanding salaries or wages; nor may such employees grant any reduction in the debt.

If the court does ratify the composition agreement, it will appoint a judge to supervise the future proceedings (*juge-commissaire*) and may also appoint an administrator (*syndic*) and/or controllers to ensure the proper performance of the composition agreement[23].

The judgment ratifying the agreement and opening the next stage of the preventive settlement proceedings must be published in the RCCM and in a legal journal[24]. Although these publications are an important source of information for the company's creditors, they may have the unfortunate side effect of discouraging other companies from continuing to trade with the company concerned.

D. Effects of composition agreement

Once the composition agreement has been ratified by the court, it becomes binding upon all the creditors declared by the debtor whose debts existed at the time of the judgment[25]. Some effects of the ratification are similar to those of the suspension order: secured creditors cannot realize their security, but they do not lose it; and deadlines after which the creditors would lose their rights by reason of the passage of time remain suspended[26]. On the other hand, the debtor recovers its freedom to dispose of its assets[27].

Guarantors of the debtor cannot rely upon the composition agreement to delay or reduce payment of any debts they have guaranteed, nor can they seek payment from the debtor once they have paid off a creditor

---

[22] Article 15.2.
[23] Article 16.
[24] Articles 17 and 36–37.
[25] Article 18.
[26] Article 18.
[27] Article 18.

under their guarantee. Instead, like other creditors, they are bound by the provisions of the composition agreement[28].

If an administrator has been appointed, he monitors the performance of the composition agreement and notifies any breaches of the agreement to the supervising judge. In addition, he submits a quarterly report to the judge, which the debtor has the right to comment upon or challenge[29].

If the debtor so requests, the court may modify the composition agreement, on condition that the modification is more favourable to the creditors than the original agreement[30].

In certain circumstances, such as a serious failure by the debtor to comply with its provisions, the agreement may be cancelled by the court. It may also be annulled if it is discovered that it was obtained by fraud, for example if the debtor had concealed certain assets or exaggerated the extent of its liabilities[31].

If the agreement is cancelled or annulled and the debtor is found to be insolvent, the court will order the debtor to be put into either administration or liquidation[32]. If the debtor is not found to be insolvent, or if the agreement is annulled, the decision suspending individual proceedings is annulled. In addition, in the event of an annulment for fraud, the debtor's management are subject to personal bankruptcy[33].

E. Appeals

No appeals are admissible against the decision ordering suspension of individual proceedings[34].

On the other hand, appeals are open against the judgment ratifying the composition agreement and opening the next phase of the preventive settlement. Any such appeals must be filed within fifteen days of the judgment, and the court of appeal must give its decision within one month thereafter. The appeal does not suspend implementation of the judgment[35].

---

[28] Article 18.
[29] Article 20.
[30] Article 21.
[31] Articles 21 and 139–140.
[32] Article 141.
[33] Article 196.
[34] Article 22.
[35] Article 23.

The court of appeal may either confirm the first judgment or, if it finds that the debtor is insolvent, declare the company to be in administration or liquidation, and refer the proceedings back to the competent court[36].

Third parties may also object to decisions by the President of the court authorizing the debtor to divest itself of assets or to pay debts incurred prior to the date of suspension of individual proceedings. Such objections must be filed before the full court within eight days of the decision, and the court must issue its judgment within eight days thereafter. These judgments are not subject to ordinary appeal and, if it is wished to

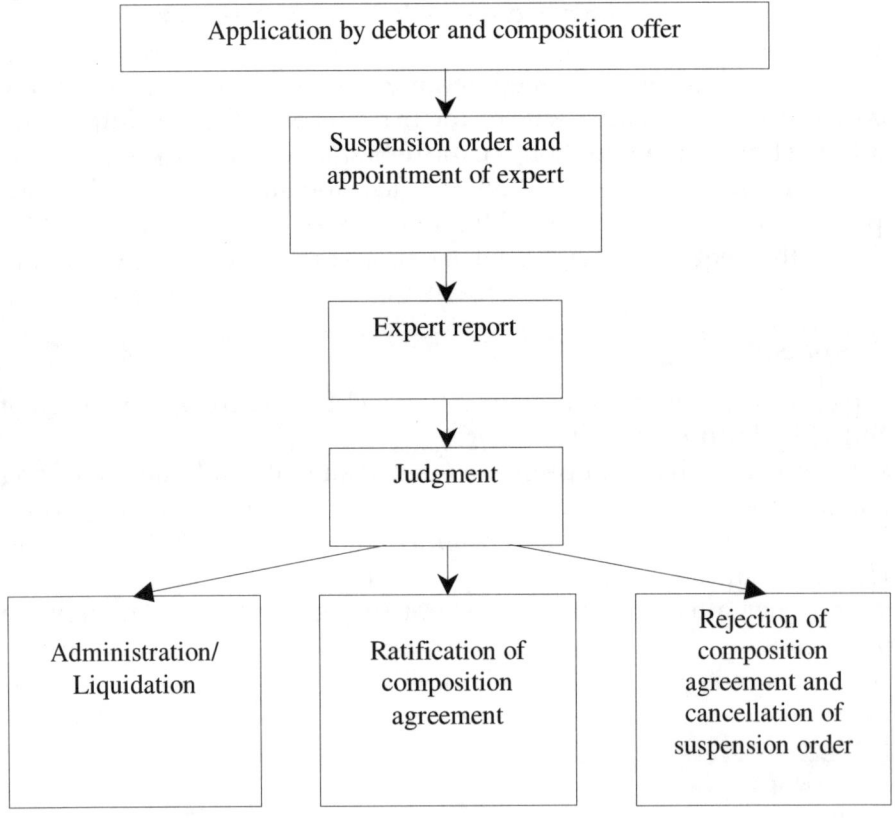

Figure 7.1 Summary of Preventive Settlement Proceedings

---

[36] Article 23.

challenge them, this must be done at the highest appellate level before the CCJA[37].

SECTION 2: ADMINISTRATION (*REDRESSEMENT JUDICIAIRE*)

A. Definition

The French term *redressement* is difficult to translate precisely into English. In the present context of collective proceedings for businesses that are in difficulties, it means the taking of measures to restore the economic and financial health of a business, with a view to its continued survival. For the sake of convenience, the word administration has been used in this Chapter, this being the most similar type of proceedings under English law. However, it should be borne in mind that these are not exact equivalents and that there are a number of substantial differences between *redressement judiciaire* under the Uniform Act and administration under English law.

Article 2 of the Uniform Act defines administration as a proceeding designed to save the company and to clear its debts by means of a composition with creditors (*concordat de redressement*).

B. Conditions

Like preventive settlement proceedings, administration is applicable to any individual exercising a commercial activity, and to any corporate body exercising a commercial or non-commercial activity, including publicly owned companies[38].

The basic criterion for determining whether preventive settlement or administration proceedings are appropriate is whether the company concerned is insolvent. Insolvency is defined for purposes of the Uniform Act as a situation where it is impossible for a debtor to meet all its due liabilities with its available assets[39].

---

[37] Article 24.
[38] Article 2.
[39] Article 2.

C. Procedure

As in the case of preventive settlement, the competent court in matters relating to administration is the court having jurisdiction for commercial matters at the place where the debtor has its principal place of business or registered office[40].

A debtor who is insolvent as defined above must file a declaration with the court registry within 30 days of the date of insolvency[41]. The declaration must be accompanied by various documents including the company's financial statements, a statement of cash flow, a list of assets and liabilities, a list of creditors and debtors, and details of the work force[42]. If it is impossible to produce all the required documents within the 30-day deadline, as many as possible should be produced and the debtor must indicate why it has been unable to produce the remainder within the deadline[43]. The debtor should not delay making the declaration at the proper time, since this may lead to personal civil or criminal liability[44].

Within 15 days of making the declaration, the debtor must also file an offer of composition along the same lines as the offer to be made in connection with preventive settlement proceedings[45]. There is no explanation why only 15 days are allowed in administration proceedings, instead of the 30 days allowed in preventive settlement proceedings, and this may simply have been an oversight in drafting.

Another difference between preventive settlement and administration is that in the latter case the proceedings may be begun by a creditor, on condition that the debt owed to that creditor is certain, liquidated and due. In such an event, the creditor serves a summons upon the debtor, indicating the nature and amount of the debt and its legal basis. The debtor may then within one month make its own declaration of insolvency and file a composition offer[46].

It is also possible for the court itself to take the initiative of opening proceedings on the basis of information that may have been provided to it by the auditors or shareholders of a debtor, or by employees' representatives. In such a case the debtor is summoned to appear before

---

[40] Articles 3–4.
[41] Article 25.
[42] Article 26.
[43] Article 26.
[44] See Section 4 of this chapter.
[45] Article 27.
[46] Article 28.

the court and, if it acknowledges a situation of insolvency or financial difficulties, or if the President of the Court is convinced that it is in such a situation, the debtor is given a period of 30 days within which to make a declaration and a composition offer[47].

The administration itself is opened by a judgment. Before the judgment is given, the President of the court may appoint a judge or any other suitable person to prepare a report on the situation and on the composition offer[48].

If the court finds that the debtor is insolvent, the judgment must order either that the debtor be put into administration or that it be liquidated, depending upon whether the court considers that the composition offer put forward by the debtor is a serious offer[49]. This judgment is subject to appeal. If the court of appeal subsequently quashes the judgment, it may itself order the debtor to be put into administration or liquidation[50].

The Uniform Act does not lay down any criteria for determining whether the composition offer is serious or not. It seems, however, that in order to be considered serious, an offer should put forward realistic solutions both for improving the financial situation of the company and for making at least a reasonable payment to creditors.

The judgment is registered as soon as possible with the RCCM[51]. Extracts from the judgment must also be published in a legal journal, together with an invitation to creditors to declare their claims, and in the OHADA legal journal with a view to making the situation known to creditors in all the Member States[52]. The administrator is responsible for ensuring that these formalities are complied with[53].

D. Effects of administration judgment

1. Appointments

The judgment must appoint a judge to supervise the ensuing proceedings (*juge-commissaire*), and one to three administrators (*syndics*)[54].

---

[47] Article 29.
[48] Article 32.
[49] Article 33.
[50] Article 33.
[51] Article 36.
[52] Articles 36–37.
[53] Article 38.
[54] Article 35.

The supervising judge ensures that the proceedings are carried forward with proper speed, and that the various contending interests are protected[55]. He collects any information that he considers necessary, and can interview any interested parties. Like the expert in preventive settlement proceedings, he is allowed access to information, which otherwise would be confidential, from the auditors, accountants, employees, social security bodies, banks, credit information companies, etc, and which is of such a kind as to give him a proper understanding of the economic and financial state of the company. He also reports to the court on any objections that may arise in connection with the proceedings[56].

The supervising judge has jurisdiction to rule upon certain requests, objections and claims that arise in the course of the proceedings, which he must do within eight days. Third parties may file objections with the court against his rulings, again within eight days[57].

The role of the administrator is to represent the creditors and to assist the debtor in its activity[58]. He must report to the supervising judge from time to time on the progress of his task and on the state of the proceedings[59].

Controllers may be appointed to assist the judge in supervising the proceedings and to watch over the interests of the creditors[60]. They are appointed from among the creditors by the supervising judge, either at his own initiative or upon the request of creditors representing more than 50 per cent of the total amount of the debtor's debts[61]. They are entitled to examine the debtor's accounts and in general to be kept informed of events occurring during the proceedings, including any actions by the administrator and any income and expenditure of the debtor[62].

2. Effects on the debtor

The debtor's activity continues, with the assistance of the administrator, for an indefinite period unless the supervising judge decides otherwise[63].

---

[55] Article 39.
[56] Article 39.
[57] Article 40.
[58] Articles 43 and 52.
[59] Article 43.
[60] Articles 48–49.
[61] Article 48.
[62] Article 49.
[63] Article 112.

The administrator keeps the judge informed of the debtor's situation at least every three months, and reports upon any income received[64]. The judge decides whether the existing members of the management of the debtor should participate in the continuation of its activity and, in the affirmative, determines their remuneration[65].

If it is decided that the existing management should not continue to participate, the court may authorize a management lease (*contrat de location-gérance*) to be entered into with a third party[66], on condition that a cessation of activity, even if only provisional, would jeopardize the debtor's recovery or would cause serious difficulties for the national, regional or local economy in the production and distribution of goods and services.

Once the judgment ordering administration has been issued, it is obligatory for the debtor to be assisted in all its actions relating to the administration and disposal of its assets, except that it may continue to perform everyday activities in the normal course of business, on condition that it reports on all such activities to the administrator[67].

Within three days of the judgment, the debtor must present its accounting records to the administrator, who will examine them and close the accounts, in order to determine the extent of the debtor's assets[68]. The administrator must also prepare an inventory of the debtor's assets[69].

When the debtor is a company, the management cannot transfer their shares in the company once the judgment has been delivered, except with the authorization of the supervising judge. The share certificates representing such shares are held by the administrator pending the outcome of the proceedings[70].

Various declarations must be made by the debtor to the tax, customs and social security authorities. The administrator ensures that this is done promptly, and in the event of failure by the debtor to make the proper declarations, the administrator must inform the supervising

---

[64] Article 112.
[65] Article 114.
[66] Article 115. See Chapter 4 for details of this type of arrangement.
[67] Article 52.
[68] Article 55.
[69] Article 63.
[70] Article 57.

judge and himself supply any available information to the relevant authorities[71].

Within one month of his appointment, the administrator must submit a summary report on the debtor's apparent situation and its causes and nature, including a social and economic status report and an evaluation of the prospects for an improvement on the basis of the proposed composition arrangement. If controllers have also been appointed, their opinion is attached to the report[72].

3. Determination and effects of date of insolvency

The judgment ordering the debtor to be put into administration must determine, at least provisionally, the date of insolvency, which may be no more than eighteen months earlier than the date of the judgment[73]. The period between this date and the date of the judgment is known as the 'suspect period' (*période suspecte*). Depending upon their nature, transactions performed by the debtor during this suspect period either must or may be held not to be valid as against the creditors[74]. A similar rule is to be found in Anglo-Saxon insolvency laws.

The following types of transaction must be declared not to be valid as against the creditors.

- all transfers of assets made free of charge;
- all contracts providing for reciprocal obligations, where the debtor's obligations have far outweighed those of the other party;
- all payments of debts that were not due, except in relation to transferable bills;
- all payments of due debts by other than ordinary means of payment;
- the granting of any securities on the debtor's assets for debts that had been contracted prior to the suspect period; and
- any provisional registration of a mortgage or pledge ordered by a court in the context of provisional measures[75].

---

[71] Article 65.
[72] Article 66.
[73] Article 34.
[74] Article 67.
[75] Article 68. With regard to provisional measures, see Chapter 9.

The aim of this provision is to avoid any preferential treatment of certain creditors and any fraudulent transfer of the debtor's assets.

Furthermore, the following types of transactions may be declared not to be valid as against the creditors, on condition that it can be shown that they have caused damage to the creditors:

- any transfers of assets free of charge which occurred during the six months preceding the suspect period;
- any registration of securities for debts when the beneficiary was aware at the time that the debtor was insolvent;
- any transactions against payment where the other party was aware at the time that the debtor was insolvent;
- any payment of due debts where the beneficiary was aware at the time that the debtor was insolvent; and
- certain payments of transferable bills or cheques, for example where the beneficiary was aware of the debtor's situation[76].

In the event that such transactions have occurred, the administrator may request the court to declare them invalid as against the creditors. The right to make such a request expires when the administrator submits to the court the final list of debts after he has verified all the creditors' claims[77]. The creditors themselves have no separate right to make such a request. If the transaction concerned is declared to be invalid, this is for the benefit of the whole body of creditors and not any particular creditor[78]. The third party concerned must reimburse the debtor but, unless he was the beneficiary of a transfer of assets free of charge, he may declare a claim against the debtor[79].

4. Effects of the administration judgment on the creditors

(a) Creation of the masse and suspension of claims

The judgment opening administration proceedings has the effect of constituting a single body of creditors, known as the *masse*[80]. The

---

[76] Article 69.
[77] Article 70.
[78] Article 71.
[79] Article 71.
[80] Article 72.

creditors concerned are those whose claims against the debtor arose prior to the date of the judgment, even if they were not yet payable. These creditors can no longer act individually, even if it is simply to obtain a formal recognition of their rights; they are represented as a body by the administrator[81]. They are bound by actions of the administrator, who acts in their collective interest[82].

Once the judgment has been issued, creditors can no longer publish any securities they may have obtained from the debtor[83]. However, they are given a collective mortgage on all the real assets of the debtor, either present or future[84].

Moreover, the judgment putting the debtor into administration halts any accrual of interest or delay penalties, with the exception of interest on loan agreements having a term of more than one year, or where the contract provides for payment to be deferred for at least one year[85].

(b) Declaration and verification of claims

All the creditors belonging to the body of creditors must declare their claims against the debtor within a period of 30 days following publication of the second legal notice of the administration proceedings, or within 60 days if they are located outside the country where the proceedings have been opened[86]. Failure to do so will result in foreclosure, unless the creditor concerned can demonstrate that the failure is not due to his negligence[87]. When there is foreclosure, the debt is deemed to be wiped out, unless special provision has been made for it to be reinstated in the event of the debtor's recovery[88].

The claims are verified by the administrator in the presence of the debtor and controllers, if any. Verification must be completed within three months of the opening of administration[89]. Any objections to claims or to related securities are notified by the administrator to the supervising

---

[81] Article 75.
[82] Article 72.
[83] Article 73.
[84] Article 74.
[85] Article 77.
[86] Article 78. The common law concept of insolvency set-off is not applied. As a result, even if a creditor owes money to the debtor, he must pay what he owes and declare a claim for the total amount owed to him by the debtor.
[87] Article 83.
[88] Article 83.
[89] Article 84.

judge and the creditor concerned. If the creditor does not provide the judge with explanations within 15 days (or 30 days if he is located outside the country), he can no longer object to any proposal that may be made by the administrator for rejecting the claim or reducing its amount[90].

At the end of the verification procedure, the administrator prepares a list of all the claims, together with his recommendations for their final or provisional acceptance or rejection. This list is verified and signed by the supervising judge, who indicates the amount of each claim and decides whether it should be accepted finally or provisionally. If he wishes to reject any part of a claim, he must first hear the creditor, debtor and administrator. Once he has signed the list, it is filed in the court registry[91].

The creditors are informed of the filing of the list[92]. If those whose claim has been totally or partially rejected wish to object to the rejection, they can do so by filing proceedings within 15 days[93]. In addition, they recover their right to file proceedings with a view to obtaining recognition of the existence of the portion of the claim that has been rejected[94]. The debtor or any other interested party may also file proceedings to object to the acceptance of a particular creditor's claim[95].

(c) Preferential rights

Employees of the debtor have a preferential right in relation to other creditors, for claims for unpaid amounts due under their employment contracts[96]. The amount to which the preferential right attaches is determined by the relevant national employment law and the law relating to securities. Within ten days of the debtor being put into administration, the administrator must pay all such claims. If the funds at his disposal are not sufficient, further payments are made from any subsequent income of the debtor before any other claims are paid[97].

Creditors whose claim is for the return of property, including goods sold under a contract providing for retention of title until full payment

---

[90] Article 85.
[91] Article 86.
[92] Article 87.
[93] Article 88.
[94] Article 75.
[95] Article 88.
[96] Article 95.
[97] Article 96.

has been made, and on condition that notice of the retention of title has been published in the RCCM, must declare their claims to the administrator[98]. If the claim is accepted, it must then be exercised individually by the creditor concerned, within three months of the filing in the court registry of the list of verified claims, or of the judgment accepting the claim, as the case may be[99].

(d) Continuation of contracts

As regards contracts that were entered into before the debtor had been put into administration, the general rule is that they should continue in force. Article 107 of the Uniform Act provides that only such contracts as have been entered into *intuitu personae* or as may be expressly specified by the national laws of the Member States may be terminated when the debtor is put into administration[100]. Otherwise, any contractual clause providing for termination in the event of administration is deemed to be null and void.

The administrator is the only person who may require the continued performance of such contracts. If however he fails to furnish the due consideration, the other party may suspend performance. If that party nevertheless does perform the contract, he joins the body of creditors with regard to his entitlement to consideration[101].

As regards employment contracts, the administrator may decide to resort to redundancies if these appear to be urgent and indispensable[102]. These redundancies must be authorized by the supervising judge, and must comply with certain rules regarding notice periods, compensation, order of priority, and information of the employees concerned. It is possible for the employees concerned to file proceedings objecting to any decision regarding redundancies. The court's judgment in such proceedings is not subject to appeal[103].

---

[98] Articles 101 and 103.

[99] Article 101.

[100] An example of termination because of administration proceedings may be found in the Uniform Act on General Commercial Law, where Article 157 provides for automatic termination of a commercial intermediary's agency agreement in the event of collective proceedings affecting either the intermediary or his principal.

[101] Article 108.

[102] Article 110.

[103] Article 111.

Any debts that arise after the judgment putting the debtor into administration are deemed to be debts owed by the body of creditors, on condition that they are validly incurred by the debtor in the continuation of its activity. There is an exception to this rule in the event that the debtor's activity is being continued under a management lease, in which case the manager under that lease is solely liable for the debts[104].

E. Closure of administration

1. Ratification of composition agreement

It will be recalled that the debtor is required to make a proposal for a composition with his creditors within 30 days of the declaration of insolvency. The administrator and the creditors are informed of this proposal and, at the same time as the claims are being verified, the administrator also seeks to reconcile the positions of the debtor and the creditors as to composition[105].

Once the claims have been verified and there is a final list of claims that have been accepted, a meeting of the creditors whose claims have been accepted either definitively or provisionally is called[106]. The meeting is attended by the supervising judge and by the debtor or its management[107]. The administrator reports upon the progress of the proceedings and the results of the company during the continuation of its activity, providing an account of the current situation, including the available or realizable assets, the secured and unsecured liabilities, and his opinion as to the proposed composition agreement[108]. After the court has heard the observations of the supervising judge as to the results of the administration and the admissibility of the composition proposal it takes delivery of the administrator's report[109].

The court then organizes a vote on the composition proposal. If a majority of the creditors whose claims have been finally or provisionally admitted, representing at least 50 per cent of the total value of such claims, votes in favour of the proposal, it is considered as ratified. If only

---

[104] Article 117.
[105] Article 119.
[106] Article 122.
[107] Article 123.
[108] Article 124.
[109] Article 124.

one of these two conditions as to majority is met, a further meeting takes place a week later[110].

When both conditions have been met, this is officially recorded by the court, and the composition agreement is ratified. The court can only ratify the composition agreement if:

- the conditions for its validity have been complied with;
- there is no reason of collective interest or public policy that militates against it;
- there is a serious possibility that the composition will permit the recovery of the debtor and the clearing of its liabilities; and
- the management is no longer in the hands of persons whose replacement has been proposed in the composition offer or by the administrator, or of persons who have been declared in personal bankruptcy or have been prohibited from managing a company.

2. Performance of composition agreement

The court may decide that performance of the composition agreement should be supervised by controllers or by the administrator[111].

The composition agreement may provide for a partial divestiture of the debtor's assets, in the form of a sale of tangible or intangible, real or movable property, or of a branch of the business. In such an event, once the divestiture has been approved by the supervising judge, the administrator must publish an offer of sale of the assets concerned[112]. Unlike French law, the Uniform Act does not provide for a total divestiture of assets, a system that is often used in France by companies which wish to expand by taking over the business of other companies, or to restructure insolvent companies by methods such as cost-cutting or simplifying structures or synergies. Moreover, in the event of a partial divestiture, the purchaser will not bear the insolvent company's liabilities, since as a rule no balance sheet (or off-balance sheet) commitments will be undertaken.

When offers of purchase have been received, the creditors are informed and vote upon which offer to accept, on the same conditions as to majority as for their decision whether to accept the composition pro-

---

[110] Article 125.
[111] Article 128.
[112] Article 131.

posal[113]. The court confirms the partial divestiture of assets on condition that the price is sufficient to pay off all creditors holding real securities on the assets that are sold (unless they waive this condition), and that payment is to be made either on a cash basis or within no more than two years and against a bank guarantee[114]. The price obtained for the assets becomes part of the debtor's assets[115].

3. Effects of composition agreement

Once the composition agreement has been ratified by the court, it is in principle binding upon all the creditors existing before the administration judgment[116]. There are however exceptions to this rule. First, various administrative bodies which may be under a statutory obligation not to grant reductions or grace periods are not bound by the composition agreement. Moreover, creditors with special real securities are bound only by grace periods or reductions that they have themselves granted, unless the composition agreement specifies a grace period of less than two years, in which case they are bound by this period. In general, creditors holding real securities do not lose the benefit of such securities, but may realize them only in the event of nullification or cancellation of the composition agreement. A further exception relates to employees of the debtor, upon whom no reduction whatsoever and no grace period of more than two years may be imposed. Finally, the composition agreement cannot be relied upon by any guarantors of the debtor, who remain bound by the terms of their guarantee[117].

Once the decision confirming the composition agreement has become final, the administration proceedings are closed, and the debtor recovers its freedom to administer and dispose of its assets[118]. However, in cases where controllers may have been appointed to supervise performance of the composition agreement, they must report on any delay or other failure in performance and the President of the court may order an investigation of the matter by the administrator.

---

[113] Article 132.
[114] Article 132.
[115] Article 133.
[116] Article 134.
[117] Article 134.
[118] Article 136.

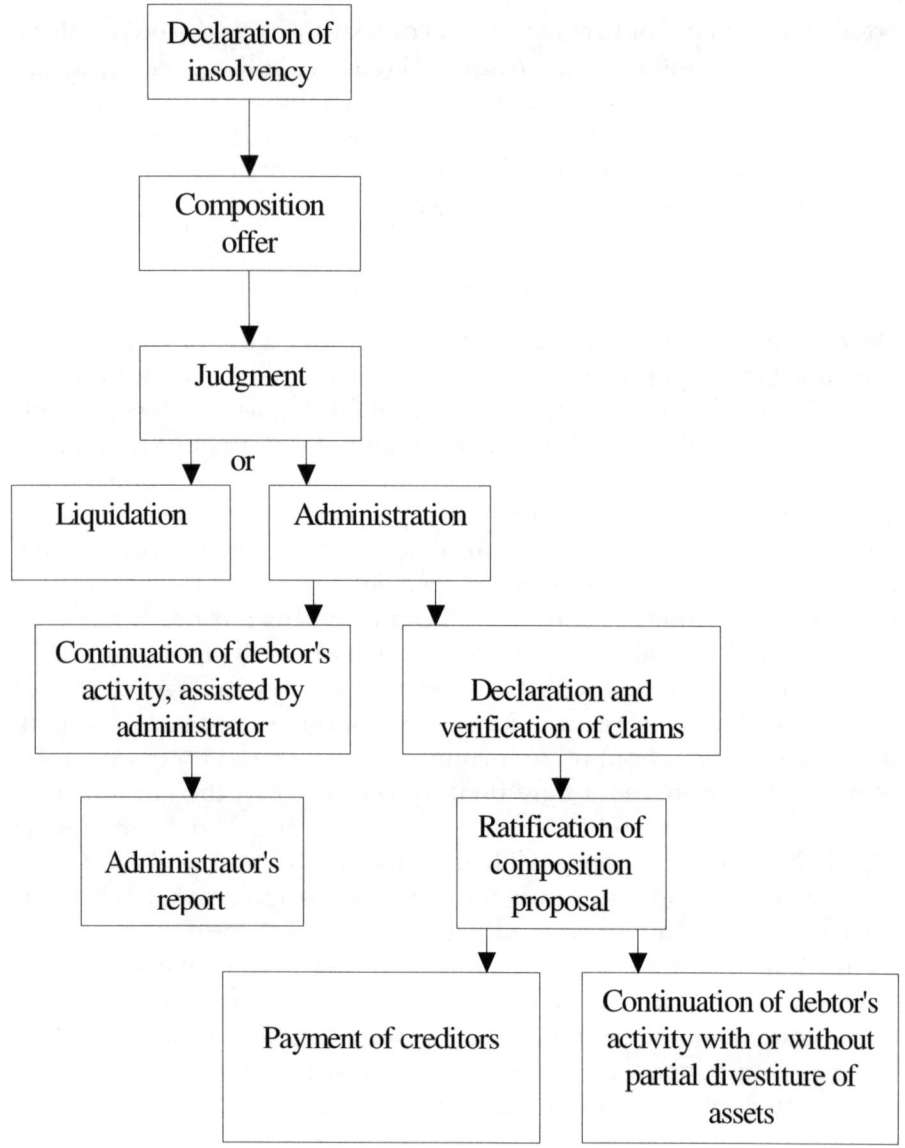

Figure 7.2 Administration Proceedings

4. Cancellation or nullification of composition agreement

The composition agreement may be cancelled by the court in the event of a serious breach by the debtor of its obligations under the agreement or if management functions are being exercised by persons who have been prohibited from assuming such functions or who have been declared in personal bankruptcy[119].

The composition agreement may be declared null and void if it has been obtained on the basis of a fraudulent concealment of assets or an exaggeration of the extent of the debtor's liabilities[120].

If the composition agreement is either cancelled or declared null and void, the court converts the administration proceedings into liquidation proceedings and appoints a liquidator. In such an event the creditors who were bound by the composition agreement and any new creditors form a single body of creditors for purposes of the liquidation[121].

SECTION 3: LIQUIDATION

A. Definition

Article 2 of the Uniform Act defines liquidation as a procedure for the purpose of realizing the debtor's assets in order to clear his liabilities.

B. Conditions

Like administration, liquidation proceedings may be applied to any individuals exercising a commercial activity and any corporate bodies exercising a commercial or non-commercial activity, including public companies, which are in a situation of insolvency[122].

C. Procedure

The court having jurisdiction in matters relating to liquidation is the court having jurisdiction over commercial matters at the principal place of business or registered office of the debtor[123].

Liquidation proceedings are begun in the same way as administration proceedings. If the court finds that the debtor is insolvent, it decides whether to order administration or liquidation proceedings. It will order liquidation when it appears that the debtor has not made a serious

---

[119] Article 139.
[120] Article 140.
[121] Article 141.
[122] Article 2.
[123] Articles 3 and 4.

proposal for composition which will allow its financial recovery and the clearing of its liabilities[124]. The court may also order liquidation during the course of administration proceedings if it becomes apparent that the debtor is not, or is no longer, in a position to make a serious composition proposal[125]. As in administration proceedings, the judgment ordering liquidation determines the date of insolvency, which in turn determines the duration of the suspect period[126].

The first stages of the procedure for liquidation are similar to those of the administration procedure. Here again, a supervising judge is appointed, together with up to three liquidators (*syndics*[127]) and controllers may also be appointed[128].

D. Effects of the liquidation judgment

1. Effects on the debtor

The judgment which orders liquidation of a company automatically entails the winding-up of the debtor's business and the removal of the debtor from involvement in any administration or disposal of its assets[129]. Instead, the debtor is represented by the liquidator for all such acts. All non-personal correspondence addressed to the debtor is handed to the liquidator, although the debtor may be present when it is opened[130].

2. Effects on the creditors

As in the case of administration, the creditors existing prior to the date of the judgment form a body (*masse* or *union*) which is represented by the liquidator acting in the creditors' collective interest[131]. Here again, they must declare their claims for verification by the liquidator[132].

---

[124] Article 33.
[125] Article 33.
[126] Article 34.
[127] No distinction is made in the Uniform Act between the terminology applied to an administrator and a liquidator.
[128] Articles 35 and 48.
[129] Article 53.
[130] Article 56.
[131] Article 72.
[132] Article 78.

However, contrary to what happens in administration proceedings, when liquidation is ordered, all the debtor's debts that were not yet due become immediately due[133].

3. Continuation of activity

The liquidator may require the continued performance of ongoing contracts, in the interests of the debtor[134].

While continuation of the debtor's activities is a necessary component of administration proceedings, in cases where liquidation has been ordered, the activity may be continued only with the authorization of the court and when it is necessary for the purposes of liquidation, on condition that it does not endanger the public interest or the creditors' interests[135]. If authorized, the activity may continue for a renewable period of three months and for a maximum of one year after the judgment ordering liquidation, unless there are serious and exceptional circumstances requiring a longer period[136].

4. Liquidation of assets

Within a month of his appointment, the liquidator must provide the supervising judge with an estimate of the available or realizable assets, the secured and unsecured debts, and any possible financial liability of the debtor's management[137].

The liquidator sells the debtor's stocks and movable property, pays its debts and pursues its claims against third parties. All sums received are paid into a special account[138].

The debtor's immovable property is sold at auction in accordance, *mutatis mutandis*, with the proceedings laid down for enforcement measures against such property (*saisie immobilière*[139]), the opening price being determined by the supervising judge[140]. Alternatively, the judge may authorize the property to be sold by private contract if appro-

---

[133] Article 76.
[134] Article 108.
[135] Article 113.
[136] Article 113.
[137] Article 146.
[138] Article 147.
[139] See Chapter 9.
[140] Article 150.

priate[141]. If the liquidator has not begun proceedings for the sale of real property within three months of the liquidation judgment, any creditor who has a mortgage on the property may exercise his individual rights, on condition that he reports to the liquidator[142].

The liquidator may also sell all of the debtor's assets as a single business, or assets making up a branch of the business. In such an event he invites offers from any person other than the management of the company or their close family members[143]. He then chooses the offer which seems to be the most serious, and submits it to the supervising judge, along with the observations of the debtor and the controllers[144].

When the assets have been realized, the supervising judge may order the proceeds to be distributed among the creditors whose claims have been accepted[145]. Payment is made after deduction of all costs and expenses relating to the liquidation[146]. When there has not yet been a final decision as to whether a claim is accepted, the corresponding amount is held in reserve[147]. Different categories of creditors are attributed different ranks for the distribution of proceeds[148]. Payment is made in full to each category in turn, until there are insufficient proceeds to pay in full all the debts appertaining to a particular category. In such an event, and when the creditors concerned do not have a security over a particular asset, the proceeds are distributed among the creditors in that category in proportion to their respective claims, and creditors in subsequent categories will receive no payment[149].

5. Closure of liquidation

When all the winding-up operations have been completed, the liquidator gives a final accounting to the supervising judge, who minutes the completion of operations. The minutes are then transmitted to the court, which declares the liquidation closed and decides upon any objections to the liquidator's accounting that might have been raised by the debtor

---

[141] Article 150.
[142] Article 150.
[143] Article 160.
[144] Article 161.
[145] Articles 164–165.
[146] Article 165.
[147] Article 165.
[148] Articles 166–167.
[149] Articles 166–167.

or the creditors. The union of creditors is dissolved, and the creditors recover their individual rights[150].

The proceedings may also be closed if there are insufficient funds to undertake or to complete the liquidation operations[151]. In such an event, any interested party may request the court to declare the proceedings closed, or the court may itself decide to do so of its own motion.

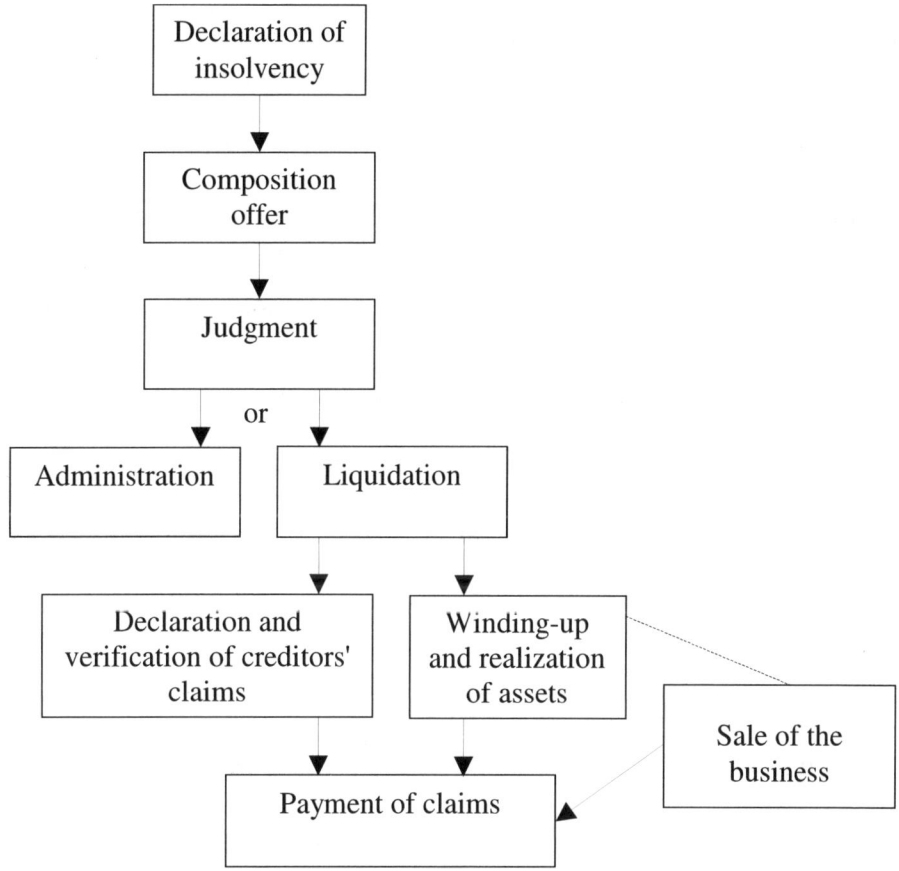

Figure 7.3 Liquidation Proceedings

---

[150] Article 170.
[151] Article 173.

However, if closure is declared for this reason, the decision may be withdrawn at the request of the debtor or of any other interested party if it can be demonstrated that the funds necessary to cover the costs of the liquidation have been deposited with the liquidator[152].

SECTION 4: MANAGEMENT LIABILITIES

The Uniform Act provides for various liabilities that may be incurred by the management of a company that has become insolvent and has been put into administration or liquidation.

In this context, the 'management' has to be understood as including not only persons who are officially directors or managers of the company, whether their functions have been remunerated or not, but also persons who have had *de facto* management control within the company, and the permanent representatives of other companies on the board of directors[153].

A. Liability for the company's debts (comblement du passif)

When there are insufficient assets to meet the company's liabilities, and when bad management has contributed to this insufficiency, the court may decide, at the request of the administrator or liquidator or of its own motion, and within a maximum period of three years from the date upon which the final list of debts is established, that the company's liabilities should be borne in whole or in part by one or more of the members of the management[154]. In such circumstances, the court may also order the managers to sell their shares, with the proceeds of the sale being used in payment of the portion of the debts for which they have been held liable[155].

B. Extension of administration or liquidation to members of the management

In the event their company is put into administration or liquidation, the members of the management may be declared personally in administra-

---

[152] Article 175.
[153] Article 180.
[154] Article 183.
[155] Article 185.

tion or liquidation if they have exercised a personal commercial activity under cover of the company, have used the company's credit or assets as if they were their own, or pursued the company's loss-making activity in their own personal interest when it was inevitable that this would lead to insolvency[156]. The same persons may also be put into administration or liquidation if they have failed to discharge their liability for the company's debts as determined in the previous paragraph[157].

When personal administration or liquidation proceedings are opened against members of the management, creditors have their claims automatically admitted in these proceedings if their claims have been admitted in the proceedings concerning the company itself[158].

C. *Personal bankruptcy* (faillite personnelle)

Individual commercial operators, individuals who are members of the management of a company subject to administration or liquidation proceedings, and permanent representatives of companies sitting on the board of a company subject to such proceedings may be put into personal bankruptcy by the court at any time during the proceedings[159].

Personal bankruptcy may be ordered when the person concerned has:

- removed the accounts from the company, embezzled or concealed part of the company's assets, or fraudulently acknowledged non-existent debts;
- exercised a commercial activity in his own personal interest;
- used the credit or assets of the company as if they were his own;
- fraudulently obtained a composition agreement which has subsequently been declared null and void; or
- committed certain acts in bad faith or has been guilty of inexcusable negligence or has seriously infringed commercial rules and practices[160].

The latter category of acts includes the exercise of a commercial activity or management functions when under a prohibition to do so; failure to

---

[156] Article 189.
[157] Article 189.
[158] Article 191.
[159] Articles 194 *et seq.*
[160] Article 196.

keep proper accounts; the deliberate delaying of a declaration of insolvency by using methods that cause further damage to the company, etc[161].

In addition, the court may declare members of the management to be in personal bankruptcy when they have committed other serious faults or are blatantly incompetent; when they have failed to make a declaration of insolvency within 30 days, or when they have failed to pay debts of the company that they have been ordered to pay[162].

When personal bankruptcy is ordered, the national rules of criminal procedure may require a publication to be made in the criminal record of the person concerned, and a publication must also be made in the RCCM, the OHADA legal journal, and a local legal journal[163].

When a member of the management has been declared in personal bankruptcy, he is automatically prohibited from:

- engaging in commerce and in particular from managing, administering or controlling companies;
- exercising any public elective function or voting in such elections;
- exercising any administrative or judicial function, or any representative functions within a professional organization[164].

The court determines the duration of such prohibitions, which cannot be less than three years or more than ten years[165]. On certain conditions the prohibitions may be lifted before they have run their term; for example, when all the company's liabilities have been paid off or when there is unanimous consent of the creditors[166].

D. Criminal bankruptcy (banqueroute)

Finally, the Uniform Act provides for two types of criminal bankruptcy – simple and fraudulent – for particularly serious acts committed either by individual commercial operators or by shareholders in certain types of companies who are indefinitely and jointly and severally liable for their company's debts[167]. The management may be made subject to

---

[161] Article 197.
[162] Article 198.
[163] Article 202.
[164] Article 203.
[165] Article 203.
[166] Articles 204–205.
[167] Article 227.

criminal bankruptcy even if they have also been made subject to the extension of administration or liquidation proceedings.

Criminal proceedings may be begun by the State, by the administrator or liquidator, or by any creditor acting in his own name or, if so authorized by the supervising judge, on behalf of the body of creditors[168]. The penalties applicable to criminal bankruptcy are defined in each Member State's national criminal law.

1. Simple bankruptcy (*banqueroute simple*)

Simple bankruptcy is incurred when the business is insolvent and when the person concerned has:

- made undertakings which are too onerous in view of the financial situation and has not received sufficient consideration in exchange;
- in an attempt to delay a determination of insolvency, made purchases with a view to reselling the goods at less than market value or has used ruinous methods to obtain funds;
- failed, without any legitimate reason, to declare insolvency within 30 days;
- prepared incomplete or improper accounts; or
- has twice been in a situation of insolvency within five years, and the proceedings have been terminated for insufficiency of assets[169].

Other management members may be found guilty of offences that are assimilated to simple bankruptcy and that give rise to the same penalties, if the person concerned has:

- used funds belonging to the company in hazardous or fictitious operations;
- after the company has become insolvent, paid off one creditor to the detriment of others;
- concealed or removed his own assets, or has fraudulently acknowledged non-existent debts, with a view to removing some or all of his assets from the scope of any proceedings against him in the context of the proceedings involving the company; or

---

[168] Article 234.
[169] Article 228.

- been guilty of any of the other actions mentioned above for other categories of persons subject to simple bankruptcy[170].

2. Fraudulent bankruptcy (*banqueroute frauduleuse*)

Fraudulent bankruptcy, for which the penalties are more severe, is incurred by individual commercial operators and by shareholders who are indefinitely and jointly and severally liable for the company's debts, when the business is in a situation of insolvency and the person concerned has:

- concealed the accounts;
- embezzled or squandered some or all of the assets;
- fraudulently acknowledged non-existent debts;
- exercised a commercial profession while prohibited from doing so;
- paid off a creditor after the business has become insolvent, to the detriment of the other creditors; or
- given a creditor particular advantages, for example in exchange for his vote in the creditors' meeting[171].

Fraudulent bankruptcy is also incurred when the business is not insolvent but is subject to preventive settlement proceedings[172], if the person concerned has:

- in bad faith presented accounts that are inaccurate or incomplete; or
- performed certain prohibited acts without authorization from the President of the court[173].

Other management members may be held to be guilty of offences assimilated to fraudulent bankruptcy on grounds similar, *mutatis mutandis*, to those applicable to individual operators and shareholders with unlimited liability[174].

---

[170] Articles 230–231.

[171] Article 229.

[172] The article refers to *règlement judiciaire*. The Uniform Act does not provide for *règlement judiciaire* proceedings, and it therefore seems that this was a slip of the pen, and that *règlement préventif* was meant.

[173] Article 229.

[174] Article 230.

The criminal court, and not the commercial court, has jurisdiction with regard to criminal bankruptcy. Proceedings may be commenced by the public prosecutor, by a private plaintiff, by the administrator or liquidator, or by any creditor acting in his own name or on behalf of the body of creditors[175].

SECTION 5: INTERNATIONAL COLLECTIVE PROCEEDINGS

A very useful feature of the Uniform Act is the possibility it has created of international collective proceedings. This type of system has been recommended in reports by international financial institutions such as the International Monetary Fund and the Asian Development Bank, and also by the United Nations Commission on International Trade Law (UNCITRAL), which has drawn up a model law on cross-border insolvency, the aim of which is to facilitate coordination between States in this regard.

A. Effects of collective proceedings in other Member States

The Uniform Act provides that once they have become irrevocable, any judgments opening or closing collective proceedings, and any decisions upon disputes arising in the course of such proceedings, or decisions upon which the collective proceedings have a legal influence, are final and binding in all the Member States[176].

At the request of the administrator or liquidator, the contents of the decision concerned are published in any Member States where it is considered that publication may promote legal security or protect creditors' interests. The court may also decide of its own motion to make the publication[177].

The administrator or liquidator may exercise all his powers derived from the Uniform Act in any other Member State, so long as no other collective proceedings have been opened against the debtor in question in that Member State[178].

---

175 Article 234.
176 Article 247.
177 Article 248.
178 Article 249.

If a creditor obtains total or partial payment against assets of the debtor situated in a different Member State, he must hand this over to the administrator or liquidator, without prejudice to any retention of title that he may be able to rely upon.

B. Secondary collective proceedings

There is no obstacle to the opening of another collective proceeding concerning the same debtor in another Member State[179]. In such an event, the administrators or liquidators appointed in each Member State are bound by a reciprocal duty to keep each other informed[180]. The proceeding opened in the country where the debtor has its main establishment or registered office is referred to as the principal proceeding; proceedings in any other Member States are secondary proceedings[181]. The administrator or liquidator in charge of a secondary proceeding must allow the administrator or liquidator in charge of the principal proceeding to make proposals relating to liquidation or any use of the assets in the secondary proceeding[182].

Any creditor may declare his claim in the principal proceeding and in any secondary proceeding[183]. However, a creditor who has obtained a partial payment of his claim in one proceeding cannot participate in the distribution of further payments in another proceeding until creditors of the same rank have obtained an equivalent payment in that other proceeding[184].

A secondary proceeding cannot be terminated by a composition agreement or by liquidation without the agreement of the administrator or liquidator in the principal proceeding. Such agreement may be refused only if it can be shown that the proposed solution jeopardizes the financial interests of the creditors in the principal proceeding[185].

If the liquidation of assets in one proceeding is sufficient to pay off all the accepted claims in that proceeding, any surplus assets are transferred to the administrator or liquidator in the other proceedings[186].

---

[179] Article 251.
[180] Article 252.
[181] Article 251.
[182] Article 252.
[183] Article 253.
[184] Article 255.
[185] Article 254.
[186] Article 256.

These modern provisions should simplify the clearing of debts incurred by persons or companies operating in several Member States. If the various administrators or liquidators work properly together as envisaged by the Uniform Act, the proceedings will be centralized and this should facilitate the assessment of the real financial situation of the debtor, its proper restructuring, and the payment of its debts.

8

Securities

The Uniform Act on Securities provides for various guarantees which protect creditors, including banks, by securing the enforcement of their debtors' obligations. This is an essential piece of legislation for those engaged in business although, as will be seen, it oversteps the bounds of pure business law and provides for a number of securities which are available to creditors who are not necessarily engaged in business. It provides for both personal and real securities, dealing in turn with:

- surety-bonds and letters of guarantee, in Articles 3 to 38;
- real securities over movable assets (rights of retention, pledges and preferential rights), in Articles 39 to 116; and
- mortgages, in Articles 117 to 146.

Finally, in Articles 147 to 149, the Uniform Act lays down rules for the distribution of proceeds from the sale of secured assets and the ranking of different types of securities.

The Uniform Act abrogates only those provisions in the laws of the Member States which are contrary to its provisions[1]. Hence, in some countries, there are a number of other laws and regulations which remain in force[2], and it is necessary to determine for each individual country

---

[1] Article 150.

[2] For example, in Côte d'Ivoire, Decree No. 83-501 of 2 June 1983 on surety-bonds or guarantees granted by the State; Law No. 94-620 of 18 November 1994 and Decree No. 99-43 of 20 January 1999 concerning coffee and cocoa held by third parties; and Decree No. 92-08 of 8 January 1992 enacting the Public Procurement Code.

whether its laws provide for additional or special requirements to be complied with.

The Uniform Act is designed to provide creditors with greater protection, in particular by requiring the registration of certain types of securities with the RCCM, which allows third parties to inform themselves of any such securities and of the degree of indebtedness of the person or entity concerned. This protection will, of course, depend upon the effectiveness and efficiency of the RCCM of the Member State in question, and it is to be hoped that the RCCM system will be fully functioning in the near future.

The availability and enforceability of different types of security will be of great relevance in project and structured finance operations in Africa, for example in the energy, telecommunications and transportation sectors where bankers commonly require security to be taken over assets or cashflows during the period of operation.

One question which has already been raised is whether other securities, not specifically mentioned in the Uniform Act, could be created in the future. The Uniform Act does not appear to exclude this possibility, and in this regard it will be necessary to examine practical developments over the coming years.

Because of their importance in obtaining financing, real securities will be dealt with first, in Section 1 below, before personal securities in Section 2.

SECTION 1: REAL SECURITIES (*SÛRETÉS RÉELLES*)

The Uniform Act contains provisions relating to real securities over both movable and immovable property. In practice, securities over movable property will be preferred by business creditors, because of their greater flexibility and relative simplicity of enforcement if the debtor fails to pay the debts they guarantee.

A. Securities over movable property (sûretés mobilières)

Article 39 of the Uniform Act defines securities over movable property as comprising rights of retention, pledges with or without dispossession, and preferential rights.

1. Rights of retention (*droit de rétention*)

(a) Definition

A right of retention is the right of any creditor who is legitimately in possession of an asset belonging to his debtor to retain that asset pending full payment of the sums due to him, notwithstanding any other security[3].

(b) Conditions

The right of retention can be exercised only if the asset concerned is not already subject to a seizure. In addition, the debt owed to the creditor must be certain, liquidated and payable, and there must be a link between the cause of the debt and the asset itself[4]. A link is deemed to exist where both the possession of the asset and the debt are the consequence of a business relationship between the creditor and the debtor[5].

A creditor must waive his right of retention if the debtor gives him in exchange another equivalent real security (on either movable or immovable assets) of a sufficient value to cover the amount of the debt[6]. There is also nothing to prevent the debtor from proposing a personal security if the creditor is prepared to waive his right of retention in exchange[7].

If the debtor neither makes payment nor provides any guarantee, and if the creditor has an enforceable right as defined in the Uniform Act on Enforcement Measures[8], the creditor may then have a formal demand for payment served on the debtor by bailiff. Failing payment within an eight-day period, the creditor may enforce his rights, either by organizing a sale at auction of the retained assets or by seeking a court order attributing the asset to himself, up to the value of the debt[9]. In the event of competing claims, a creditor with a right of retention has the same rank as a creditor with an ordinary pledge, which is higher than that of

---

[3] Article 41.
[4] Article 42.
[5] Article 42.
[6] Article 42.
[7] Article 42.
[8] See Chapter 9, sub-section 2.A.3.
[9] Articles 43 and 56, and Articles 120 *et seq* of the Uniform Act on Simplified Recovery Procedures and Enforcement Measures.

certain other categories of creditors, including those who are secured by pledges without dispossession[10].

2. Pledges (gage)

The classic type of pledge is a contract whereby a movable asset is handed over to the creditor or to an agreed third party as security for a debt[11].

A pledge is an efficient form of security as it enables a creditor to retain possession of the pledged asset (or have it held by a third party) until full payment of the debt, including interest and related costs[12]. Moreover, even in the absence of any contractual stipulation to this effect, if the debtor incurs any new debts vis-à-vis the creditor after the pledge has been created, and if such new debts are payable before payment of the original debt, the creditor may retain the pledged asset until all the debts have been paid in full[13]. For this reason, pledges are often used in project financing operations, in particular pledges over third-party debts, bank accounts or specific contractual rights. For example, a pledge over third-party debts will enable a bank to obtain a guarantee in the form of specific identified third-party debts that will be payable to it in the event of default by the project company.

(a) Creation of the pledge

A pledge may be given for any debts, whether existing or future or even only potential. The pledge, however, becomes null and void if the debt it is to guarantee is itself declared null and void[14]. The asset may be pledged either by the debtor or by a third party who in either case must be the owner of the asset[15].

Any movable asset, be it tangible or intangible, may be pledged[16]. If the parties so agree, during the course of the pledge agreement another asset may be substituted for the asset originally pledged[17].

---

[10] Articles 43 and 149.
[11] Article 44.
[12] Article 54.
[13] Article 54.
[14] Article 45.
[15] Article 47.
[16] Article 46.
[17] Article 46.

The pledge agreement is effective as between the parties once the asset has been handed over to the creditor or the agreed third party[18]. In order to be valid as against third parties, the pledge agreement must be made in writing and registered, unless the amount of the debtor's obligation is below a certain threshold and when, for this reason, the national law of the relevant Member State allows it to be proven by any means and not necessarily by written evidence[19].

(b) Specific formalities

In certain circumstances specific formalities will have to be complied with, depending upon the nature of the assets that are pledged.

If the debtor pledges a third-party debt, he must provide the creditor with any document entitling him to payment of the debt, and must serve upon the third-party debtor notice of the transfer of the debt. If he fails to do so, the creditor himself may serve such notice[20]. The creditor may also request an undertaking from the transferred debtor to make payment directly to him. This undertaking must be made in writing, otherwise it will be void. Once the undertaking has been made, the transferred debtor cannot make any objection to payment for any reason arising out of his relations with the transferring debtor. If the transferred debtor has not undertaken to pay the creditor upon the due date, he must nevertheless do so if on that date he has no valid reason not to pay either the transferring debtor or the beneficiary of the pledge. Moreover, the transferring debtor remains jointly and severally liable with the transferred debtor for the payment of the debt[21].

If transferable securities are to be pledged, the debtor may do so by providing the creditor with a receipt for their deposit with the third party who holds them on his behalf. The creation of the pledge must also be notified to the depositary of the securities, who must not return them to their owner unless on presentation of the receipt or of an enforceable judgment ordering their return[22].

The pledging of goods which may be at the debtor's disposal by virtue of a pledge certificate, a bill of lading or other transport or customs

---

[18] Article 48.
[19] Article 49.
[20] Article 50.1.
[21] Article 50.1.
[22] Article 50.4.

document is subject to the particular rules laid down for such matters[23]. In addition to the rules relating to the pledging of stocks under a pledge certificate which are laid down by the Uniform Act[24], specific national or other rules may apply to pledges such as pledges over stock held by marine or air carriers.

Finally, intangible assets are pledged in accordance with any specific rules that may be applicable[25]. For example, pledges of patents and trademarks registered with OAPI[26] are also required to be registered with OAPI if they are to be valid as against third parties. If there are no specific rules, intangible assets are pledged by handing over to the creditor the document that evidences title to them.

(c) Effects of the pledge

The pledge has the effect of removing from the debtor's possession the asset (or the documentary title to that asset) which is provided as security to the creditor. Unless otherwise agreed between the parties, the creditor may not use the pledged asset, nor may he take the revenues from it. If he is allowed to take such revenues, he must set these off against the amount of his claim unless otherwise stipulated[27].

If there is a risk that the pledged asset will be lost or damaged, the creditor or third party in whose possession it is may seek urgent authorization from the court to sell it. In such an event, the proceeds of the sale are pledged to the creditor[28]. If the pledged asset is sold or lost or destroyed, the creditor has a preferential right over the proceeds of the sale or over any insurance payment. This preferential right covers the capital of the secured debt plus interest and costs[29].

In the event of default, a creditor who has an enforceable right to payment may arrange for the forced sale at public auction of the pledged asset eight days after notice has been served on the debtor and if need be on the third party who has granted the pledge[30]. The sale is organized in accordance with the Uniform Act on Enforcement Measures[31]. Alterna-

---

[23] Article 52.
[24] Articles 100 *et seq*. See sub-section 3(d) of this section.
[25] Article 53.
[26] See Chapter 12.
[27] Article 58.1.
[28] Article 58.2.
[29] Article 57.
[30] Article 56.1.
[31] Articles 120 *et seq* of that Uniform Act. See Chapter 9.

tively, the creditor may request the court to attribute the asset to him, within the limits of the value of his claim[32]. These formalities are mandatory, and the pledge agreement may not provide for the sale or attribution of the asset in any other way.

When the pledged asset is a third-party debt, payment to the creditor is made as follows:

- If the due date of the third-party debt is earlier than the due date of the transferring debtor's own debt, the creditor may receive payment of the amount in capital and interest immediately;
- If the due date of the transferring debtor's own debt is earlier than the due date of the third-party debt, the creditor must wait until the later date before receiving payment[33].

In either case, the creditor receives the whole amount of the third-party debt, and acts as his own debtor's agent with regard to any amount received in excess of his own claim.

(d) Termination of the pledge

A pledge is indivisible even if the debt itself is divisible. Therefore in the event of the death of the debtor, if one of the heirs pays his portion of the secured debt, that heir is not entitled to request the return of a portion of the pledged asset, even if division is physically possible. Similarly, in the event of the death of the creditor, if one of his heirs has received payment of his portion of the secured debt, that heir cannot return any portion of the pledged asset to the debtor[34].

The pledge terminates when the debt for which it has been granted has been paid in full[35], or if the creditor voluntarily returns the pledged asset or is ordered to do so by the court[36]. Following complete satisfaction of the debt, the creditor must return the asset to the debtor, who must reimburse the creditor for any expenses that have been necessary for its safekeeping[37].

---

[32] Article 56.1.
[33] Article 56.2.
[34] Article 60.
[35] Article 61.
[36] Article 62.
[37] Article 59.

3. Pledges without dispossession (*nantissement*)

Alongside the classic type of pledge where the asset is removed from the debtor's physical possession, there is a category of pledges where the debtor is not dispossessed. These pledges may be decided contractually or by court order, and may be obtained only over the following types of assets:

- transferable securities and other partnership rights or shareholdings;
- a business (*fonds de commerce*) or any of its components, excluding real property rights;
- professional equipment;
- motor vehicles;
- stocks of raw materials and goods[38].

This type of pledge is very convenient in practice, since it allows the creditor to obtain security over assets which may have a very high value, while not depriving the debtor of the use of these assets which may be essential for his business.

(a) Pledges over transferable securities and other partnership rights or shareholdings

This type of pledge is an innovation in most of the Member States. It allows a creditor to obtain security over any type of shares (either negotiable or non-negotiable) in any type of company or any bonds held by his debtor, and is likely to be used more and more frequently over financial instruments in the Member States, with the development of financial markets such as the BRVM in West Africa and the future BVMAC and BCVM in Central Africa. In particular, in the context of project finance initiatives, the shares of any special purpose vehicle created for the project are often pledged in favour of financial institutions.

If the pledge is made by agreement, this must be done either by notarized deed or by a private contract which must be registered. The agreement must include certain information as specified in Article 65 of the Uniform Act, such as the identities of the debtor and creditor, the RCCM registration number of the company whose securities are pledged, its registered office and the amount of the secured debt.

---

[38] Article 63.

Article 66 states that if a creditor wishes to obtain a court-ordered pledge, the conditions laid down for court-ordered mortgages in Articles 136 to 144 are applicable. These conditions seem unnecessarily cumbersome, however, and it would seem possible for a creditor to proceed, *mutatis mutandis,* in accordance with the provisions of the Uniform Act on Enforcement Measures regarding the seizure of shareholdings[39]. If the pledge is given not by agreement but pursuant to a court order, the court order must contain the same information as required under Article 65.

The pledge is only effective once it has been registered with the RCCM[40]. This registration is valid for five years and is renewable.

The pledge must also be notified to the issuing company of the shares or other interests which have been pledged[41]. In accordance with Article 747 of the Uniform Act on Commercial Companies, if the pledge covers shares which are registered shares of a *société anonyme,* it should be registered in the company's corporate books, and in particular in the share transfer ledger. The pledged shares themselves must be transferred to a special account in the name of their holder. Furthermore, the pledging creditor would be well advised to obtain a transfer form and share certificates for the pledged shares, as a guarantee in the event of enforcement of the pledge.

If the creditor has an enforceable right, the pledge over shares or other interests entitles him to organize their sale at auction in the event the debtor does not pay his debt on the due date and after a notice period of eight days has elapsed following a formal demand for payment, or he may seek a court order attributing the shares to himself, up to the value of the debt[42]. The pledge also gives the creditor a preferential right over certain other creditors in the event of competing claims[43].

(b) Pledges over a business (fonds de commerce) *and seller's preferential right*

(i) Pledges

In principle, a pledge over a business may cover all or part of the components of the business, provided that it covers at least the clientele,

---

[39] Articles 85–90 and 236–245 of that Uniform Act.
[40] Article 67.1.
[41] Article 67.2.
[42] Articles 56 and 68.
[43] Article 149.

the commercial name and logo, the commercial lease and any operating licences[44]. However, it cannot include real rights over property which require registration with the land registry such as mortgage rights or leases with a term that is so long that they are considered as conferring real rights (*baux emphytéotiques*)[45].

This type of pledge is very useful as it gives the creditor security over assets which generally have a high value and which may extend to all the assets comprised in the business. In this respect, it can be assimilated to the common law concept of a floating charge.

The pledge is required to be made in writing, either by notarized deed or registered private contract. It must include similar information as for pledges over shares, together with a description of the components of the business which are being pledged[46]. As is the case for the court-ordered pledging of shares, Article 71 provides for the conditions laid down for court-ordered mortgages to be applicable. Here again, this seems unnecessarily cumbersome.

The pledge is effective once it has been registered with the RCCM[47]. It secures the rights of the creditor for a five-year period, which is renewable[48]. Any modification of the beneficiary of the pledge is effective only once it has been registered alongside the initial registration in the RCCM[49].

In addition to registration with the RCCM, certain other measures may need to be taken[50]. For instance, when the pledge covers intellectual property rights which are registered with OAPI, OAPI requires the pledge also to be registered. If the pledge covers equipment, the specific rules of the Uniform Act relating to the pledging of such equipment must be complied with, as described below. In addition, if the business is operated in rented premises the creditor must notify the registration to the lessor of the premises once the pledge has been registered[51].

If there are unsecured creditors whose claims have arisen prior to the registration of the pledge in connection with the operation of the pledged

---

[44] Articles 69.1 and 69.2. The various components are described in Chapter 4, Section 4.A.
[45] Article 69.3.
[46] Article 70.
[47] Article 72.
[48] Article 83.
[49] Article 80.
[50] Article 77.
[51] Article 81.

business, these creditors may seek a court order declaring their claims immediately payable. The same right is available to such creditors in the event the pledged components of the business are sold[52].

The beneficiary of the pledge may apply to the court for the secured debt to be declared immediately payable if the owner of the business informs him of his intention to relocate the business and if the creditor considers that the relocation would reduce the value of his security[53]. If the owner of the business relocates it without properly notifying the creditor, the debt becomes immediately payable without the need for a court order[54].

If the lessor of the premises from which the pledged business is operated wishes to terminate the lease, and if he has been properly informed of the pledge, he must serve notice of his intention upon any beneficiaries of the pledge. The termination cannot be effective until after expiry of a two-month period following such service[55].

If the owner sells the business, the beneficiary of a pledge may, within one month of publication of the deed of sale, force a new sale of the business by making a bid one-sixth higher than the price for which the business has been sold[56].

Failure by the debtor to pay his debt on the due date gives the creditor the right to organize the forced sale by auction of the pledged components of the business and to receive payment of his claim, including up to two years of interest, out of the proceeds[57]. The creditor also has a preferential rank in relation to certain competing creditors[58].

(ii) Seller's preferential right

As has been noted in Chapter 4, if the owner of a business sells his business he may, on certain conditions, seek cancellation of the sale if the purchaser does not pay the purchase price[59].

---

[52] Article 85.

[53] Article 86.2.

[54] Article 86.1.

[55] Article 87.

[56] Article 88, and Articles 131 *et seq* of the Uniform Act on General Commercial Law. See also Chapter 4, Section 4.D.

[57] Articles 56 and 89.

[58] Articles 90 and 149.

[59] Article 75, and Uniform Act on General Commercial Law, Articles 135–136. See Chapter 4, Section 4.D.

In addition to this right, and on condition that he registers the deed of sale with the RCCM, the seller obtains a preferential right which is, in many ways, similar to a pledge over the business[60]. This preferential right is valid for a renewable five-year period; its registration has the same effects as registration of a pledge over the business; and the seller enjoys the same rank as the beneficiary of a pledge in the event of competing claims[61].

(c) Pledges over professional equipment and vehicles

Professional equipment and motor vehicles may be pledged. If they form part of a business, all or part of them may be pledged, either separately or with other components of the business[62].

The value of this type of pledge will depend to a large extent on its duration and the nature of the equipment, which may be such as to depreciate rapidly and thus to diminish the value of the pledge over time.

The pledge is recorded either in a notarized deed or in a registered private contract, which must include certain information including a description of the equipment which is pledged[63]. The security is effective once it has been registered with the RCCM, and is valid for a renewable five-year period[64]. A pledge over a vehicle must also be recorded on the vehicle's registration document[65].

If the owner of the equipment wishes to sell it, this may be done only with the prior consent of the secured creditor or, failing such consent, with the authorization of a court. In the absence of authorization, and if the debtor nevertheless proceeds with the sale, the debt becomes payable immediately upon the sale[66]. In the event that the debtor fails to make payment in such circumstances, administration or liquidation proceedings may be commenced against him (to the extent that such proceedings may be applicable to him)[67]. In addition, the debtor may be declared in personal bankruptcy, and he may be subject to criminal penalties if he is found to have fraudulently reduced his secured creditor's rights.

---

[60] Article 74.

[61] Articles 77 *et seq* and 85 *et seq*.

[62] Article 91.

[63] Article 94.

[64] Article 95.

[65] Article 96.

[66] Article 97.

[67] Such proceedings are not applicable to individuals without commercial status (*non commerçants*). See Chapter 7.

If the debtor fails to make payment of the secured debt on the due date, and after a notice period of eight days following a formal demand for payment, the creditor may arrange for the forced sale at auction of the pledged equipment. Alternatively, he may seek a court order attributing the pledged equipment to himself, up to the amount of his debt[68]. Whichever method is chosen, the creditor is entitled to receive the amount of his debt together with up to two years of interest[69]. The pledge also gives the creditor a preferential rank in relation to certain other categories of creditors[70].

(d) Pledges over stock

Article 100 of the Uniform Act provides that stocks of raw materials, agricultural or industrial products or other goods which are to be sold may be pledged without dispossession of their owner, on condition that they form a defined collection of fungible goods. This again may provide security on assets of a high value, which could include, for example, minerals, crude oil or petroleum products.

The pledge is recorded by notarized deed or by registered private contract. The deed or contract must contain certain information, including a precise description of the stock concerned, allowing it to be identified as to its nature, quality, quantity, value and location, and indicating the bank where the pledge will be payable[71].

The pledge becomes effective only upon registration with the RCCM, and is valid for a renewable one-year period[72]. Once it has been registered, the RCCM issues a pledge certificate (*bordereau de nantissement*) which the debtor then endorses in favour of the creditor[73]. This certificate has the same effect as a bill of exchange, and may be endorsed in the same way and on the same conditions. It is valid for a renewable three-year period from the date of issue[74].

The debtor is responsible for the safekeeping of the pledged stock. He undertakes not to reduce its value, and to insure it against loss or destruction. The debtor must also keep at the creditor's disposal a

---

[68] Articles 56 and 98.
[69] Article 99.
[70] Article 99.
[71] Article 101.
[72] Article 102.
[73] Article 103.
[74] Article 103.

statement of the pledged stock and the accounts relating to any operations affecting the stock, and the creditor may inspect the stocks at any time at the debtor's expense. In the event the value of the stock falls below the value of the pledge, the debt becomes immediately payable[75].

Nevertheless, the debtor retains the right to sell the pledged stock, but if he does so he may only make delivery to the purchaser after deposit of the proceeds with the bank where the pledge certificate is payable.

If the debtor fails to pay, either on the due date or if the value of the stock has fallen below the value of the pledge, the creditor or the bearer of the pledge certificate may realize the stock in the same way and on the same conditions as holders of other types of pledge[76].

Failure by the debtor to deposit the proceeds after a sale of the stock similarly allows the creditor or bearer of the pledge certificate to realize the pledge.

4. General or special preferential rights (*privilèges généraux ou spéciaux*)

Certain categories of creditors automatically enjoy preferential rights, which are classified by the Uniform Act as real securities over movable assets. General preferential rights, defined under Articles 106 to 108, may be exercised by their beneficiaries with regard to any assets of the debtor, whereas special preferential rights, defined under Articles 109 to 116, may be exercised only with regard to particular assets. Articles 148 and 149 then determine the rank of such preferential rights in the event there are competing claims[77].

(a) General preferential rights

Article 107 identifies a number of preferential rights which benefit the creditor without the need for any publications to be made in the RCCM or elsewhere. Most of these rights benefit creditors of a deceased debtor or a debtor whose assets have been seized or who has been put into administration or liquidation. In descending order of rank, the debts to which general preferential rights are attached are as follows:

---

[75] Article 104.
[76] Articles 56 and 104–105.
[77] See Section 3 of this chapter.

- burial costs and medical costs incurred during the debtor's last illness before any seizure of assets;
- means of subsistence provided to the debtor during the year preceding his death, the seizure of his assets or the opening of administration or liquidation proceedings;
- amounts owed to the debtor's employees under their employment contracts during the year before his death, the seizure of his assets or the opening of administration or liquidation proceedings;
- amounts owed by the debtor for the use of intellectual property rights during the three years before his death, the seizure of his assets or the opening of administration or liquidation proceedings;
- within the limits of the maximum amount laid down by the relevant national law for the provisional enforcement of court decisions, amounts owed by the debtor to the tax, customs and social security authorities.

In the event subsequent legislation creates general preferential rights which are not specifically provided for under the Uniform Act, that legislation must specify the rank of such rights in relation to the above rights[78]. If it fails to do so, the new right will be ranked last after all the other rights already provided for by Article 107.

The tax, customs and social security authorities may also benefit from general preferential rights with regard to debts of a higher amount than the limit specified in Article 107, but such rights are effective only if they are registered with the RCCM within six months of the debt falling due[79]. In such an event the registration is valid for a renewable three-year period from the date of registration.

(b) Special preferential rights

Holders of special preferential rights may exercise their rights after first seizing the assets to which these rights are attached[80]. In general, there is a connection between the source of the debt and the assets concerned, as follows[81]:

---

[78] Article 106.
[79] Article 108.
[80] Article 109. See Chapter 9.
[81] Articles 110 *et seq.*

- The seller of a movable asset who has not been paid the full sale price has a preferential right to that asset or, if the asset itself has been sold on to another purchaser, to the proceeds of that subsequent sale if the price has not yet been paid;
- The lessor of immovable property has a preferential right over the furniture of the lessee which is located in the rented premises, as security for payment of the rent and any damages which might be awarded to him in relation to the 12 months preceding and the 12 months following the seizure of the furniture;
- A carrier has a preferential right over the goods carried, as security for any sum owed to him, provided that there is a link between those goods and the debt;
- Employees and suppliers of a contractor have a preferential right over the amounts due to the contractor for their work or supplies, with employees being ranked ahead of suppliers;
- A factor has a preferential right over the goods held by him on behalf of his principal, as security for the payment of his commission;
- A person who has incurred costs or performed services to protect a particular movable asset has a preferential right over that asset.

B. Securities over immovable property (sûretés immobilières)

The Uniform Act provides for only one form of security over real property, which is the mortgage. Property which may be mortgaged is determined by Article 119, according to which land, with or without constructions, and any subsequent improvements or constructions on the land may be mortgaged, as may other real property rights (which would include for example rights of usufruct or a long-term lease (*bail emphytéotique*)). In principle only property and other real rights which are registered with the land registry may be mortgaged, unless there are particular national laws which allow a mortgage to be provisionally registered pending registration of those rights, in which case a final registration of the mortgage must be made following the final registration of the rights to which it relates. As a result, before a mortgage is taken out on a property, it should be verified whether the property is registered with the land registry.

The mortgage registration process is relatively complex and costly, as it is generally a notarized process requiring the payment of tax and registration fees. In addition, the enforcement of a mortgage may sometimes be time-consuming and difficult, with various safeguards being put in place to protect the debtor, and with appeals being admissible.

For these reasons, business creditors will generally prefer to obtain more flexible securities.

1. General provisions

A mortgage may be agreed contractually or ordered by a court, or may simply result from operation of the law. Whichever type of mortgage is concerned, a number of general provisions are applicable.

A mortgage may only be granted over property that exists and is identified. It is indivisible, and its scope cannot be reduced either when there is a partial payment of the debt that it secures or in the event of an inheritance affecting the property concerned[82]. If the owner of the mortgaged property has only a conditional right to the property, the mortgage will be similarly conditional[83].

The Uniform Act has not laid down a complete set of rules for mortgages, but leaves considerable scope to the national law of the country where the property is situated. As a result, the mortgage must be established in accordance with the national law, and must be duly registered with the land registry in accordance with any rules that may be laid down by the national law[84]. The rights resulting from registration are those defined by the national law and, while the Uniform Act provides that in principle creditors with mortgages are ranked in accordance with the date of registration of the mortgage, this is subject to any exceptions that may exist in the national law[85].

When the mortgage is given over a real right which is other than full title to the property (such as usufruct, for example), the existence of the mortgage must be notified by bailiff to any other person having a real right to the property concerned[86].

If, as a result of destruction or damage affecting the property, its value becomes insufficient to guarantee the payment of the debt, the creditor may either seek payment before the due date or obtain a new mortgage[87].

The registration of the mortgage is valid for a period of time which may be decided by the parties or by the court, as the case may be[88]. It

---

[82] Article 120.
[83] Article 121.
[84] Article 122.
[85] Article 122.
[86] Article 122.
[87] Article 145.
[88] Article 123.

may also be renewed before expiry, for a determined period. The mortgage terminates by virtue of:

- termination of the main obligation in respect of which the mortgage has been given;
- release of the mortgage by the creditor;
- expiry and non-renewal of its registration with the land registry, as certified by the land registrar; or
- release of the mortgage following an expropriation of the property for public use, and the payment or deposit of the related compensation[89].

The mortgage is discharged in accordance with the rules of the relevant Member State's land registry. If the conditions for discharge have been fulfilled, but if the creditor refuses to agree to discharge or if the land registrar fails to effect it, the debtor may obtain a court order for the release of the mortgage[90].

If the debtor fails to pay the debt that is secured by the mortgage, the creditor is entitled to pursue payment against the mortgaged property, in accordance with the rules laid down by the Uniform Act on Simplified Recovery Procedures and Enforcement Measures[91]. The creditor has a preferential right over the proceeds of the sale of the mortgaged property to guarantee payment of the principal amount of the debt, related costs, and up to three years of interest[92]. This preferential right also attaches to any insurance payment made as a result of damage to the property or its destruction.

2. Contractual mortgages (*hypothèques conventionnelles*)

A contractual mortgage may be granted by the holder of real rights in order to guarantee certain identified debts for a defined amount[93]. It may be granted either by notarized deed or by any administrative or judicial authority that is empowered to draw up such deeds, or by private contract drawn up in accordance with a standard form approved by the

---

[89] Article 124.
[90] Article 125.
[91] Articles 246 *et seq* of that Uniform Act. See also Chapter 9, sub-section 2.C.6.
[92] Articles 117 and 148.
[93] Article 127.

land registry, depending upon the national law of the Member State concerned[94].

The mortgage may be relied upon as against third parties only once it has been registered with the land registry[95]. The amount of the debt must be indicated when the mortgage is registered, and may thus be made known to third parties. This information may have a serious effect on the debtor's apparent creditworthiness and therefore, if the debt is reduced after registration, the debtor may have the registration amended to reflect the reduction, in accordance with the rules laid down by the national law[96].

3. Statutory or court-ordered mortgages (*hypothèques légales ou judiciaires*)

Statutory mortgages are granted by law while court-ordered mortgages are granted by a court decision. Both are granted without any need for the prior consent of the debtor. They are compulsory mortgages which can only be granted over identified real property as security for identified debts for a determined amount[97]. In addition to the statutory and court-ordered mortgages provided for by the Uniform Act, each Member State may permit other types of compulsory mortgage, which will be governed by the national law[98].

(a) Statutory mortgages

One type of statutory mortgage is provided for in the Uniform Act on Collective Proceedings for the Clearing of Debts[99]. It is given in favour of an insolvent debtor's creditors (the *masse des créanciers*) when administration or liquidation proceedings are opened against the debtor, and must be registered within 10 days of the opening of those proceedings, at the request of the court registrar or the administrator or liquidator.

The Uniform Act on Securities provides for statutory mortgages in favour of two other categories of persons: sellers or other assignors of real property; and architects and contractors employed for the construc-

---

[94] Article 128.
[95] Article 129.
[96] Article 127.
[97] Article 132.
[98] Article 132.
[99] Article 74 of that Uniform Act. See Chapter 7, sub-section 2.D.4.

tion or repair of buildings[100]. In either case, a mortgage may be given by agreement to cover debts arising out of the sale or the work performed; but failing such agreement, the person concerned is entitled to obtain a court-ordered mortgage on the property in question. Although these are technically court-ordered mortgages, they are categorized as statutory mortgages because the court order is a mere formality, which cannot be refused.

(b) Court-ordered mortgages

A creditor may obtain a court-ordered provisional mortgage over the real property of his debtor in order to secure a debt before it is enforceable[101]. The judgment must indicate the amount of the debt for which the mortgage is authorized, and determine a deadline within which the creditor must file proceedings to validate the provisional mortgage or proceedings on the merits, failing which the mortgage will lapse[102]. The decision may also require the creditor to provide evidence of his solvency or to provide a surety-bond before the mortgage is granted[103]. The court order is immediately enforceable, notwithstanding any appeal or third-party objections[104].

Article 139 of the Uniform Act lists certain information that must be contained in the court order, including details of the debt guaranteed (the amount in principal plus interest and costs), and the designation of each property over which the mortgage has been granted, with its land registration number.

The creditor must notify the debtor of the court order by serving upon him a summons to appear in the proceedings for validation of the mortgage or the proceedings on the merits, as the case may be, within the deadline fixed by the court[105]. He must also notify the debtor of the registration of the mortgage within two weeks of registration.

Release of the mortgage or a reduction of its amount may be obtained in urgent summary proceedings before the president of the court which gave the original order, on condition that the debtor deposits with an escrow agent the amount of the debt in principal, interest and costs, and

---

[100] Articles 134 and 135.
[101] Article 136.
[102] Article 136.
[103] Article 137.
[104] Article 138.
[105] Article 140.

that this amount is specifically set aside for payment of the debt concerned[106]. Such summary proceedings must be filed within one month of service of the creditor's summons. If the debtor's request is granted, and if the creditor subsequently obtains a final judgment in his favour in respect of the debt in question, he has an overriding preferential right to the sums held in escrow, which are specifically allocated to payment of the debt. These sums are frozen throughout the proceedings on the merits[107].

The debtor may also obtain from the court, at any time, a partial or total release of the mortgage, on condition that he can show that there are serious and legitimate reasons for such a release[108]. In practice this would appear to mean either that the debt does not appear to be well founded in principle or that there are no circumstances that jeopardize its recovery.

It is possible for the debtor to limit the scope of the mortgage if he can show that the value of the mortgaged property is more than twice the amount of the debt. In such an event, he may request that the mortgage be limited to certain property within the original scope of the mortgage[109].

In addition, if the creditor fails to bring the validation proceedings or the proceedings on the merits within the deadline fixed by the court, or if he lets such proceedings lapse or withdraws them, the court which authorized the registration of the mortgage may order its discharge if the creditor does not agree to it voluntarily[110]. In such an event, the discharge is made by filing the court's judgment with the land registry, once it has become final and binding.

If during the court proceedings on the merits the existence of the debt is confirmed, the judgment may either maintain in full or in part the provisional mortgage as already registered, or grant a final mortgage[111]. The creditor must register the mortgage resulting from the judgment within six months after the judgment has become final and binding. If he fails to do so or if the debt is not confirmed by a final judgment, the provisional registration of the mortgage becomes void retroactively and

---

[106] Article 141.
[107] Article 141.
[108] Article 142.
[109] Article 143.
[110] Article 142.
[111] Article 144.

any interested party may apply to the court which ordered it to seek its de-registration, at the expense of the party who registered it[112].

SECTION 2: PERSONAL SECURITIES (*SÛRETÉS PERSONNELLES*)

Personal securities are undertakings by a person or entity to guarantee an obligation undertaken by another person or entity. The Uniform Act provides for two types of personal security: the surety-bond (*cautionnement*) and the letter of guarantee (*lettre de garantie*).

A. *Surety-bonds* (cautionnement)

A surety-bond is a contract between a guarantor (*caution*) who stands surety for the debtor's obligation, ie who undertakes to perform that obligation if the debtor fails to perform it himself, and the creditor of that obligation, who accepts the guarantor's undertaking[113]. In order for the contract to be made, there is no need for the consent of the principal debtor, and the surety-bond may even be given without his knowledge.

Under a surety-bond, the guarantor is deemed to be jointly and severally liable with the debtor for the guaranteed debts, unless otherwise provided under the contract or by the national law of the Member State concerned[114].

1. Creation of the surety-bond

(a) General

Because a surety-bond can be a very serious undertaking, certain formalities must be complied with in order to ensure that the guarantor is properly aware of his obligations. The agreement must be made expressly between the creditor and the guarantor, failing which it will be null and void. It must be given in writing and signed by both parties, and the guarantor must indicate in handwriting, in both words and

---

[112] Article 144.
[113] Article 3.
[114] Article 10.

numerals, the maximum amount guaranteed. If there is a difference in the two amounts, the amount in words will prevail[115].

If the debtor is obliged by contract, by law or by a court order to provide his creditor with a surety-bond, and if the guarantor under that surety-bond subsequently becomes insolvent, the debtor must find another guarantor to provide a surety-bond or must furnish real security providing the creditor with the same guarantees[116].

A surety-bond may not be contracted on conditions that are more onerous than those of the obligation that it guarantees, nor may it be for an amount greater than the amount owed by the debtor including any costs and interest attached to the debt, although it may be for a lesser amount[117]. In order for the surety-bond to be valid, the debt to which it relates must also be valid[118].

A general surety-bond may be given to cover all the debts contracted by the debtor. In such an event, it is deemed to cover only direct contractual debts, except if otherwise provided by contract, and a maximum guaranteed amount must be indicated if the bond is to be valid[119]. The bond may however be renewed once the maximum amount has been reached. It may also be revoked by the guarantor before that amount has been reached, but the revocation will affect only such obligations of the debtor which arise after the date of revocation. Similarly, a general surety-bond does not, unless otherwise provided, cover any debts which arose before it was entered into[120].

The guarantor may provide security for the performance of his own obligations under the surety-bond by giving real security over one or more of his assets[121]. In such an event, and if the creditor agrees, he may limit his exposure under the surety-bond to the value of such assets if they are realized.

Alternatively, the guarantor may have his obligations under the surety-bond underwritten by a further guarantor, who must be designated as such in the bond. Unless otherwise indicated in the bond, the

---

[115] Article 4.
[116] Article 6.
[117] Articles 7 and 8.
[118] Article 7.
[119] Article 9.
[120] Article 9.
[121] Article 12.

underwriting guarantor does not have joint and several liability with the principal guarantor[122].

(b) Surety-bonds given by commercial companies

The granting of a surety-bond by an SA or an SARL to members of their management or their close relatives is prohibited[123]. However, this prohibition does not apply if the surety-bond is granted to a member of the board which is a legal entity, nor does it apply if the company concerned is a banking or other financial institution.

When a surety-bond is granted by an SA to a third party, the Uniform Act on Commercial Companies and Economic Interest Groups requires that prior authorization be given by the board of directors or the shareholders, as the case may be, depending on the management structure of the company[124]. However, a general authorization may be given by the board of directors to the chairman and general manager or to the general manager (or by the shareholders to the managing director, as the case may be) to grant surety-bonds not exceeding a maximum total amount or a maximum amount for each bond. If the authorized amount is exceeded, a new authorization will be required. In any event, the general authorization cannot be granted for a duration exceeding one year.

If the maximum authorized amount has been exceeded, this cannot be relied upon as against third parties unless it can be shown that the third parties were aware of the fact, or unless the amount of the commitment itself exceeds the authorized limit.

2. Effects

(a) Information requirements

When the surety-bond is a general bond as defined above, the creditor must deliver certain information to the guarantor. In addition to informing him of any failure of the debtor to pay, or any debt which has become immediately payable or whose term has been extended, he must deliver

---

[122] Article 11.

[123] Uniform Act on Commercial Companies and Economic Interest Groups, Article 356 (SARL) and Articles 450 and 507 (SA).

[124] Uniform Act on Commercial Companies and Economic Interest Groups, Articles 449 and 506.

to the guarantor within one month of the end of each calendar quarter, a statement of all the debts of the debtor, with an indication of their due dates and their amounts as of the end of the quarter together with a reminder that the guarantor remains free to revoke the surety-bond[125]. This requirement puts a very heavy constraint on the creditor, especially by comparison with French law, which requires such information to be communicated only once a year and then only if the guarantor is an individual. However, the precaution is understandable, given the importance of the guarantor's obligation under a general surety-bond. In the event of non-compliance with these requirements, the creditor is not entitled to claim interest from the guarantor for the period between the date for which such information was last communicated until the date further information is communicated[126].

(b) Enforcement

The guarantor is liable to pay the debts of the debtor only if the debtor himself defaults after having been formally put on notice to pay[127]. In such an event, the creditor cannot commence proceedings against the guarantor alone, but must also involve the debtor in any such proceedings[128]. This is because a guarantor under a surety-bond is entitled to raise any defences against payment that are inherent to the debt itself and that the debtor himself may raise, and it is therefore essential that the guarantor should be properly informed of such defences[129]. These defences might include in particular any reasons for the debt to be reduced, extinguished or deferred.

As has already been mentioned, unless the surety-bond or the applicable national law provides otherwise, the guarantor is jointly and severally liable with the debtor for payment of the debt. As a result, he cannot require the creditor first to pursue the debt against the debtor's assets before seeking payment under the surety-bond[130]. On the other hand, if joint and several liability has been excluded, and unless there has been a waiver by the guarantor, the guarantor may require the creditor to pursue the debt against the debtor's assets, on condition that

---

[125] Article 14.
[126] Article 14.
[127] Article 13.
[128] Article 15.
[129] Article 18.
[130] Article 16.

he indicates any such assets which may be seized in the Member State concerned, and advances the necessary costs for such proceedings[131]. If the creditor then fails to take the required action, he will be liable towards the guarantor for any insolvency of the debtor, up to the value of the debtor's assets that have been indicated by the guarantor.

Where there are several guarantors who have provided surety-bonds to cover the same debtor for the same debt, the guarantor who is first approached by the creditor for payment may require the creditor to divide the burden of the debt among all the guarantors who are solvent as of that date, unless the guarantors have waived the benefit of this provision or unless joint and several liability has been stipulated among the guarantors[132].

The guarantor must inform the debtor before he makes any payment under the surety-bond. If he fails to do so, he will lose his right to claim against the debtor if, subsequent to payment, the debtor would have been in a position to obtain a decision that the debt no longer existed, or if the debtor pays the debt without being aware that the guarantor has already made payment[133]. Nevertheless, in such circumstances the guarantor remains entitled to claim reimbursement from the creditor of all sums that have been unduly paid.

If the guarantor has properly informed the debtor and has made payment to the creditor, he is subrogated in all the rights and guarantees of the creditor against the debtor for the sum paid[134]. The guarantor may also claim against the debtor for any damage that he might have suffered as a result of his pursuit by the creditor[135]. In addition, if several debtors were jointly and severally liable for the same debt, the guarantor is subrogated in all the creditor's rights against each of them for the whole amount that he has paid, even if he provided a surety-bond only on behalf of one of them. If several guarantors have provided surety-bonds for the same debt, the guarantor who pays the debt may seek reimbursement from the other guarantors, in proportion to their undertakings[136].

The guarantor may seek payment from the debtor or may secure his rights to payment, even before he has himself made payment to the creditor, in the following circumstances:

---

[131] Article 16.
[132] Article 17.
[133] Article 19.
[134] Article 20.
[135] Article 21.
[136] Article 23.

- when the creditor seeks payment under the surety-bond;
- when the debtor becomes insolvent or otherwise cannot meet his obligations;
- when the debtor has not released him from the surety-bond within the agreed time period; or
- when the debt has become payable upon expiry of its contractual term[137].

(c) Termination

If the main obligation is wholly or partially extinguished, the surety-bond will be extinguished to the same extent. If there is a novation of the main obligation by means of a change in the object of the obligation or the consideration, the guarantor is freed from his surety-bond unless he agrees to transfer his guarantee to the new debt[138].

Furthermore, the surety-bond may be extinguished independently from the main debt in the following circumstances:

- when, in the context of proceedings brought by the creditor for payment under the surety-bond, the guarantor can rely upon a set-off between his debt under the surety-bond and a debt owed to him by the creditor;
- when the creditor waives the guarantor's debt under the surety-bond; or
- when the guarantor also becomes the creditor, for example if the guaranteed debt is assigned to him[139].

B. *Letters of guarantee or counter-guarantee* (lettre de garantie ou de contregarantie)

The letter of guarantee or counter-guarantee is a legal instrument that has been derived from contractual practice and case law. The letter of guarantee is defined in the Uniform Act as an agreement whereby, at the request or on the instructions of a principal, a guarantor (*garant*) undertakes to pay a defined amount to a beneficiary, upon the beneficiary's first call[140]. The counter-guarantee is defined in turn as an agreement

---

[137] Article 24.
[138] Article 25.
[139] Article 26.
[140] Article 28.

whereby, at the request or on the instructions of a principal or a guarantor, a counter-guarantor (*contregarant*) undertakes to pay a defined amount to the guarantor, upon the guarantor's first call.

The system of a back-to-back guarantee and counter-guarantee is frequently used in international contracts where a performance bond is required from a foreign contractor. In such cases, the party for whom the work is being performed will usually require the contractor to furnish a performance bond (*garantie de bonne fin*) given by a local bank. That bank will in turn generally require a counter-guarantee to be given by a bank in the contractor's own country, under which it can seek payment if a call is made on the guarantee that it has itself issued. As a result, in practice the contractor will first approach its own bank to act as counter-guarantor, and that bank will then arrange for the guarantee from the local bank.

Letters of guarantee can also be used to guarantee an overdraft on a bank account (*garantie de découvert*) or for the payment of customs duties, and in open bid procedures, bidders will sometimes be required to provide a tender guarantee (*garantie de soumission*) in order to demonstrate the seriousness of their tender.

The Uniform Act has been innovative in creating a specific legal regime applicable to both guarantees and counter-guarantees. It has created harmonized rules that can be used by practitioners to draft guarantees more efficiently, even though the existence of a legislative framework does not always solve all the legal issues which may arise in practice. The rules laid down for letters of guarantee are largely derived from the definition of a guarantee upon first demand in the Uniform Rules on Demand Guarantees (URDG) of the International Chamber of Commerce.

An essential characteristic of the letter of guarantee or counter-guarantee is that it creates obligations that are independent from the main contract in relation to which it has been given[141]. This means that a guarantor under a letter of guarantee, unlike a guarantor under a surety-bond, is not entitled to raise defences inherent to the debt that might be available to the principal under the main contract. Instead, he must pay immediately, without argument, upon the first call.

Unless where otherwise stated, the provisions of the Uniform Act are applicable, *mutatis mutandis*, to letters both of guarantee and of counter-guarantee.

---

[141] Article 29.

1. Creation of the letter of guarantee

The letter of guarantee is an agreement between the guarantor and the beneficiary. It is given upon the instructions or at the request of a principal, and it is therefore advisable for the principal also to be a party to the letter of guarantee to ensure that it corresponds properly to his instructions.

The letter of guarantee must be made in writing and must contain the following required information, failing which it will be null and void: an indication that the agreement is a guarantee upon first demand (*lettre de garantie à première demande*); the names of the principal, beneficiary and guarantor; identification of the main agreement in relation to which the guarantee is given; the maximum amount guaranteed; the date of expiry or any event which will cause the guarantee to expire; the conditions which must be fulfilled for payment to be made under the guarantee; and a statement that the guarantor may not rely on any defences that would be available to a guarantor under a surety-bond[142].

These precautions are laid down so that the guarantor is aware of the nature of his undertaking, which is even more serious under a letter of guarantee than under a surety-bond. For this reason, the Uniform Act prohibits the giving of a letter of guarantee by an individual, and provides that any letter of guarantee that is given in contravention of this prohibition will be null and void[143].

In practice, a distinction must be made between several types of guarantee. In particular, (i) the guarantee may require that reasons be given when the beneficiary demands payment, (ii) it may require the presentation of specific documents, or (iii) it may be absolutely unconditional, with no more than the statutory requirement that a call upon the guarantee must be made in writing and state that the principal is in default of his obligations or, when a call is made upon a counter-guarantee, that the guarantor must state in writing that he has received a demand for payment from the beneficiary[144]. Because of these variations, special attention should be paid to the definition of the conditions of payment when drafting a letter of guarantee and when demanding payment under the guarantee.

---

[142] Article 30.
[143] Article 29.

2. Effects

Since under the Uniform Act the letter of guarantee is defined as a guarantee upon first demand which is independent from the principal's obligations, it is a very powerful and efficient instrument for the beneficiary, especially when it guarantees the obligations of contractors undertaking major projects such as infrastructure constructions or engineering assessments, where no specific assets are available as real security, for instance during the construction period.

Letters of guarantee are effective as of the date of their issue, unless otherwise provided. They are irrevocable unless the principal has instructed otherwise[145].

A letter of guarantee is valid only for the amount stated in the agreement, as may be reduced from time to time by payments made by the guarantor or the principal which are not disputed by the beneficiary. It may also be stipulated that the amount will be reduced by a determined or determinable amount on particular dates or upon presentation to the guarantor of certain documents[146].

A letter of guarantee is personal to the beneficiary, and therefore cannot be assigned, unless otherwise provided in the guarantee. However, this does not prevent the beneficiary from assigning the benefit of the corresponding obligations under the main contract[147].

3. Enforcement

Any request for payment under the letter of guarantee must be made in writing by the beneficiary, who must be careful to comply with any conditions stipulated in the guarantee for making a call under it[148].

If the beneficiary calls the guarantee, the guarantor must be allowed a reasonable time period within which to verify the conformity of any documents supplied by the beneficiary as against the requirements of the letter of guarantee[149]. Since the Uniform Act does not contain any indication of what is meant by a reasonable time period, this will no doubt be determined in the future by the CCJA.

---

[144] Article 34.
[145] Article 32.
[146] Article 33.
[147] Article 31.
[148] Article 34.
[149] Article 35.

Before making any payment under the letter of guarantee, the guarantor must also inform the principal of the call and transmit to him a copy of the demand and all accompanying documents[150].

If the guarantor decides to refuse the demand for payment, he must inform the principal and the beneficiary as soon as possible. He must also inform the principal of any reduction in the amount of the guarantee and of any event causing the guarantee to terminate.

Article 36 provides that the principal cannot order the guarantor not to make payment under the guarantee, unless the call for payment is obviously abusive or fraudulent. This provision will doubtless give rise to numerous court proceedings, since in practice a principal will often try to block payment under a letter of guarantee because of a contractual dispute, even though the guarantee is independent of the main contract. The decision of the courts – and in particular of the CCJA – as to what constitutes an abusive or fraudulent call will determine whether the letter of guarantee remains an efficient security or whether its efficiency will be diminished by too liberal a definition.

If payment has been properly made under the letter of guarantee, the guarantor may seek reimbursement from the principal[151]. Although this is not expressly provided for in the Uniform Act, there also seems to be nothing to prevent the principal or the beneficiary from claiming against each other or against the guarantor. For example, the principal could claim against the beneficiary in the event payment has been made upon an abusive or fraudulent request, or against the guarantor in the event payment has been made in contravention of a court order. Also, the beneficiary might claim against the guarantor in the event of a refusal to pay or a delay in payment when the call upon the guarantee has been properly made.

SECTION 3: DISTRIBUTION OF PROCEEDS AND RANKING OF SECURITIES

Articles 148 and 149 of the Uniform Act organize the order in which proceeds from the sale of secured immovable assets and movable assets, respectively, are to be distributed among competing creditors. These

---

[150] Article 35.
[151] Article 37.

articles are very useful in that they establish a clear and definite order of priority.

A. *Immovable assets*

Article 148 provides for distribution of the proceeds of a sale of immovable assets to the following categories of creditors in the following order:

- creditors for legal costs incurred in organizing the procedure for the sale of the assets and distribution of the proceeds;
- employees for their wages and salaries;
- mortgage-holders, in chronological order of the dates of registration of their respective mortgages;
- beneficiaries of general preferential rights which are subject to registration with the RCCM (i.e. the tax, customs and social security authorities), in chronological order of the dates of registration);
- beneficiaries of general preferential rights which are not subject to registration with the RCCM, in the order defined in Article 107 of the Uniform Act[152]; and
- unsecured creditors with an enforceable right who have obtained seizures or filed third-party objections.

If there are not sufficient proceeds to satisfy all the creditors, payment is made in full to each category until a category is reached where there are not sufficient proceeds to satisfy all the creditors in that category. If the category is one where registration with the land registry or the RCCM is required, the same procedure is followed within that category, ie the creditors are satisfied in full in chronological order of their registrations until the proceeds are exhausted. If on the other hand the category is one where no registration is required, the remaining proceeds are shared out among the creditors in that category in proportion to the amounts owed to each of them, respectively.

B. *Movable assets*

Article 149 provides for a similar system with respect to proceeds realized from the sale of movable assets, with the following categories of creditors in descending order of rank:

---

[152] See sub-section 1.A.4 (a) of this chapter.

- creditors for legal costs incurred in relation to the sale of the assets concerned and the distribution of the proceeds;
- creditors for expenses incurred in safeguarding the assets concerned in the interests of creditors having a prior entitlement;
- employees for their wages and salaries;
- beneficiaries of a pledge, in chronological order of the creation of the pledge;
- beneficiaries of a pledge without dispossession or a preferential right that is subject to registration, in chronological order of registration with the RCCM;
- beneficiaries of special preferential rights, who are entitled to the proceeds realized on the asset to which the right attaches; in the event of competing claims to the same asset, the first creditor to have seized the asset has a preferential right;
- creditors who are beneficiaries of a general preferential right that is not subject to registration, in the order established by Article 107 of the Uniform Act; and
- unsecured creditors with an enforceable right who have obtained seizures or filed third-party objections.

If the proceeds are insufficient to satisfy all the creditors, they are distributed according to the same principles as under Article 148.

9

Simplified recovery procedures and enforcement measures

The Uniform Act on Simplified Recovery Procedures and Enforcement Measures was issued on 10th April 1998. Like the Uniform Act on Securities, this Act oversteps the bounds of pure business law in that it effects a general reform of civil procedure in relation to recovery and enforcement.

The reform was indispensable; of the OHADA Member States, only Mali had, in 1994, put in place a modern system that was suited to present-day economic and social conditions. Otherwise, the relevant legislation dated, at best, from the 1970s and in several cases from colonial times.

The new OHADA legislation should go some way towards reassuring investors and lenders that, if the need arises, procedures exist that will allow them to recover what is due to them. However, the procedures are not always as efficient or simple as might be wished.

SECTION 1: SIMPLIFIED RECOVERY PROCEDURES

The first part of the Uniform Act is devoted to what it calls simplified recovery procedures. These are in fact two types of order: the traditional order to make payment, and the more innovative order to deliver or to return an object. As their names indicate, the idea is that both these procedures should be simple and inexpensive, and should allow a creditor quickly to obtain what is due to him. So long as there is no serious dispute as to whether the debt or obligation is due (or so long as the debtor refrains from raising any spurious objections), this should be the case.

A. Conditions for orders to make payment

A creditor may seek an order to make payment if the following conditions are met:

- the debt is certain, liquidated and due[1], and
- the debt is a contractual debt or arises out of the issuance or acceptance of any negotiable instrument or of a cheque for which there is insufficient cover[2].

B. Conditions for orders to deliver or return an object

Fewer conditions are laid down for orders to deliver or return an object. Here, all that is required is that:

- the object concerned should be identifiable, tangible and movable, and
- the applicant should consider that he is owed an obligation to deliver or return this particular object[3].

C. Procedure

The procedure for either type of order is similar. The first step is for the creditor to make an application to the court having jurisdiction at the place of domicile or actual residence of the debtor, or to the court that may otherwise have been designated by the parties' contract. The proceedings are *ex parte*, ie the debtor does not participate in them, and does not need to be informed that they are taking place[4].

---

[1] Article 1.
[2] Article 2.
[3] Article 19.
[4] Articles 3 and 20.

If the court decides that the conditions have not been met and the application is unfounded, it will refuse to issue an order. This decision is not subject to appeal, but the creditor remains free to file ordinary proceedings to seek recovery of the debt or object[5].

If the court decides on the other hand that the application is well founded, it will issue an order[6]. In the case of an order to make payment, this may be for a fraction of the amount claimed, if the court considers that the application is only partially well founded. As in the case of an outright rejection of the application, the creditor may then pursue the balance of the debt in ordinary proceedings[7].

The aim of the Uniform Act is to make these simplified recovery proceedings as rapid as possible, and it therefore sets relatively short deadlines for the subsequent steps once an order has been issued.

The order must be served upon the debtor within three months of its issuance, failing which it will lapse[8]. The deed of service will be null and void if it does not contain certain indications. For an order to make payment, these include in particular a demand that the debtor pay to the creditor the amount indicated in the order, together with interest and filing fees, and notice that, if the debtor intends to set aside the order, he must file an objection with the court[9]. For an order to deliver or return an object, the deed of service must contain a demand that the debtor transport the object at his own cost to a designated place of delivery and must again put the debtor on notice to file an objection with the court if he intends to request setting-aside of the order[10].

The onus is then on the debtor either to pay the claim or deliver the object, or to take steps to set aside the order. If the debtor neither complies with the order nor raises objections within a 15-day period from the date of service of the order, the creditor may apply to the court for the order to be made absolute and enforceable[11]. This must be done within two months of expiry of the deadline, failing which the order will lapse[12]. Obtaining the declaration of enforceability is a mere

---

[5] Articles 5 and 24.
[6] Articles 5 and 23.
[7] Article 5.
[8] Articles 7 and 25.
[9] Article 8.
[10] Article 25.
[11] Articles 16 and 27.
[12] Articles 17 and 27.

formality, which then allows enforcement of the order without further appeals[13].

If on the other hand the debtor decides to defend against the claim, he has 15 days within which to file a summons commencing proceedings, and the parties must appear in court within 30 days of the date of the summons[14].

The court must then make an attempt at conciliation. No time limit is specified for this stage of the proceedings. If the attempt at conciliation fails, the court must give immediate judgment on the claim[15]. This judgment supersedes the original order, and is subject to appeal within a 30-day time limit[16]. Such appeals are governed by the national procedural law of the Member State concerned[17].

D. Practical problems

If a debtor does not defend against an order, the whole process, from application for an order to enforcement, should take only a few weeks. In reality, however, a debtor is more than likely to defend against an order, even if he has no valid grounds for defence. In such an event, simplified recovery proceedings could paradoxically last longer than ordinary proceedings on the merits of the claim. This is essentially due to two facts. First, there is the requirement to have conciliation proceedings. These may take months if not years to complete, because of the number of cases to be dealt with and the insufficient number of judges available, leading to the courts being saturated with pending cases. Second, there is the right of ordinary appeal (and subsequently ultimate appeal before the CCJA) that is open to a debtor following the failure of conciliation proceedings. These seem to be serious flaws in the Uniform Act which would merit reconsideration if the Uniform Act were to be amended.

---

[13] See sub-section 2.C of this chapter.

[14] Articles 10–11 and 26.

[15] Articles 12 and 26.

[16] Articles 14–15 and 26.

[17] This has been confirmed by the CCJA in its judgment No. 002/2001 of 10 January 2002, which held that an appeal filed before the CCJA against a judgment of the commercial court in Bamako (Mali) which had confirmed an order to pay was inadmissible, and that the appeal should have been filed in accordance with the national law of Mali.

SECTION 2: ENFORCEMENT MEASURES

The enforcement measures that are provided for by the Uniform Act fall into two separate categories: (i) provisional or conservatory measures, whereby a creditor may secure a debt pending a final judgment on the merits of his claim; and (ii) measures of execution (or enforcement measures in the strict sense of the term), whereby a creditor can enforce a judgment against the assets of his debtor. These two main categories can then be broken down into sub-categories of different types of measures, depending upon the type of assets seized or the nature of the debt.

The Uniform Act contains a series of general provisions which are applicable to all types of enforcement measures. It is therefore useful to review these first, before turning to the individual types of measures.

A. General provisions

1. Principles

Article 28 of the Uniform Act lays down the general principle that, failing voluntary performance by the debtor of any kind of obligation, a creditor may force the debtor to perform, or may take provisional measures in order to preserve his rights.

The article further states that, unless the debt is specifically guaranteed by a mortgage or other privilege, any measures must first be taken against the movable assets of the debtor. It is only if such assets are insufficient to cover the debt that measures may be taken against the debtor's immovable assets. This rule has advantages for both the creditor and the debtor. For the creditor, it means that the procedures for obtaining enforcement are less cumbersome, and for the debtor it means that to the extent possible he will avoid the type of measure that is likely to have the most serious consequences for him.

2. Liability of the State

The Uniform Act provides further support for the creditor by stating expressly that the State – ie the Member State where enforcement is sought – must lend its assistance in enforcing decisions, and that if it fails or refuses to do so it may be held liable[18].

---

[18] Article 29.

Whether this liability of the State constitutes realistic and enforceable protection for a creditor is however a different question, to which the answer depends upon whether there can be any set-off against debts due by the creditor to the State. This is because Article 30 of the Uniform Act lays down the principle that enforcement measures cannot be taken against entities and persons who enjoy immunity from execution. This would generally include not only the State and its various agencies, but might also cover public companies. The prohibition is however tempered by the next paragraph of the same article, according to which the debts of public entities, including public companies, which are certain, liquidated and due, may be offset against debts owed to them which are similarly certain, liquidated and due, subject to reciprocity. The debts of a public entity or company are deemed to be certain only if they arise out of an acknowledgement of the debt or a judgment or other right that is enforceable in the State where the public entity or company is located[19].

3. Definition of enforceable right (*titre exécutoire*)

The term *titre exécutoire* – or enforceable right – appears throughout the Uniform Act. Article 33 provides a definition of this term, which is important to note, since certain enforcement measures are possible only if the creditor has such an enforceable right. Within the context of the Uniform Act, only the following are defined as enforceable rights:

- a court decision which has been declared enforceable;
- a foreign deed or court decision or an arbitral award that cannot be suspended by any type of appeal and that has been declared enforceable by a court decision in the State where enforcement is sought;
- official minutes of conciliation, signed by a judge and the parties;
- a notarized deed that has been declared enforceable; or
- a decision which, under the national law of the Member State concerned, has the same effect as a court decision.

In every case the enforceable right is evidenced by a written document which will need to be produced by the creditor for enforcement.

---

[19] Article 30.

4. Effects of provisional and enforcement measures

Any type of seizure of assets under the Uniform Act has the effect of making the assets inalienable[20]. It also interrupts the statute of limitations applicable to the claim[21].

Third parties may not seek to impede enforcement measures but, on the contrary, must assist in them when legally required to do so. Failure to assist may lead to liability to pay damages, and a third party holding assets which are to be seized may be ordered to make payment to the creditor out of his own assets in the event he impedes or fails to assist in the enforcement measures[22]. If the assets concerned have already been seized by another creditor, the debtor and any third party holding those assets must inform the new creditor of the existing seizure[23].

The debtor cannot force the creditor to accept partial payment of the debt. However, he may apply to the court for a postponement or for authorization to make payment in instalments. He may also request the court to order that any payments will be imputed first against the capital of the debt rather than the interest. Such measures of leniency in favour of the debtor may not however be ordered when the debt arises out of a negotiable instrument. In deciding whether to grant the debtor's request, the court will take into consideration both the debtor's own situation and the needs of the creditor. If the court does grant the debtor's request, it may require the debtor to provide guarantees, and the measures granted cannot have a duration of more than one year[24]. These rules are more protective of the creditor than were the corresponding rules in the superseded national laws.

5. Procedure

A series of detailed provisions lays down the procedure to be followed by the bailiff in implementing the enforcement measures[25]. In particular, the Uniform Act provides that the bailiff may enter the premises where the assets are held, assisted if necessary by the police or other public authority[26]. However, unless this is necessary and unless he is author-

---

[20] Article 36.
[21] Article 37.
[22] Article 38.
[23] Article 36.
[24] Article 39.
[25] Articles 41 *et seq.*
[26] Articles 41–42.

ized by the President of the court, the bailiff may not do so on Sundays or public holidays, or between 6 pm and 8 am[27]. If difficulties arise, the bailiff may apply to the court for an urgent order[28]. In principle, the costs of enforcement measures are borne by the debtor[29].

6. Seizable assets

As regards the assets that may be seized, these comprise all assets of the debtor, including those held by a third party, unless the national law of the Member State concerned has declared them to be immune from seizure[30]. In practice, immune assets tend to be those that are necessary for the personal life of the debtor and his family, such as salaries (or a portion thereof), and certain items of furniture and utensils.

In addition to tangible assets, a creditor may seize debts owed by a third party to the creditor's own debtor. Such debts do not need to be certain or due, but may be simply conditional or due in the future or by instalments[31].

B. *Provisional or interim measures* (saisies conservatoires)

Provisional or interim measures, which allow a creditor to obtain a provisional seizure of assets belonging to his debtor, serve a dual purpose. First, they can be used as a means of putting pressure on a recalcitrant debtor and second, and perhaps more importantly, they provide protection against the possible future insolvency of a debtor. As a consequence, such measures are very often used by creditors as soon as any payment difficulties arise.

1. Conditions

Two fundamental substantive conditions must be fulfilled if a creditor is to be allowed to take provisional measures:

- the claim must appear to be well-founded in principle; and

---

[27] Article 46.
[28] Article 48.
[29] Article 47.
[30] Article 50.
[31] Article 50.

- circumstances must exist which are such as to jeopardize recovery of the debt[32].

If the creditor does not have an enforceable right as defined in sub-section 2.A.3 of this chapter, he must apply to the court for an *ex parte* order authorizing the measures to be taken by means of a seizure of assets[33]. The measures must be taken within three months of the date of the order, which will otherwise lapse[34]. Proceedings on the merits of the claim must then be instituted by the creditor within one month of the seizure[35].

No court order is necessary, however, if the creditor does have an enforceable right, or if the claim is for failure to make payment under an accepted bill of exchange, a promissory note or a cheque, or for rent resulting from a written rental agreement which has remained unpaid after a formal demand[36]. Likewise, in such circumstances, it is not necessary to institute proceedings on the merits, since the creditor already has an enforceable right[37].

2. Effect of provisional measures

Provisional measures have the effect of freezing those assets of the debtor to which they are applied, and of making them inalienable[38]. The assets concerned must be movable assets, but may be either tangible or intangible[39]. If the asset seized is a sum of money owed to the debtor by a third party, the third party must indicate the extent of his obligations towards the debtor; however, the amount seized is limited to the amount authorized by the court or, if authorization is not necessary, to the amount of the creditor's claim[40].

---

[32] Article 54.
[33] Article 54.
[34] Article 60.
[35] Article 61.
[36] Article 55.
[37] Article 61.
[38] Article 56.
[39] Article 56.
[40] Articles 57, 80 and 156.

3. Procedures

The Uniform Act goes into a great deal of detail regarding the procedures to be followed for the following different types of provisional measures:

- seizure of tangible movable assets[41];
- seizure of debts owed to the debtor[42] (excluding wages or salaries owed by the debtor's employer, which may not be seized as a provisional measure, but only as a measure of execution[43]); and
- seizure of transferable securities and other partnership rights or shareholdings[44].

In all cases, the measures must be taken by a bailiff, who must in particular prepare a formal report of the seizure and take the necessary steps to inform the debtor of his rights. Failure by the bailiff to comply with the detailed requirements laid down by the Uniform Act may result in the seizure being declared null and void.

4. Lifting of seizure

A debtor whose assets have been seized may apply for the seizure to be lifted. In order to obtain a lifting, the debtor must show that one or more of the conditions for the seizure, as outlined above in sub-section B.1, have not been fulfilled[45].

5. Conversion of provisional measures

Once the creditor has obtained an enforceable right, he may convert the provisional measure into a measure of execution. The type of measure will depend upon the nature of the assets seized, and will be either a forced sale (*saisie-vente*) if the assets are tangible assets, transferable securities or other partnership rights or shareholdings, or a forced attribution to the creditor (*saisie-attribution*) if the assets consist of a debt owed by a third party to the debtor. The creditor effects the conversion by serving upon the debtor a conversion deed which, on penalty of being

---

[41] Articles 64 *et seq.*
[42] Articles 77 *et seq.*
[43] See sub-section 2.C.3 of this chapter.
[44] Articles 85 *et seq.*
[45] Article 62.

declared null and void, must contain certain indications including the identity of the parties and the amount of the debt in principal, interest and costs[46].

In the case of a conversion into a forced sale, the debtor has a period of eight days within which to make voluntary payment, and a further month within which to sell the seized assets himself, subject to the agreement of the creditor[47].

In the case of conversion into a forced attribution, the debtor is allowed a period of fifteen days within which he may file court proceedings objecting to the conversion deed. Failing objection by the debtor, payment is made to the creditor by the third-party debtor[48].

Both these measures are discussed further in the following sub-section.

C. *Measures of execution* (mesures d'exécution)

In the event the creditor has an enforceable right, he is not obliged to obtain provisional measures before seeking enforcement against his debtor's assets. The Uniform Act provides for various categories of measures that may be taken by a creditor with an enforceable right. The type of measure will depend upon both the type of assets seized and the nature of the creditor's right.

1. Forced sale of tangible movable assets (*saisie-vente*)

(a) Conditions

Under the Uniform Act, any creditor with an enforceable right relating to a liquidated and payable claim may seize his debtor's tangible movable assets, whether such assets are in the possession of the debtor or of a third party (or indeed in the creditor's own possession) and may cause such assets to be sold, taking payment of his claim from the proceeds of the sale[49].

---

[46] Articles 69 and 82.
[47] Article 70.
[48] Article 83.
[49] Article 91.

(b) Procedure

The creditor must first make a formal demand for payment. This must be served on the debtor at least eight days before the seizure[50].

This precaution allows the debtor to avoid what may be serious consequences of a compulsory sale of his assets by making payment voluntarily. However, from the creditor's point of view it has the disadvantage of warning the debtor of impending measures of execution, and thus giving him time to organize his own insolvency. For this reason, and although the procedure is more cumbersome, a creditor would be well advised to take provisional measures and then to convert such measures into a forced sale.

Detailed procedures are laid down for the actual seizure of the assets, which must be performed and officially reported by a bailiff[51]. In particular, the debtor must be informed of his rights, and must also be instructed to reveal the existence of any prior seizure affecting the same assets[52].

A special régime is provided for the seizure of standing crops[53]. Such seizures are possible only during a maximum period of six weeks before the usual date of ripeness of the crop concerned, and the official report must be signed not only by the bailiff but also by the local mayor or other head of the local administrative authority[54]. The crops remain under the responsibility of the debtor, unless at the request of the creditor the court appoints a manager[55]. Otherwise, the formalities for the ordinary type of forced sale are followed.

(c) Effects

Unless the seized assets are consumable, or unless the court orders them to be placed in the keeping of a third party, the debtor retains the right to use them[56]. If the seizure relates to a motor vehicle, the court may order it to be immobilized by any means that do not harm the vehicle, until it is taken away to be sold[57].

---

[50] Article 92.
[51] Articles 95 *et seq.*
[52] Articles 100–102.
[53] Articles 147 *et seq.*
[54] Articles 147–148.
[55] Article 149.
[56] Article 103.
[57] Article 103.

If cash funds which are in the possession of the debtor are seized, this can only be in an amount not exceeding the amount of the debt. The funds are removed from the debtor's possession and are held by the bailiff or by the court registry, at the creditor's option[58]. If court proceedings are not brought by the debtor to object to such seizure within 15 days, the funds are paid immediately to the creditor. If the debtor does object, the court may either order payment to be made to the creditor or return of the funds to the debtor, or it may order the funds to be held by a third party pending the final outcome of the enforcement proceedings[59].

(d) Assets in the possession of a third party

A few additional rules apply if the assets to be seized are not in the possession of the debtor[60].

When the assets are held at the third party's place of residence, the seizure must be authorized by the local court[61]. The Uniform Act also allows a creditor to seize assets of his debtor which are legitimately in his own possession[62]. In such an event, and although this is not specified, it is presumably unnecessary for the creditor to obtain authorization from the court.

If the third party refuses to cooperate – either by refusing to declare the assets in his possession that belong to the debtor, or by making an inaccurate or deliberately untruthful declaration – he may be ordered to pay the debt himself, with or without additional damages[63].

If the third party claims a right of retention over the seized assets, he must inform the bailiff of this. In such an event the creditor may file court proceedings to contest the alleged right, during which time the assets remain inalienable[64].

(e) Sale of the assets

Whether the assets seized are held by the debtor himself or by another person, including the creditor himself, the debtor has a period of one

---

[58] Article 104.
[59] Article 104.
[60] Articles 105 *et seq.*
[61] Article 105.
[62] Article 106.
[63] Article 107.
[64] Article 114.

month within which he may sell them himself[65]. If he decides to do so, he must inform the bailiff of any offers that he receives, and the bailiff must inform the creditor. The creditor may either agree to or refuse the sale, or may offer to purchase the assets himself[66]. During the one-month period and thereafter, if the creditor agrees to the private sale, the assets cannot be moved, save in cases of absolute emergency, and there is no transfer of title to the purchaser, until the proceeds of the sale have been deposited either with the bailiff or with the court registry, at the creditor's option[67].

If the sale does not take place under private contract, the assets may be sold at public auction[68]. The Uniform Act lays down various formalities that must be complied with. These include publication of details of the auction at least 15 days before it is due to take place and notification of the debtor at least 10 days in advance[69]. The sale is made to the highest bidder, and is stopped once the price of the assets sold is sufficient to cover the amount of the debt, interest and related costs. The price must be paid on cash terms[70].

(f) Procedural incidents

Various incidents may occur in the course of the proceedings. First, any additional creditor whose claim fulfils the conditions for a *saisie-vente* may join the proceedings, by filing objections and, if he has not already done so, by obtaining a seizure against the same assets[71]. In such an event, the initial creditor and the debtor are informed, and the initial creditor proceeds with the sale of the assets alone, but the additional creditor may benefit from the proceeds[72].

Second, the seizure may be extended to further assets, either by a new creditor or by the initial creditor[73]. If this happens, as a general rule all the assets are auctioned together, only after the expiry of the last deadline relating to the last assets to be seized, unless the debtor otherwise agrees or the court authorizes an earlier sale of the assets that were originally

---

[65] Article 116.
[66] Article 117.
[67] Articles 116 and 118.
[68] Articles 120 *et seq.*
[69] Articles 121 and 123.
[70] Article 125.
[71] Article 130.
[72] Articles 131 and 138.
[73] Article 132.

seized, or unless the date for the public auction of those assets has already been advertised[74].

Disputes may also arise as to title to the assets. When the debtor is not the owner of an asset that has been seized, he may apply for the seizure of that asset to be declared null and void[75]. Similarly, if a third party claims to be the owner of an asset that has been seized, he may also apply to the court for an order lifting the seizure insofar as it relates to that asset[76]. This is however no longer possible once the assets have been sold, when the only action open to the third party is in principle an action for recovery of such assets; although when the sale price has not yet been made over to the creditor, the third party may claim payment of the proceeds, with no deduction being made for the costs of the sale[77].

There may in addition be disputes as to whether the assets can legally be seized. In such a case, the debtor or the bailiff must file court proceedings against the creditor within one month of notice of the seizure[78]. As mentioned above, the Uniform Act does not define which assets may not legally be seized, and this is therefore a question that is dealt with by the laws of the Member State concerned.

Finally, the debtor may bring proceedings claiming that the seizure is null and void, for either formal or substantive reasons, at any time up to the sale of the seized assets. If the seizure is held to be null and void before the sale has taken place, and if the asset is in the possession of a third party, the debtor can require the asset to be returned to him. If the sale has taken place but the proceeds have not yet been paid to the creditor, the debtor can demand payment of such proceeds to himself[79].

2. Forced attribution of third-party debts (*saisie-attribution de créances*)

(a) Conditions

The general principle for the forced attribution of third-party debts is that any creditor who has an enforceable right relating to a liquidated

---

[74] Article 134.
[75] Article 140.
[76] Article 141.
[77] Article 142.
[78] Article 143.
[79] Article 144.

and payable debt may seize any amount owed to his debtor by a third party, in payment of his own claim[80]. This is, however, subject to any restrictions that might exist with regard to the seizure of wages and salaries.

(b) Effects

The effect of such a seizure is to attribute immediately to the creditor, within the limits of his own claim including interest and costs, the debt owed by the third party. The third party then becomes personally liable to the creditor, within the limits of his own debt to the debtor[81].

If several seizures are notified to the same third-party debtor on the same day, they are deemed to have been notified simultaneously. In cases where the amounts seized are not sufficient to pay off all such creditors, these creditors have identical rank and rights, but are privileged in relation to creditors who notify seizures subsequently, even where such creditors themselves enjoy a preferential right[82]. This is subject, however, to the statutory requirements relating to creditors with preferential rights in the event of collective insolvency proceedings. For example, as has been seen in Chapter 7, the employees of a company that becomes subject to collective insolvency proceedings enjoy a first-ranking preferential right for payment of their wages and salaries.

As in the case of provisional measures, the third-party debtor must declare the extent of his obligations towards the debtor. Failure to do so or failure to make a proper declaration may lead to the third-party being ordered to pay the debt to the creditor, with or without damages[83].

(c) Procedure

Unlike the procedure for a forced sale, there is no requirement for the debtor first to be served with a formal demand for payment. Instead, the procedure begins with service of the seizure upon the third-party debtor by bailiff[84].

Detailed procedures are laid down that must be followed by the bailiff in order for the seizure to be valid. Within eight days of service of the

---

[80] Article 153.
[81] Article 154.
[82] Article 155.
[83] Article 156.
[84] Article 157.

seizure made upon the third-party debtor, notification must also be served upon the debtor, together with an indication that he is entitled to file proceedings objecting to the seizure within a period of one month[85].

If the third-party debtor is a bank or similar establishment, it must declare the type of accounts it holds in the name of the debtor, and the balance of those accounts as of the date of the seizure. Those balances are frozen as of that date, except where it can be shown, during a period of 15 days following service of the seizure, that debits or credits had been effected but had not yet been recorded as movements on the accounts before the date of the seizure. In such an event the frozen balance may be reduced or increased accordingly[86].

The third party makes payment to the creditor upon presentation of a certificate from the court registry to the effect that no objections have been filed by the debtor against the seizure within the one-month deadline, or upon presentation of an enforceable judgment dismissing the objections, as the case may be[87]. The debtor may also consent in writing to payment being made before the deadline for objections has expired. If the debt that has been seized is to be paid in instalments, the creditor is similarly paid on the due date of each instalment[88].

In cases where the debtor does file objections to the seizure, the court will allow immediate payment of any portion of the debt which is not disputed[89]. In addition, when it appears that neither the amount of the debt nor the debt of the third-party debtor is seriously disputable, the court may order provisional payment, with or without the provision of a guarantee by the creditor[90]. As a result, the creditor should be protected against objections that are raised merely as dilatory tactics.

3. Seizure and assignment of wages and salaries (*saisie et cession des rémunérations*)

(a) Conditions

Any creditor with an enforceable right relating to a liquidated and payable debt may seize the wages or salaries owed to the debtor by his

---

[85] Article 160.
[86] Article 161.
[87] Article 164.
[88] Article 167.
[89] Article 171.
[90] Article 171.

employer[91]. However, because of the particular nature of the monies seized, and the gravity of the situation that such a seizure would be likely to create for the debtor, conciliation must first be attempted, before the local court at the place where the debtor is domiciled[92]. Seizure is possible only if this attempt fails, and after the court has verified the amount of the debt and, if necessary, decided upon any objections that may have been raised by the debtor[93].

Each Member State determines in its national law what proportion of the wages or salary may be seized, thus ensuring that the debtor is not deprived of his whole remuneration. In addition, the Uniform Act provides that all amounts included in the gross salary which are withheld by the employer for payment of tax and other obligatory contributions, all payments made to defray the employee's expenses, and all payments made as family allowances, etc, are immune from seizure, as are any allowances declared immune by the applicable national law[94].

(b) Procedure

The seizure itself is performed not by a bailiff, as is the case for the other types of seizure, but by the court registrar. This is done by notification of the seizure to the employer by registered letter, within eight days of determination by the court that efforts at conciliation have failed, or within eight days of any decision by the court as to objections raised by the debtor, as the case may be[95]. The employer must declare to the registry of the court the nature of his contractual relations with the debtor and any seizures already in existence[96]. Failure to make this declaration may lead to the employer being held personally liable for payment of the amounts seized, with or without damages[97]. The employer is also required to declare to the court registry any modification in his relations with the debtor which may have consequences for the proceedings[98].

Once the seizure has been notified, the employer must pay monthly to the court registry (or any other body that may be designated for this

---

[91] Article 173.
[92] Articles 174 and 179 *et seq.*
[93] Article 182.
[94] Article 177.
[95] Article 183.
[96] Article 184.
[97] Article 185.
[98] Article 186.

purpose by the Member State concerned), the amount withheld from the employee's salary by virtue of the seizure[99]. This is then paid onward to the creditor[100]. Failure by the employer to make payment will result in his being held personally liable for the debt[101].

If the employee changes employer during the course of the proceedings, the creditor must apply within one year for the seizure to be transferred to the new employer[102].

If other creditors having enforceable rights wish to join the proceedings and share in the proceeds, they do so by applying to the court[103]. In such an event there is no need to attempt conciliation, and all the creditors rank equally, subject to any legitimate preferential consideration[104]. For example, any debts relating to support of the employee's family would take precedence over all other debts.

Rather than having payment made through the court registry, the employee may agree to assign a portion of his salary to a creditor[105]. This is done by means of a declaration to the court registry. Thereafter, the employer pays directly to the creditor the amounts assigned by the debtor[106]. If a seizure of the employee's salary occurs subsequently, the creditor to whom a portion of the salary has been assigned is deemed to be a seizing creditor of equal rank, and payments of sums due to him are no longer to be made directly, but to the court's registry[107]. If the seizure ends before the agreed term of the assignment, the situation then reverts to the previous situation, with payments being made directly by the employer to the assignee creditor[108].

If there are strong reasons for believing that the assignment has been made in order to evade obligations due to a particular creditor, that creditor may file proceedings to have the assignment declared null and void. Pending the outcome of these proceedings, the sums in question may be deposited with the registry of the court[109].

---

[99] Article 188.
[100] Article 195.
[101] Article 189.
[102] Article 204.
[103] Article 190.
[104] Article 196.
[105] Article 205.
[106] Article 207.
[107] Articles 208–209.
[108] Article 210.
[109] Article 211.

4. Seizure of tangible movable assets (*saisie-appréhension et saisie-revendication des biens meubles corporels*)

(a) Conditions

The Uniform Act provides for two different types of seizure of tangible movable assets where the debtor's obligation is not to make payment of a sum of money, but to deliver or return the particular assets that are seized[110].

The *saisie-appréhension* procedure is available only when the creditor has an enforceable right, whereas the *saisie-revendication* is used to make the assets inalienable pending the securing of an enforceable right, although it may also be used when the creditor already has an enforceable right. Typically, the enforceable right would be an order issued in accordance with the simplified recovery procedures discussed in Section 1 of this chapter.

(b) Procedure

(i) Saisie-appréhension

Saisie-appréhension proceedings are commenced by service of a formal demand upon the debtor to deliver or to return the object concerned[111]. If the debtor is present and if he does not volunteer to make delivery at his own expense within eight days, the bailiff may seize the goods in question immediately[112].

If the goods are in the possession of a third party, that party is served directly with a demand for the goods to be handed over[113]. If he refuses, the creditor or the third party himself may seek a court order within one month of the demand being made, failing which the demand, and any prior provisional measures, will lapse[114]. If the court orders the goods to be handed over, they may be taken immediately upon presentation of the order[115].

---

[110] Articles 218 *et seq.*
[111] Article 219.
[112] Article 220.
[113] Article 224.
[114] Article 225.
[115] Article 226.

(ii) *Saisie-revendication*

Unlike *saisie-appréhension* proceedings, *saisie-revendication* proceedings are available when a creditor does not already have an enforceable right. However, they may also be used instead of a *saisie-appréhension* if it is feared that the service of the formal demand required in *saisie-appréhension* proceedings will give the debtor the opportunity to divest himself of the goods in question.

If the creditor does not already have an enforceable right, he must first obtain a court order authorizing the seizure. This is given if the claim appears to be well founded[116].

The creditor must then seize the assets concerned within three months of the order and, within a further month, take steps if necessary to obtain an enforceable right. If these conditions are not fulfilled, a lifting of the seizure may be requested[117]. Article 228 states that this is the case even if the creditor has an enforceable right. However, this provision does not seem to make sense, since if the creditor already has an enforceable right there is no need for a court order from which a deadline would start running, and there is no need to take steps to obtain an enforceable right.

The assets seized may be in the possession of either the debtor or a third party. If the seizure is to occur at the residence of a third party, it is first necessary to obtain authorization from the court[118].

The person in possession of the assets is required to indicate whether there are any previous seizures affecting the assets[119]. The debtor is informed of the seizure, and either of the parties may apply to the court for the assets to be removed and held in escrow[120]. If the holder of the assets himself claims to have rights to them, the person making the seizure must file court proceedings within one month to resolve the situation, and the assets remain inalienable pending the outcome of such proceedings[121].

Once the creditor obtains an enforceable right entitling him to the delivery or return of the assets, the *saisie-appréhension* procedure is followed in accordance with Articles 219 to 226[122].

---

[116] Article 227.
[117] Articles 60–61 and 228.
[118] Article 230.
[119] Article 231.
[120] Articles 232–233.
[121] Article 234.
[122] Article 235.

5. Seizure of transferable securities or other partnership rights or shareholdings (*saisie des droits d'associés et des valeurs mobilières*)

The Uniform Act provides for a special procedure with regard to the seizure by a creditor of a debtor's transferable securities or other partnership rights or shareholdings[123].

Transferable securities or other partnership rights or shareholdings may be seized by serving notice either on the issuing company or upon the agent who holds or manages them[124]. The seizure must be preceded by a formal demand to pay, which must have remained unhonoured for at least eight days[125].

The usual requirements apply as to informing the creditor of any prior seizures or pledges affecting the securities, and informing the debtor of his rights[126]. In addition to a right to object to the seizure, the debtor has the right to sell the securities under private contract in the same way as for a *saisie-vente*[127].

If there has been no objection to the seizure within one month, and if no private sale occurs during that period, the securities are sold at public auction[128]. A set of specifications is drawn up before the sale, including details of the procedure to date, the articles of association of the company, and any document allowing the value of the securities to be ascertained[129]. If any shareholders' agreements require new shareholders to be approved, or give existing shareholders a pre-emptive right, these must be included in the specifications. Failure to include them means that they cannot be relied upon as against the purchaser of the securities[130].

If the securities have been seized by more than one creditor, the proceeds of the sale are shared among them[131].

---

[123] Articles 236 *et seq.*
[124] Article 236.
[125] Article 237.
[126] Articles 237–238.
[127] Article 238.
[128] Article 240.
[129] Article 241.
[130] Article 241.
[131] Article 245.

6. Seizure of immovable assets (*saisie immobilière*)

(a) Conditions

The seizure of immovable assets is generally a very serious matter for the debtor. For this reason the Uniform Act states expressly that certain specified conditions must be complied with before the assets in question may be sold, and that any agreement to derogate from such procedures is null and void[132].

The first condition is that the debtor should have an enforceable right relating to a debt that is liquidated and payable[133]. If these criteria are not fulfilled, the proceedings may nevertheless be commenced in cases where there is a judgment that is provisionally enforceable even if it is still subject to appeal, or where the debt is for a sum of money that is not liquidated. However, the assets may not be sold at public auction until the entitlement has become final and until the amount has been liquidated[134].

If the property is owned by several persons indivisibly, the debtor's share cannot be sold until the property has been divided or liquidated at the request of a creditor of one of the joint owners[135]. If, however, the property is owned jointly by a husband and wife, the sale takes place as against both spouses[136].

If the creditor is the beneficiary of a mortgage on part of the debtor's property, the unmortgaged part of the property may only be sold if the sale of the mortgaged property does not meet the totality of the debt, or if all the property together forms a single business unit and if the debtor himself requires all the property to be sold[137].

In countries where the national legislation requires immovable property to be registered with the land registry, any property that is not registered must be registered by the creditor before he can pursue the seizure[138].

---

[132] Article 246.
[133] Article 247.
[134] Article 247.
[135] Article 249.
[136] Article 250.
[137] Article 251.
[138] Article 253.

(b) Procedure

Any seizure must be preceded by a formal demand for payment, with a warning that failure to pay within 20 days will lead to seizure of the property[139].

If the property is in the possession of a third party, the demand must be notified to him, putting him on notice either to pay the debt or to vacate the property or undergo expropriation proceedings[140].

The formal demand to pay is filed with the land registry for publication. If it is not filed with the land registry within three months of its service, or if filing is not followed by actual publication, the whole process must be started again from the beginning[141].

(c) Effects of registration

Once registered, the formal demand has the effect of a seizure of the property. Neither the property nor any revenues from the property can then be disposed of by the debtor, nor can any security or other charge be taken out on the property, unless a purchaser or creditor deposits an amount sufficient to pay off all the debts owed to any registered creditors[142].

Any natural fruits, industrial earnings or rent accruing from the seized property are also frozen with a view to their distribution to creditors along with the proceeds from the sale of the property[143].

(d) Requests for suspension of the sale

If the value of the property seized is far in excess of the amount of the debt, the debtor may request the court to suspend proceedings with respect to one or more of the properties mentioned in the formal demand[144]. However, if a suspension is granted and in the event the property sold at public action does not reach a price sufficient to pay the whole debt, the creditor may resume the proceedings that had been suspended with regard to the other properties[145].

---

[139] Article 254.
[140] Article 255.
[141] Article 259.
[142] Article 262.
[143] Article 263.
[144] Article 264.
[145] Article 264.

The debtor may also obtain a suspension of the sale if he can show that the net income from the properties over a period of two years will be sufficient to cover the whole debt, including interest and expenses, and if he undertakes to assign such income to the creditor[146].

(e) Procedure for sale

Within 50 days of publication of the formal demand, the creditor's lawyer must draw up and file with the registry of the court a document specifying the conditions for sale of the property[147]. Various indications must be included in this document, which otherwise will be null and void. In particular, it must indicate the price at which bidding will start, which cannot be less than one-quarter of the market value of the property[148]. The document must also indicate the date of the public sale, which must be between 45 and 90 days after the document has been filed with the registry of the court[149].

Within eight days of filing with the court registry, the creditor must serve notice upon the other creditors and the debtor to inspect the conditions of sale and to submit any observations in that regard[150].

If any observations are submitted, the parties are invited to exchange pleadings and the court will give judgment on them[151]. The court may, for example, order certain properties to be removed from the scope of the seizure if the total value of the properties is out of proportion to the value of the debt; or it may change the price at which bidding is to open[152]. If necessary, the court will also set a new date for the public auction if the date originally set cannot be met because of the court proceedings[153].

No earlier than 30 days and no later than 15 days before the public auction, notice must be published of the sale, which is to take place either at the court or before a notary[154].

---

[146] Article 265.
[147] Article 266.
[148] Article 267.
[149] Article 268.
[150] Article 269.
[151] Article 272.
[152] Article 275.
[153] Article 274.
[154] Article 276.

Bidders may represent themselves at the sale or be represented by a lawyer[155]. A detail that may seem surprising to bidders from common law countries is that, as in France, the auction is timed by the successive burning of three candles. The successful bidder is the highest bidder before the third candle has gone out. If there are no bids before the third candle has gone out, the creditor who has initiated the sale is declared the successful bidder, at the initial asking price, unless he wishes to organize a further auction[156].

Within ten days of the auction, any person may make a higher bid, on condition that it is at least 10 per cent higher than the highest bid at auction[157]. In such an event, and if the validity of the new bid is not contested, a new auction takes place. If there is no bid higher than the new bid, the new bidder is declared successful. When such a second auction has taken place, there is no longer any possibility for any further higher bids[158].

When the sale has become final, it must be registered with the land registry within two months[159].

(f) Objections

The Uniform Act provides for urgent court proceedings in the event of any objection to the seizure or sale of immovable property.

Any third party who claims to be the owner of seized property and who is not personally liable and has not provided the property as security for the debt can file proceedings requesting the removal of the property from the scope of the seizure, on condition that the national law of the Member State where the property is located provides for proceedings to claim the return of property (*action en revendication*)[160].

Within 15 days of the sale, any interested party other than the successful bidder may claim that the sale is null and void, in proceedings before the court having jurisdiction at the place where the sale occurred. The claim may be based only on circumstances arising at or subsequent to the time set for the hearing of any objection to the proceedings prior to the sale[161].

---

[155] Article 282.
[156] Article 283.
[157] Article 287.
[158] Article 289.
[159] Article 294.
[160] Article 308.
[161] Article 313.

(g) Folle enchère

A special proceeding – *folle enchère* (which translates literally as 'mad bidding') – is available to the debtor and any creditors in cases where the successful bidder fails to comply with his obligations, ie when within 20 days following the sale he has not paid the price and met any conditions to which the sale may have been made subject, or where he has failed to have the sale published by the land registry within two months of the sale[162].

In such an event arrangements are made for a new auction to be held, with a view to having the original sale cancelled. The new auction is again subject to various formalities relating to publicity and notifications to be made to various interested parties[163]. If however the previously successful bidder complies with his obligations before the new auction takes place, and if he deposits a sum of money sufficient to cover the expenses incurred in relation to the new sale, the new sale does not take place[164].

If the new sale does take place but there are no bids, the asking price may be reduced to a minimum of one-quarter of the market price of the property. If there are still no bids, the seizing creditor is declared the successful bidder, at the original asking price[165].

The purchaser at the first sale who has not complied with his obligations is not allowed to bid at this new auction. He is however liable for interest on the price he had offered at the first sale, up to the date of the second sale, and also for the difference between that price and the price offered by the successful bidder at the second auction, if the latter is lower. On the other hand, if the new price is higher, he does not receive the difference[166].

7. Distribution of proceeds

The Uniform Act lays down a series of rules governing the distribution to creditors of the proceeds obtained from a sale of seized assets[167].

---

[162] Article 314.
[163] Articles 317–319.
[164] Article 320.
[165] Article 322.
[166] Article 323.
[167] Articles 324 *et seq.*

If there is only one creditor, he receives the amount of the debt in principal, together with interest and an amount to cover expenses, within fifteen days of payment by the purchaser. The balance is paid to the debtor within the same time period[168].

Where there are several creditors with seizures of movable assets or several creditors with a mortgage or preferential rights who have seized immovable assets, they may agree upon the apportionment of the proceeds. If they fail to reach agreement within one month, any of them may file court proceedings, in which all the creditors must declare their claims and provide evidence of their rank and of the existence of the debt[169]. Failure to declare a claim within 20 days of being put on notice to do so means that the creditor concerned cannot benefit from any distribution of the proceeds[170]. The court will then decide how the proceeds are to be distributed, in a judgment which is subject to appeal within 15 days of its service[171].

---

[168] Article 324.
[169] Articles 326–327.
[170] Article 330.
[171] Articles 332–333.

10

Arbitration law

When entering into a contract for any significant value, the parties will generally want to ensure that any disputes that might arise under the contract in the future will be dealt with efficiently, rapidly and confidentially. If the parties are from different countries, each of them will generally prefer disputes to be dealt with by a neutral body rather than by the national courts of the other party. These considerations have led to the popularity of arbitration clauses, particularly in international contracts.

Arbitration allows parties to have their dispute settled by a private tribunal consisting of a sole arbitrator or a panel of arbitrators, who may be chosen by the parties concerned. The proceedings are confidential and may be more rapid than proceedings before the normal courts. They result in an arbitral award which, as a general rule, will be final and binding, subject only to limited appeals, and which on certain conditions will be easily enforceable if the losing party does not comply with it spontaneously.

Arbitrations may be either institutional, ie conducted under the auspices of an arbitration centre which administers the arbitration in accordance with its own rules, or *ad hoc*, ie conducted without the assistance of an arbitration centre and in accordance with any rules that the parties or the arbitral tribunal may choose to apply, subject to any mandatory rules laid down by the applicable law.

Arbitrations are generally subject to rules laid down by the law of the country where the arbitral tribunal has its seat. However, until 1999 very few of the OHADA Member States had legislation specifically relating to arbitration, and not all of those that did had modern legislation on the subject. For this reason, it was not always advisable to provide for the seat of arbitration to be in a Member State.

OHADA has changed this situation, and it is now possible for parties to a contract to include an arbitration clause providing for arbitration proceedings to take place in any of the Member States, in the knowledge that a modern law will apply.

Nevertheless, the parties would be well advised to be vigilant when drafting their arbitration clause. It is a truism that when a contract is negotiated, the parties deal first with all the commercial aspects of the transaction, and frequently pay only very cursory attention to the dispute resolution provisions. This often leads to unpleasant surprises when a dispute does arise, with the parties finding that the arbitration clause is inoperative, or that it has consequences that they had not anticipated. Vigilance will be particularly required when the parties envisage arbitration under OHADA law, since OHADA has created two different sets of legislation applicable to arbitration.

First, there is the OHADA Treaty, which provides for institutional arbitration under the auspices of the CCJA, in accordance with the CCJA's Rules of Arbitration (the CCJA Rules). Second, there is the Uniform Act on Arbitration, which lays down basic rules that are applicable to any arbitration where the seat of the arbitral tribunal is in one of the Member States, or which might also be chosen by the parties as the applicable procedural law even if the seat of the tribunal is not in a Member State.

In other words, if a contractual arbitration clause simply provides for arbitration under the Uniform Act, there will be no institutional framework but the Uniform Act will govern certain matters relating to the proceedings. On the other hand, if the clause states the parties' agreement to arbitration under the OHADA Treaty or under the CCJA Rules, this will establish an institutional framework for the arbitration, akin to providing, for example, for arbitration under the auspices of the International Chamber of Commerce (ICC). Finally, a clause might provide for arbitration in one of the Member States in accordance with institutional rules other than those of the CCJA, in which case the Uniform Act would apply to matters not regulated by such institutional rules.

None of the above three hypotheses would pose any particular problem in implementing the arbitration clause, even if the parties may not have been fully aware of all the consequences at the time they entered into their contract. However, a more serious situation would arise if, for example, an arbitration clause provided for "ICC arbitration in accordance with the OHADA Treaty". In such an event there would be a conflict of institutional jurisdiction between the ICC and the CCJA which could lead to the arbitration clause being held to be inoperative.

In addition to the question of whether the arbitral proceedings will be administered by the CCJA or by another institution, or whether they will be *ad hoc*, there are further essential differences between arbitration under the Uniform Act and arbitration under the Treaty and the CCJA Rules, as will be seen in further detail below. These include, in particular, matters relating to the appointment of arbitrators, and appeals and enforcement procedures. Before signing their contract, therefore, the parties should be very careful to verify the terms of any arbitration clause to ensure that it provides for the intended solution.

Section 1 of this Chapter will review the main features of *ad hoc* arbitration under the Uniform Act, it being understood, however, that some of the provisions of the Uniform Act will remain applicable but others will be derogated from if the parties have chosen to arbitrate under the rules of an arbitration centre. Section 2 will then review the main features of institutional arbitration under the Treaty and the CCJA Rules.

SECTION 1: UNIFORM ACT ARBITRATION

The Uniform Act on Arbitration Law was signed on 11 March 1999 and entered into force 90 days later. It is applicable to arbitrations that had not commenced before its entry into force[1].

Very few provisions of the Uniform Act are mandatory, and many of them may be derogated from if the parties choose to apply different rules, either as may be devised between themselves or as a result of resorting to institutional arbitration. Some provisions of the existing national laws on arbitration may also remain applicable, as a result of the CCJA's advisory opinion No. 001/2001/EP of 30 April 2001[2]. According to that advisory opinion, the Uniform Act must be interpreted as superseding the existing national laws on arbitration, but subject to any provisions of such national laws which do not conflict with the Uniform Act. Therefore, depending on the country where the arbitration is to be held, it will be necessary to determine whether any other rules will apply in addition to the Uniform Act.

---

[1] Article 35.
[2] See Chapter 3, Section 1.B.

A. Scope of application

Article 1 states that the Uniform Act applies to all arbitrations where the seat of arbitration is located in one of the Member States. This is analogous, for example, to application of the Arbitration Act 1996 to any arbitration whose seat is in England, or of the relevant provisions of the French Code of Civil Procedure to any arbitration having its seat in France. Unlike many arbitration laws, which contain different provisions for domestic and international arbitration, the Uniform Act makes no distinction between these two types of arbitration.

As a result, any *ad hoc* arbitration taking place in a Member State will be governed by the Uniform Act and by any other arrangements as may be agreed between the parties, to the extent that such arrangements are permissible under the Uniform Act. If institutional arbitration has been provided for and the seat of the tribunal is in a Member State, the Uniform Act will still apply, but only to complement the institutional rules that the parties have chosen. Thus, for example, if the parties have chosen to arbitrate in Mali under the Rules of Arbitration of the ICC, the Uniform Act will apply only where there are gaps in those Rules.

Unlike many arbitration laws, the Uniform Act does not restrict arbitration to commercial matters. Article 2 provides that arbitration may be resorted to with respect to any rights that may be freely disposed of. This means, in practical terms, that any dispute may be submitted to arbitration on condition that it does not relate to rights where intervention of the public authorities is required. The definition of such rights will depend upon the applicable national law, but in general it is likely that they will principally relate to questions of personal status. For example, a dispute arising out of the private sale of a car could be submitted to arbitration, but it is unlikely that a divorce petition could.

Article 2 also provides that both individuals and corporate bodies may submit to arbitration, and lays down the principle that States and other territorial public authorities and public companies may also submit to arbitration. It adds that such entities may not rely upon their own national laws to argue either that the dispute is not arbitrable, that they did not have the capacity to enter into the arbitration agreement, or that the arbitration agreement is invalid. This will be an important provision for foreign investors who often encounter this type of defence where their contractual partner is a public body or company, particularly in countries influenced by the French system of administrative law. It will be of particular interest to investors who are required to enter into a joint venture or participate in a privatization with a public authority or company, since it should avert defences based on sovereign immunity from jurisdiction. However, there will still remain the question of enforcement of an arbitral award, which may run into difficulties arising out of defences based on sovereign immunity from execution.

B. The arbitration agreement

The most usual form of arbitration agreement is the arbitration clause, which is inserted in the parties' contract at the outset of their contractual relationship. However, an arbitration agreement may also be entered into at any time subsequently, and typically when a dispute arises between the parties. The Uniform Act also provides that the parties may enter into such an agreement even if they have already commenced proceedings before a court[3].

The arbitration agreement must be made in writing 'or by any other means allowing its existence to be proven'[4]. It is not entirely clear how the latter part of this provision should be interpreted, although it goes on to state that such means would include, in particular, a reference to another document which itself stipulates an agreement to arbitrate. This would occur, for example, when a contract simply makes reference to the general conditions of contract of one of the parties which, in turn, specify an arbitration clause. This is in conformity with the present trend in France and other countries to validate arbitration clauses by reference, and is again an instance where the parties to a contract must be vigilant.

In addition to arbitration clauses by reference, Article 3 implies that other means of entering into an arbitration agreement might be possible, such as, for example, by oral agreement before witnesses, who could then attest to the existence of the agreement. However, even if this were possible – and the CCJA has not yet had the opportunity to express any view on this point – it would be inadvisable, since the Uniform Act itself requires a copy of the arbitration agreement to be produced in enforcement proceedings in the Member States[5]. In addition, if enforcement is sought in other countries the New York Convention may come into play, and this also requires the arbitration agreement to be in writing[6]. For these reasons, it is strongly recommended that if arbitration is the

---

[3] Article 4.

[4] Article 3.

[5] Article 31.

[6] The New York Convention of 1958 on the Recognition and Enforcement of Foreign Arbitral Awards provides for enforcement, on the territory of a State which is a party to the Convention, of arbitral awards that have been issued in a different State. There are at present some 130 parties to the New York Convention, which is therefore used very widely.

desired means of settling disputes, this should be clearly spelt out in the contract.

The Uniform Act expressly lays down the principle of autonomy of the arbitration agreement, as has been evolved by modern case law. This principle has two main consequences, both of which are spelt out in the Uniform Act. First, it means that the arbitration agreement is independent from the main contract (even if it is contained in a clause within that main contract) and that its validity is unaffected by any finding that the main contract itself is null and void. The second consequence is that the arbitration agreement is not necessarily governed by the same law as the main contract or any particular national law, but that it is to be interpreted in accordance with the common intention of the parties[7].

C. The arbitral tribunal

Article 8 of the Uniform Act provides that the arbitral tribunal must be composed of either a sole arbitrator or three arbitrators. This is a mandatory provision, since the article lists a hierarchy of methods that must be followed for the appointment of an additional arbitrator if the parties have appointed an even number of arbitrators or if a previously appointed arbitrator can no longer sit on the tribunal, for whatever reason. Although it is clear that the real prohibition under this article relates to an even number of arbitrators, there is a risk that, if the parties were to agree upon a five-member tribunal, the tribunal might be considered as having been improperly constituted, and its award might therefore be set aside[8].

The parties are free to determine by agreement the rules applicable to the appointment, dismissal or replacement of arbitrators[9]. Failing any such agreement, or if the agreement is insufficient to cover all eventualities, the Uniform Act lays down certain rules.

As regards appointments, if there are to be three arbitrators, each party is to appoint one arbitrator and those two arbitrators are to agree upon a third arbitrator; or if there is to be a sole arbitrator, the parties are to agree upon an appointment. If there is a failure at any stage of this appointing process, either through a failure of the parties or the arbitrators to agree as required, or through a party's refusal to appoint an

---

[7] Article 4.
[8] See Article 26.
[9] Article 5.

arbitrator, the appointment of the arbitrator concerned is instead made by the local court in the Member State where the seat of arbitration is located[10]. Although this is not expressly stated, the same procedure could presumably be applied, *mutatis mutandis*, if it were necessary to replace an arbitrator. The provision is useful, in particular since it prevents a party from frustrating the arbitration process by refusing to appoint its own arbitrator.

A problem may arise, however, in cases where there are more than two parties to the arbitration agreement, all having different interests, and where a three-member tribunal has been provided for. One of the fundamental principles in arbitration is that the parties must be treated equally[11], and a corollary of this is that no party must have a greater influence than the other parties on the appointment of the arbitral tribunal. However, if the parties have not made specific provision in their agreement for the appointment of an arbitral tribunal in such a way that no party has a greater influence, there is nothing in the Uniform Act to resolve the difficulty. In practice, however, it would seem that in such an event, and if they cannot otherwise agree, the parties should be able to apply to the court for the appointment of all three arbitrators, or of the two arbitrators who would normally be appointed by the parties themselves. On the other hand, this presupposes that all the parties will act in good faith in the matter, which is not always the case. This is a question that may have to be dealt with by the CCJA in the future.

The requirement for all arbitrators to be independent and impartial as regards the parties is formally laid down, and any arbitrator who considers that there may be grounds for a party to challenge his independence or impartiality is required to draw this to the attention of the parties. In such an event he may only accept the appointment if he obtains the unanimous written consent of the parties[12].

An arbitrator may also be challenged during the course of the proceedings if he is perceived as lacking independence or impartiality. If the parties have not provided for a different procedure in such an event, the challenge is referred to the local court for final settlement. As is usual in such matters, any challenge must be raised as soon as the grounds upon which it is based are known, and it will be inadmissible if these grounds were already known before the arbitrator's appointment[13]. If

---

[10] Article 5.

[11] This principle is stated in Article 9.

[12] Articles 6 and 7.

[13] Article 7.

the challenge is successful, or in the event of any other circumstances which mean that the arbitrator can no longer sit on the tribunal, a new arbitrator is chosen by the remaining arbitrators, if any, and failing this by the court, unless the parties have agreed otherwise[14].

D. The proceedings

The Uniform Act states the fundamental principle that the parties to an arbitration must be treated on an equal footing and must be allowed every opportunity to state their claims[15].

Article 10 expressly recognizes the right for the parties to submit to institutional arbitration, and states that if they do so they will be bound by the rules of the chosen institution unless they have expressly agreed that certain of those rules will not be applicable.

A number of basic rules of due process are laid down in the Uniform Act. These are classic rules which are designed to ensure that the parties receive fair and equal treatment, as follows:

- The parties have the burden of proving their respective claims, although the tribunal may direct them to provide the necessary explanations and evidence.
- The tribunal may not rely in its award on any grounds or documents with regard to which the parties have not had a proper opportunity to present their case during the proceedings. This applies both to grounds and documents that may have been relied upon by one of the parties, or legal grounds which the tribunal might have raised at its own initiative.
- Any alleged irregularity in the proceedings must be raised as soon as a party becomes aware of it, failing which that party is deemed to have waived the right to raise it[16].

In addition to these fundamental rules of procedure, the tribunal must apply any institutional rules or the rules of any national procedural law that may have been chosen by the parties. In the absence of such choices, the arbitral tribunal may itself determine appropriate rules[17].

---

[14] Article 8.
[15] Article 9.
[16] Article 14.
[17] Article 14.

The tribunal must rule upon the merits of the case in accordance with the substantive law chosen by the parties. If there has been no such choice, the tribunal itself chooses the law that it considers the most appropriate, taking into account, if necessary, the usages of international commerce. The tribunal may also rule in equity, but only if the parties have allowed it to do so[18].

The Uniform Act confirms the principle, which is now well-established in modern arbitration practice, that the arbitral tribunal has jurisdiction to rule upon issues relating to its own jurisdiction, including any questions concerning the existence or validity of the arbitration agreement[19]. Any challenge to the tribunal's jurisdiction must be raised before any defence on the merits, unless it is based on facts that have become known only subsequently. If its jurisdiction is challenged, the tribunal may either give a separate award on jurisdiction or may deal with both jurisdiction and the merits in a single award. If a separate award is given on jurisdiction and if the proceedings are to continue on the merits, that award may be submitted to setting-aside proceedings immediately, without any need to await the final outcome of the proceedings[20].

As is usual in modern laws, the Uniform Act provides for precedence to be given to arbitration over any court proceedings if there is an arbitration agreement between the parties. Consequently, if a dispute is submitted to a national court either before or after arbitral proceedings have commenced, and if the defendant relies on the existence of an arbitration agreement to challenge the court's jurisdiction, the court must decline jurisdiction unless the arbitration clause is quite clearly null and void and the arbitral proceedings have not begun[21]. However, if a party does not contest the court's jurisdiction, this may be construed as a tacit waiver of the benefit of the arbitration clause, and the court therefore cannot decline jurisdiction of its own motion[22].

Notwithstanding the existence of an arbitration clause, it remains possible for a court to order provisional or conservatory measures in the event of a recognized situation of urgency, or where the measures are to be taken in a country which is not one of the Member States, but this is

---

[18] Article 15.
[19] Article 11.
[20] Article 11. See sub-section 1.F of this chapter.
[21] Article 13. If the arbitration proceedings have already begun, the arbitral tribunal itself has jurisdiction to rule upon the question of the existence or validity of the arbitration agreement, in accordance with Article 11.
[22] Article 13.

on condition that the ordering of such measures does not involve a review of the merits of the dispute[23].

In addition, if it is necessary to obtain assistance from the courts in order to obtain evidence, the tribunal may seek such assistance from the court in the relevant Member State, either of its own motion or at the request of one of the parties[24].

If the parties have not agreed otherwise, a deadline of six months is laid down for the award to be issued, running from the date on which the last of the arbitrators has accepted his appointment[25]. Unless the case is very simple, this deadline is unrealistically short. It may however be extended, either by agreement of the parties or by the local court at the request of one of the parties or the arbitral tribunal itself. If a party has the impression during the course of the arbitration that the proceedings are not going in its favour, there is a risk that it may refuse to agree to an extension at that time. In order to avoid the inconvenience of having to apply to the court in such circumstances (and also the risk that the court may not agree to order an extension), it would be wise for the parties to provide for a longer period of time at the outset, in the arbitration agreement itself.

E. The award

The Uniform Act lays down various formal requirements that must be included in the award, such as the names of the parties and of the arbitrators. In addition to these, the award must indicate the reasoning upon which it is based[26].

The tribunal may order provisional enforcement of the award, on condition that the successful party has requested this. If such a request has been made but the tribunal refuses to order provisional enforcement, the reasons for the refusal must be indicated in the award[27].

Unless the parties have agreed otherwise, when there are three arbitrators the award is given on the basis of a majority vote[28]. It must

---

[23] Article 13.
[24] Article 14.
[25] Article 12.
[26] Article 20.
[27] Article 24.
[28] Article 19.

be signed by the arbitrators. However, if a minority refuses to sign, the award has the same effect as if it had been signed by all the arbitrators[29].

Once the award has been signed, the arbitrators no longer have any jurisdiction over the dispute. However, they may still interpret the award or modify errors or omissions where the modifications, such as corrections of typographical errors or errors of calculation, do not alter the substance of the award[30]. In addition, in cases where the arbitrators have failed to give a decision on one of the heads of claim, they may give an additional award. In any of these cases, an application must be submitted to the arbitral tribunal within 30 days of notification of the award, and the tribunal must give its interpretation or its additional or corrected award within 45 days. If it is impossible for the arbitral tribunal to be reconstituted, the local court at the seat of arbitration has jurisdiction to give the necessary decisions. No time limit is laid down for the court to issue its judgment in such circumstances, nor is there any indication of the extent to which the court must re-hear the parties. This will therefore depend upon the national procedural rules, if any, in the country concerned, and may be an issue on which the CCJA will have to be consulted in the future.

F. Appeals

There is no right of ordinary appeal against an arbitral award[31]. However, in certain limited circumstances a party may file setting-aside proceedings seeking annulment of the award. These proceedings are filed before the competent court in the Member State of the seat of arbitration. They may be filed at any time between issuance of the award and one month following service of the award after it has been declared enforceable by court order[32]. Unless the arbitral tribunal has ordered provisional enforcement of the award, the filing of setting-aside proceedings suspends enforcement[33].

Setting-aside proceedings are admissible only if they are based on one or more of the following grounds[34]:

---

[29] Article 21.
[30] Article 22.
[31] Article 25.
[32] Article 27.
[33] Article 28.
[34] Article 26.

- there was no arbitration agreement, or the arbitration agreement was null and void or had expired by the time the tribunal gave its award;
- the arbitral tribunal was improperly constituted;
- the arbitral tribunal failed to comply with its terms of reference;
- there was a lack of due process in the proceedings;
- the award does not contain reasoning; or
- the arbitral tribunal has violated a rule of international public policy (*ordre public international*) of the Member States[35].

These limited grounds mean that there can be no review of the merits of the award by the national courts, except to the extent that it may be necessary to determine whether there has been a violation of international public policy. Even in such a case, the court does not give a new decision on the merits, but merely either rejects the application for setting-aside or declares the award null and void.

When the award is declared null and void, either party may begin a new arbitration[36].

Any judgment which either dismisses the claim or declares the award null and void is subject to ultimate appeal (again on limited grounds) before the CCJA[37].

The parties also have the possibility of requesting a revision of the award by the arbitral tribunal, when a new fact has come to light since its issuance and when that fact may have had a decisive influence on the outcome of the case had it been known at the time[38]. No time limit is provided for requesting a revision, nor is any provision made for the intervention of the courts if the arbitral tribunal cannot be reconstituted. These are matters that may have to be resolved in the future by the CCJA.

Finally, any third party who has not been called to participate in the arbitration and who considers that the arbitral award is prejudicial to its own rights may file objections before the arbitral tribunal[39]. This is an unusual provision, since arbitration is personal to the parties to the arbitration agreement, and there is generally no possibility to join third

---

[35] The wording of this ground suggests that the international public policy in question is not that of the Member State in which the court is located, but of all the Member States as a whole. This may lead to problems in determining the extent of such public policy. In any event, fraud would no doubt be covered by this provision.

[36] Article 29.

[37] Article 25.

[38] Article 25.

[39] Article 25.

parties to the proceedings. Moreover, the Uniform Act does not specify the procedure that must be followed by a third party who wishes to file objections against an arbitral award, nor does it lay down any time-limits or provide for the possibility of filing the objections before a court in cases where the arbitral tribunal cannot be reconstituted. Here again, the CCJA may in the future be called upon to provide an answer.

G. Enforcement

In order to be enforceable, the award must be submitted to the national court for an enforcement order (*exequatur*)[40]. This provision is rather ambiguous, since it does not specify whether the national court concerned is the court in the Member State where the award was issued or the Member State where enforcement is sought, which may not be the same. However, it should doubtless be assumed that it is the court in the State where enforcement is sought that is intended, since judgments of a national court in one Member State cannot have extraterritorial effect in another Member State.

The party applying for the enforcement order must produce an original of the award and of the arbitration agreement, or certified copies of these documents. If the documents are not in French, a translation into French must also be produced, certified by a translator registered with the court[41]. This is an unfortunate provision, given that there are Member States with English, Portuguese or Spanish as their official language. The intention can surely not have been, for example, to oblige a party who has obtained an arbitral award in Spanish to have that award translated into French for enforcement in Equatorial Guinea by a Spanish-speaking court. As a result, the provision should presumably be read as requiring the award to be translated, if necessary, into the official language of the court where the enforcement order is sought, but this would merit clarification.

Enforcement will be refused only if the award is clearly contrary to a rule of international public policy of the Member States[42]. Any judgment refusing enforcement is subject to appeal before the CCJA. On the other hand, if an enforcement order is given, this is subject to no appeals whatsoever, other than in the context of setting-aside proceedings

---

[40] Article 30.
[41] Article 31.
[42] Article 31.

against the award, which are deemed also to be an appeal against the enforcement order[43]. If such proceedings fail, both the award and the enforcement order are validated[44].

Provision is also made for the recognition of arbitral awards based on rules other than those of the Uniform Act[45]. This would appear to mean foreign arbitral awards, ie those where the seat of the tribunal was not in a Member State. Article 34 states that such awards are recognized in the Member States in accordance with any international conventions that may be applicable or, failing any such conventions, in accordance with the provisions of the Uniform Act[46].

A difficulty may arise in this regard because the Uniform Act uses the word 'recognized' and not 'enforced', whereas the intention was presumably to provide not only for recognition but also for enforcement. While this is not a problem if enforcement is sought under the New York Convention, which binds the States who are parties to it both to recognize and to enforce foreign awards on certain limited conditions, it may be a problem if enforcement is sought in a Member State which is not a party to the New York Convention. In such an event, the question arises of whether it should be assumed that the Uniform Act applies not only to recognition but also to enforcement, or rather that the pre-existing national legislation on the enforcement of arbitral awards (if any) remains applicable. This is clearly another question that merits clarification.

SECTION 2: CCJA ARBITRATION

Unusually for a treaty establishing an international organization, the OHADA Treaty contains a separate chapter devoted to arbitration, not between Member States in connection with the Treaty itself, but laying down a procedural framework for the arbitration of private contractual disputes under the auspices of the CCJA.

These provisions have been incorporated in and supplemented by a set of Rules of Arbitration (the 'CCJA Rules') which were adopted on 11

---

[43] Article 32.

[44] Article 33.

[45] Article 34.

[46] The international convention that is most commonly relevant in this context is the New York Convention of 1958 on the Recognition and Enforcement of Foreign Arbitral Awards. Nine of the Member States are parties to this Convention: Benin, Burkina Faso, Cameroon, Central African Republic, Côte d'Ivoire, Guinea, Mali, Niger and Senegal.

March 1999 (the same date as the Uniform Act on Arbitration) and which entered into force 30 days later. The CCJA Rules are in many ways very similar to the ICC Rules, although there are some fundamental differences relating in particular to enforcement and appeals, as will be seen below. A decision given by the CCJA on 3 February 1999 complements the CCJA Rules, laying down provisions relating to the costs of arbitration for this type of proceeding[47].

As of the summer of 2002, three CCJA arbitrations were pending, one between a Member State and a private company and the other two between private companies, but no awards had yet been issued.

A. Scope of application

CCJA arbitration is possible only if there is a certain link with one or more Member States. Article 21 of the Treaty states the principle that, in application of an arbitration clause or other agreement to arbitrate, a contractual dispute may be submitted to CCJA arbitration where:

- one of the parties is domiciled or has its usual place of residence in one of the Member States; or
- the contract has been or is to be performed, in whole or on part, on the territory of one or more Member States[48].

These are the only conditions for submission of a dispute to CCJA arbitration. In particular, there is no express requirement for the seat of arbitration to be in a Member State. As a result, there would seem to be no obstacle to the parties to a contract agreeing to CCJA arbitration with the seat of the tribunal outside the Member States. For practical reasons relating in particular to appeals, this may however not be advisable, as will be discussed further below.

B. The CCJA as an arbitration centre

Like the now familiar International Court of Arbitration of the ICC, the CCJA does not itself perform judicial functions as an arbitral tribunal. Instead, it performs an administrative function as an arbitration centre. Unlike the ICC Court, however, the CCJA also plays an important role

---

[47] Decision No. 004/99.
[48] The provision is reproduced in Article 2.1 of the CCJA Rules.

in the enforcement of awards, as will be seen in sub-section 2.I of this Chapter.

In its role as an arbitration centre, the CCJA appoints arbitrators (or confirms their appointment when not called upon to make the appointment itself); deals with challenges to arbitrators; is kept informed of the progress of the arbitral proceedings; and reviews draft awards before they are issued[49]. The decisions taken by the CCJA in this role are administrative, not judicial decisions. They are subject to no appeal, and the reasons upon which they are based are not communicated to the parties[50].

A Secretary-General is in charge of the administrative functions of the CCJA in its role as an arbitration centre, and in particular ensures that all relevant notifications are made. This office is filled by the Chief Registrar of the CCJA[51].

C. The arbitration agreement

Neither the Treaty nor the CCJA Rules provide that the agreement to arbitrate must be made in writing. However, if the parties' real intention is to have CCJA arbitration, it is advisable for this to be stated in writing to avoid any misunderstanding[52]. When there is no *prima facie* arbitration agreement between the parties providing for application of the CCJA Rules, and if the defendant objects to CCJA arbitration or fails to respond to the request for arbitration within 45 days, the CCJA may decide that the arbitration cannot take place[53]. As of the summer of 2002, two requests for arbitration had been refused by the CCJA on this basis. When the CCJA considers that there is a *prima facie* agreement to resort to CCJA arbitration, but when one of the parties subsequently refuses to participate in the proceedings, the arbitration takes place nonetheless[54].

As a consequence of the principle of autonomy of the arbitration clause, the arbitral tribunal may rule upon a dispute even if it determines

---

[49] Article 2.2 of the CCJA Rules.
[50] Article 1.1 of the CCJA Rules.
[51] Article 1.1 of the CCJA Rules.
[52] See also the discussion at sub-section 1.B of this chapter. While the absence of a written agreement may not be an obstacle to enforcement of a CCJA award in the Member States, problems might arise in other countries where enforcement is sought.
[53] Article 9 of the CCJA Rules.
[54] Article 10.2 of the CCJA Rules.

that the contract is null and void, on condition that it considers that the arbitration clause itself is valid[55].

D. The arbitral tribunal

Like the Uniform Act, the CCJA Rules provide for either a sole arbitrator or a three-arbitrator tribunal. If the parties have not opted for either solution, the CCJA will appoint a sole arbitrator unless the circumstances of the case appear to warrant the appointment of three arbitrators[56]. Therefore if, as is frequently the case, a party wishes to have the right to appoint an arbitrator on its own behalf, or if it believes that any dispute likely to arise under the contract would be better dealt with by three arbitrators, it would be well advised to ensure that three arbitrators are provided for in the arbitration agreement.

The rules governing the appointment of arbitrators are otherwise similar to the Uniform Act rules, giving priority to the parties' choice. However, if there is a failure by the parties or by one of them at any stage of the appointing process, the necessary appointments are to be made by the CCJA and not by the national court[57].

Unlike the Uniform Act, the CCJA Rules make provision for the possibility of multi-party arbitration. Article 3.1 states that when several claimants or defendants are required to make a joint proposal for the appointment of an arbitrator, and when they fail to do so within the given deadline, the Court may appoint all the members of the tribunal. In this way any inequality of treatment between the parties in the appointment of arbitrators can be avoided.

The arbitrators may be chosen from a list of arbitrators that is drawn up by the CCJA and updated annually[58]. In drawing up this list, the CCJA may consult with experts in the field of international commercial arbitration. The current list contains some 70 arbitrators of both African and other nationalities[59].

When the CCJA appoints an arbitrator, it is required to take into account the parties' nationalities and places of residence, the places of residence of the other arbitrators and counsel, the parties' languages, the

---

[55] Article 10.4 of the CCJA Rules.
[56] Article 3.1 of the CCJA Rules.
[57] Article 3.1 of the CCJA Rules.
[58] Article 3.2 of the CCJA Rules.
[59] CCJA decision No. 02/2002 of 20 March 2002.

type of questions in dispute and any governing law or laws that may have been chosen by the parties[60].

Article 49 of the Treaty is an unusual provision, according to which any arbitrators who have been designated by the CCJA enjoy diplomatic privileges and immunities in the exercise of their functions. This appears to mean that such arbitrators – but not arbitrators who have been designated by the parties themselves – will be immune from any suit by the parties. While this might protect arbitrators and the arbitral process from certain actions taken by a party in bad faith, it is unfortunate that it would also protect arbitrators who have, for example, acted dishonestly in the course of the arbitration. Moreover, the provision creates an unjustified inequality between arbitrators chosen by the CCJA and those chosen by the parties.

The Rules require all arbitrators to be independent of the parties and to inform the CCJA of any circumstances which might cause the parties to question their independence. In such an event the CCJA informs the parties and invites them to comment[61]. Any challenges of an arbitrator are dealt with by the CCJA. A party who intends to challenge an arbitrator must do so within 30 days of being notified of the arbitrator's appointment, or within 30 days of discovery of the fact giving rise to the challenge, if this occurs subsequently. The other party or parties, the arbitrator concerned and the other arbitrators are all invited to comment in writing on the challenge[62].

In principle an arbitrator cannot resign, but must undertake to participate in the proceedings until their conclusion[63]. However, the CCJA may accept a resignation if there are good reasons for it.

In the event of a successful challenge or the death or accepted resignation of an arbitrator, the arbitrator must be replaced[64]. If an arbitrator resigns but his resignation is not accepted, and he refuses to continue to sit on the tribunal, he will be replaced if he is the sole arbitrator or if he is the president of the tribunal. If he is an ordinary member of a three-arbitrator tribunal, the CCJA will decide whether he should be replaced, taking into account the status of the proceedings and the opinion of the two remaining arbitrators. In cases where the CCJA decides that he

---

[60] Article 3.3 of the CCJA Rules.
[61] Article 4.1 of the CCJA Rules.
[62] Article 4.2 of the CCJA Rules.
[63] Article 4.1 of the CCJA Rules.
[64] Article 4.3 of the CCJA Rules.

should not be replaced, the proceedings continue and the award is rendered without his participation[65].

An arbitrator may also be replaced if it is impossible for him, *de jure* or *de facto*, to continue to sit as arbitrator or if he is not performing his obligations properly. In such an event the parties and arbitrators, including the arbitrator concerned, are invited to submit their comments. When the arbitrator to be replaced is a party-appointed arbitrator, the party which appointed him is allowed to express an opinion on the appointment of the new arbitrator, but the CCJA is not bound by that opinion[66].

Once the tribunal has been reconstituted in any of the above circumstances, the tribunal itself determines to what extent there has to be a repetition of the earlier proceedings, after consulting with the parties[67].

E. The proceedings

The CCJA Rules lay down detailed procedures to be followed during the course of the arbitration.

Proceedings are initiated by the submission by the claimant to the Secretary-General of a request for arbitration[68]. The request must contain certain information as specified in Article 5 of the Rules, including a summary statement of the claims and of the grounds upon which they are based, and must be accompanied by payment of a deposit of 200,000 FCFA[69].

Unlike the ICC, the CCJA does not forward a copy of the request to the defendant. Instead, the claimant must do this. However, the Secretary-General notifies all parties of receipt of the request by the Secretariat, and it is that date of receipt that is deemed to be the date upon which the arbitration has been commenced[70].

The defendant must file an answer to the request within 45 days of receiving notification of the commencement of proceedings from the Secretary-General[71]. The Rules lay down various requirements for the

---

[65] Article 4.3 of the CCJA Rules.
[66] Article 4.4 of the CCJA Rules.
[67] Article 4.5 of the CCJA Rules.
[68] Article 5 of the CCJA Rules. For CCJA arbitration, unlike court proceedings before the CCJA, there is no need for the parties to make an election of domicile in Abidjan.
[69] The amount of the deposit is fixed by Article 1 of Decision No. 004/99 of the CCJA of 3 February 1999 relating to costs of arbitration.
[70] Article 5 of the CCJA Rules.
[71] Article 6 of the CCJA Rules.

contents of the answer. In addition to a brief response outlining its position on the claims, the defendant must also indicate whether or not it confirms the existence of an arbitration agreement between the parties which provides for CCJA arbitration[72]. At the same time, the defendant may file a counter-claim, to which the claimant may respond within 30 days[73].

Once these pleadings have been exchanged (or after expiry of the deadline for their filing), the CCJA determines the amount of the advance to be paid on the costs of arbitration, decides the seat of arbitration if it has not been decided by agreement of the parties, and sets the proceedings in motion[74].

Notwithstanding any previous agreement of the parties or decision of the CCJA as to the seat of the tribunal, the proceedings may take place in any other location if the tribunal so decides after consultation with the parties[75]. In the event of disagreement in this regard, the CCJA will give a binding decision. It should be noted that a change in the location of the proceedings does not *ipso facto* cause a change in the seat of the tribunal. On the other hand, when circumstances make it impossible or difficult to hold the proceedings in the place that has been determined, the Court may choose another seat, at the request of one or more of the parties or of the arbitral tribunal[76].

Within 60 days of receipt by the tribunal of the file of the pleadings exchanged to date, a meeting between the tribunal and the parties is held and minutes are drawn up to determine the object of the arbitration and certain procedural matters[77]. These minutes must include a summary of the respective claims of the parties; any agreement of the parties as to

---

[72] Article 6 of the CCJA Rules.

[73] Article 7 of the CCJA Rules.

[74] Article 8 of the CCJA Rules.

[75] Article 13 of the CCJA Rules.

[76] The distinction between the seat of the tribunal and the location of the proceedings is of little importance if the award is to be enforced only in the OHADA region since, as will be seen in sub-section 2.I of this chapter, the CCJA gives supranational enforcement orders, allowing awards issued under its auspices to be enforced easily in any of the Member States. However, if the seat were moved from a State which is a party to the New York Convention (Benin, for example) to a State which is not (Togo, for example), this might make enforcement more difficult in other countries, such as France, which apply the New York Convention only to foreign arbitral awards issued in States which are also parties to the Convention.

[77] Article 15 of the CCJA Rules.

the seat and language of the arbitration, the applicable procedural and substantive laws, and the law applicable to the arbitration clause; and any agreement or disagreement of the parties as to the existence of a CCJA arbitration clause.

If there is no agreement as to the language of arbitration, the tribunal will give an immediate decision on the question, after consulting with the parties[78].

At the same meeting, the tribunal must ask the parties whether they wish to have the tribunal act as *amiable compositeur* and give an award in equity[79].

Finally, the tribunal will take any measures that seem appropriate for the conduct of the proceedings, and will fix a provisional calendar, including the date of a hearing (unless the parties agree not to have a hearing), which will also be the date of closure of the proceedings. Unless the parties agree otherwise, the date of the hearing must be no later than six months after the date of the meeting[80]. However, if necessary, the provisional calendar may be modified by the tribunal, either at its own initiative or at the request of the parties. In such an event the modified calendar is communicated to the CCJA[81]. The award must be signed within 90 days of the date of the closure of the proceedings, but this deadline may be extended by the CCJA at the request of the tribunal[82]. This means that proceedings under the CCJA Rules may be somewhat longer than under the Uniform Act, where the whole procedure from the date of constitution of the tribunal to the issuance of the award is supposed not to exceed six months.

The applicable procedural rules are those contained in the CCJA Rules. In the event the Rules are silent, the applicable rules are those agreed by the parties or, failing such agreement, by the tribunal. Reference may be made to a national procedural law, but this is not obligatory[83].

The tribunal must apply the substantive law chosen by the parties. If the parties have made no such choice, the tribunal must apply the law designated by the rule of conflict that it considers to be the most appropriate, taking into account any relevant usages of international

---

[78] Article 15.1(b) of the CCJA Rules.
[79] Article 15.1(b) of the CCJA Rules.
[80] Article 15.1(d) of the CCJA Rules.
[81] Article 15.3 of the CCJA Rules.
[82] Article 15.4 of the CCJA Rules.
[83] Article 16 of the CCJA Rules.

commerce[84]. If necessary, the tribunal may appoint one or more experts and define their terms of reference[85].

If one of the parties wishes to challenge the jurisdiction of the tribunal, it must do so, at the very latest, during the first meeting with the tribunal[86]. The tribunal may also, of its own motion, look into the question of its jurisdiction at any point in the proceedings, if reasons of public policy arise[87]. In such an event the parties are invited to comment. In cases where its jurisdiction is questioned, the tribunal may decide upon the question either in a preliminary award or in a final or partial award after it has heard pleadings on the merits[88].

Unless otherwise agreed by the parties, the arbitral tribunal has jurisdiction to order any provisional or conservatory measures during the course of the proceedings[89]. If an enforcement order is necessary in relation to the implementation of such measures, it may be applied for immediately, in proceedings before the President of the CCJA or the specially delegated judge at the CCJA[90].

If the need arises at a time when the case is not yet before the tribunal, or in exceptional situations of urgency thereafter, the party concerned may apply to the national courts for provisional or conservatory measures. In such an event the CCJA must be informed of the application and of any measures that are ordered by the national court, and the CCJA must in turn inform the arbitral tribunal[91].

F. Costs of arbitration

As mentioned above, once the initial written pleadings have been exchanged the CCJA determines the amount of the advance to be paid by the parties to cover the anticipated costs of arbitration[92]. These costs include the arbitrators' fees and expenses, the CCJA's administrative costs, the costs incurred in the functioning of the tribunal, and the fees and expenses of any experts. The arbitrators' fees and the CCJA's

---

[84] Article 17 of the CCJA Rules.
[85] Article 19.3 of the CCJA Rules.
[86] Article 21.1 of the CCJA Rules.
[87] Article 21.2 of the CCJA Rules.
[88] Article 21.3 of the CCJA Rules.
[89] Article 10.5 of the CCJA Rules.
[90] Articles 10.5 and 30.2 of the CCJA Rules.
[91] Article 10.5 of the CCJA Rules.
[92] Article 11.1 of the CCJA Rules.

administrative costs are determined on the basis of the amounts in dispute, in accordance with a scale drawn up by the CCJA in general assembly and approved by the Council of Ministers by Decision No. 004/ 99 of 12 March 1999. On the basis of this scale, if for example the amount in dispute is 1,000 million FCFA, the CCJA's administrative costs will be 7.75 million FCFA and the fees of one arbitrator will be between 7.75 million and 27.5 million FCFA depending upon various considerations and in particular the complexity of the dispute, making a total of between 15.5 million and 35.25 million FCFA. If there is a three-arbitrator tribunal, the total amount of the arbitrators' fees will be a maximum of three times the amount allowed for a sole arbitrator.

The advance may be adjusted during the course of the proceedings if the amounts in dispute vary by more than 25 per cent, or if new events make an adjustment necessary[93].

If a party so requests, separate advances may be fixed for the claim and counter-claim. In principle, the parties pay equal shares of the advance. However, if a party refuses to pay its share, the other party may pay the whole advance. The advances must be paid in full before the case file is delivered to the arbitral tribunal, although if a party so wishes, it may instead pay only 25 per cent of the advance and provide a bank guarantee for the remainder of the amount[94].

The tribunal will not hear any claims or counter-claims with respect to which the advance has not been paid (or secured) in full. Similarly, the tribunal will suspend the proceedings until any additional amount has been paid, in the event of an adjustment during the course of the proceedings[95].

G. The award

Unless otherwise agreed by the parties in cases where the applicable law allows such an agreement, the award must contain reasoning[96]. Since the Uniform Act, which requires awards to be reasoned, is applicable to all arbitrations taking place in the Member States, it is likely that the great majority of awards in CCJA arbitration will have to contain reasoning.

---

[93] Article 11.1 of the CCJA Rules.
[94] Article 11.2 of the CCJA Rules.
[95] Article 11.3 of the CCJA Rules.
[96] Article 22.1 of the CCJA Rules.

Before they are signed by the tribunal, drafts of all awards on jurisdiction, partial awards which put an end to the proceedings, and final awards are to be submitted to the CCJA for review[97]. Other awards are not subject to review, but are nonetheless to be sent to the CCJA for information.

When it reviews a draft award the CCJA may only propose purely formal modifications[98]. If the award is a final award, the CCJA advises the tribunal of the final amount of the costs of arbitration and determines the amount of the arbitrators' fees. The final award must indicate the costs of arbitration and decide in what proportion they are to be borne by each of the parties[99].

The award must be signed by the arbitrators[100]. If there are three arbitrators, the award may be given by majority. If there is no majority (for example, if an arbitrator refuses to sign, or an arbitrator has not been replaced, as discussed above, and if the remaining two arbitrators hold opposing views), the award is given by the president of the tribunal alone[101]. Any separate or dissenting opinion may be attached to the award at the request of the arbitrator concerned[102].

Once the costs of arbitration set forth in the award have been paid in full, the Secretary-General delivers the signed award to the parties[103].

Any request for rectification of non-substantive errors in the award, for interpretation, or for a supplemental award on a claim which the tribunal has failed to rule upon may be submitted to the CCJA within 45 days of delivery of the award to the parties[104]. The request is transmitted immediately to the arbitral tribunal, which must then hear both parties on the issue in question and must draft a further award for examination by the CCJA within 60 days. If it is impossible to reconstitute the same tribunal, the CCJA will appoint a new arbitrator or arbitrators after consultation with the parties[105]. It is not clear whether, if the original

---

[97] Article 23.1 of the CCJA Rules.
[98] Article 23.2 of the CCJA Rules.
[99] Article 24.1 of the CCJA Rules.
[100] Article 22.3 of the CCJA Rules.
[101] Article 22.3 of the CCJA Rules.
[102] Article 22.4 of the CCJA Rules.
[103] Article 25.1 of the CCJA Rules.
[104] Article 26 of the CCJA Rules.
[105] Under the Uniform Act, a new tribunal is not constituted in such circumstances, but the matter is submitted to the national court. The requirement that a new tribunal be constituted under the CCJA Rules seems rather cumbersome and even illogical, especially when the issue is interpretation of the original tribunal's award.

tribunal had three members, a completely new tribunal must be constituted, or whether only the arbitrator or arbitrators who are no longer able to sit on the tribunal must be replaced.

If a new arbitrator is appointed, a fee will be payable. In all other cases no additional fee is payable[106]. It is, however, not clear what would happen if the tribunal comprises a new arbitrator and two of the original arbitrators, assuming such a situation would be possible. In these circumstances it would be logical to suppose that only the new arbitrator would receive a fee, but this is not specified.

If costs of arbitration are incurred, and if the new request is dismissed in its entirety, such costs are to be borne by the party who made the request. Otherwise, they are shared between the parties in the proportions determined in the original award[107].

Arbitral awards given under the CCJA Rules are deemed to have final *res judicata* effect on the territory of all the Member States, with the same authority as judgments given by the national courts, and they may be enforced on the territory of any Member State[108]. As will be seen below, however, an enforcement order will be required if it is necessary to seek forced execution in a Member State[109].

H. Appeals

Ordinary appeals are not available against a CCJA arbitral award. Instead, a party may contest the validity of the award on a limited number of grounds, unless this possibility has been waived by the parties in their arbitration agreement[110]. Although the terminology used is not the same, proceedings where the validity of an award is contested have essentially the same effects as setting-aside proceedings under the Uniform Act and other arbitration laws.

If a party wishes to contest the validity of the award, it does so in proceedings before the CCJA, which may be filed at any time after issuance of the award until two months after its delivery to the parties[111]. The only grounds upon which such proceedings may be based are the following:

---

[106] Article 26 of the CCJA Rules.
[107] Article 26 of the CCJA Rules.
[108] Article 27 of the CCJA Rules.
[109] Article 30 of the CCJA Rules.
[110] Article 29 of the CCJA Rules.
[111] Article 29.3 of the CCJA Rules.

- absence, nullity or expiry of the arbitration agreement;
- failure by the tribunal to comply with its terms of reference;
- failure to comply with due process; and
- failure of the award to comply with international public policy[112].

These are more limited grounds than under the Uniform Act, which allows setting-aside proceedings on all of these grounds and also if the award does not contain reasoning or if the tribunal has been improperly constituted. As regards absence of reasoning, it is logical that this should not be a ground for challenging the validity of an award under the CCJA Rules, since the Rules do not necessarily require a reasoned award. On the other hand, if the agreement of the parties or the applicable law requires reasoning, any absence of reasoning could doubtless be considered as a failure by the tribunal to comply with its terms of reference, and the award could therefore be challenged on this ground.

The absence of a provision allowing the parties to contest the validity of an award if the tribunal has been improperly constituted is more troubling. The logic behind this provision is presumably that application of the CCJA Rules, with appointments being made by the CCJA itself if necessary, should ensure that the tribunal is properly constituted. However, this presupposes the infallibility of the CCJA in such matters, which may not always be the case.

If the CCJA finds that the challenge to the validity of the award is well founded, it will declare the award null and void. It may then give a new judgment on the merits, on condition that the parties have allowed it to do so. Otherwise, either party may request a resumption of the arbitral proceedings, as from the last event in such proceedings, if any, that has been recognized as valid by the CCJA[113].

The Rules do not specify what will happen in connection with appeals if the seat of arbitration is not in a Member State. In such an event conflicts of jurisdiction and of laws may arise. For example, if the seat of arbitration is in France, the parties are entitled to file proceedings with a French court of appeal seeking the setting-aside of the award on certain limited grounds which are analogous to the grounds listed in the CCJA Rules but which also include the improper constitution of the arbitral tribunal. If the French court of appeal finds that the request for setting-

---

[112] Articles 29.2 and 30.6 of the CCJA Rules. Unlike the Uniform Act, the CCJA Rules do not refer to the international public policy "of the Member States". Fraud, for example, would be covered by this concept.

[113] Article 29.5 of the CCJA Rules.

aside is well founded, it will declare the award null and void but cannot issue a new judgment on the merits. Since under French law the parties cannot waive the right to file such proceedings in advance, it must therefore be assumed that in a CCJA arbitration having its seat in France, the parties would retain the right to seek the setting-aside of the award before a French court, on the grounds specified by French law. It is however not clear whether proceedings could also be filed before the CCJA, or how the situation would be resolved if such proceedings were filed concurrently.

In addition to proceedings contesting the validity of the award, a party may request revision either of the award itself or of a judgment of the CCJA ruling upon the merits following the setting-aside of the award[114]. Such a request is admissible only in the event of discovery of a fact which may have had a decisive influence on the decision in question and which was unknown to the tribunal or the CCJA, as the case may be, and to the party making the request, at the time of issuance of the decision. Any request for revision must be filed with the CCJA within a period of three months from discovery of the new fact, and requests are no longer admissible more than ten years after the date of the award or judgment concerned[115].

Third-party objections are also possible before the CCJA (but not before the arbitral tribunal, as under the Uniform Act) in the event that a third party who has not been joined to the proceedings considers that the award or judgment is prejudicial to its own rights[116].

I. Enforcement

If a party wishes to enforce a CCJA award, an *ex parte* application for an enforcement order is made to the CCJA[117]. Enforcement orders are issued by the President of the CCJA or a specially delegated judge, and may only be refused on the basis of one or more of the grounds listed above for challenges to the validity of the award[118].

Any refusal on such grounds may be appealed before the CCJA[119]. Unlike the proceedings where the enforcement order is applied for, these

---

[114] Article 32 of the CCJA Rules.
[115] Article 49 of the CCJA Rules of Procedure.
[116] Article 33 of the CCJA Rules of Arbitration and Article 47 of the CCJA Rules of Procedure.
[117] Article 30.1 of the CCJA Rules.
[118] Articles 30.2 and 30.6 of the CCJA Rules.
[119] Article 30.4 of the CCJA Rules.

Table 10.1 Summary table of *ad hoc* arbitration under the Uniform Act and CCJA arbitration

	Uniform Act	**CCJA**
1. Scope	Seat of arbitration in Member State	Party resident in Member State <u>or</u> contract performed in Member State
2. Tribunal	1 or 3 arbitrators Appointment by local court if necessary No provision for multi-party arbitration Challenge before local court	1 or 3 arbitrators Appointment by CCJA if necessary Provision for multi-party arbitration Challenge before CCJA
3. Proceedings	Procedural rules chosen by parties or tribunal	CCJA Rules: – Request for arbitration – Answer and, if applicable, counterclaim within 45 days – Response to counterclaim, if applicable, within 30 days – Meeting of tribunal and parties within 60 days – Minutes – Further proceedings as may be determined – Hearing and closure
4. Provisional or conservatory measures	May be ordered by national court	May be ordered by tribunal; enforcement order by CCJA if necessary May exceptionally be ordered by national court
5. Time limit for issuance of award	Six months from appointment of last arbitrator, extension possible	90 days from closure of proceedings, extension possible
6. Costs	As may be determined by tribunal	According to CCJA scale of costs
7. Appeals	No ordinary appeal Setting-aside proceedings before national court Ultimate appeal before CCJA	No ordinary appeal Setting-aside proceedings before CCJA No further right of appeal
8. Enforcement	Enforcement order from national court	Enforcement order from CCJA, enforceable in all Member States

take place before the full court and the other party may participate in them. Similarly, if the enforcement order is granted, any appeal is filed before the full CCJA, and both parties may participate in the proceedings[120]. The grounds for appeal against the enforcement order are again the same as for a contestation of the validity of the award.

An enforcement order will also be refused for procedural reasons if the award is already the subject of proceedings in which its validity is contested. In such an event, the CCJA will order a joinder of the two proceedings and the full court will rule upon both validity and enforcement at the same time. There is no further right of appeal if the enforcement order is refused in such circumstances[121].

When an enforcement order is granted, the award is enforceable in all the Member States[122], although it will be necessary to have the award stamped as enforceable by the national authorities of the State where enforcement is sought[123]. This is, however, a mere formality, which cannot be refused.

---

[120] Article 30.6 of the CCJA Rules.
[121] Article 30.3 of the CCJA Rules.
[122] Article 30.2 of the CCJA Rules.
[123] Article 31.2 of the CCJA Rules.

11

Future Uniform Acts

Article 2 of the OHADA Treaty defines the scope of business law with a view to its harmonization in the Member States. The definition covers the law relating to companies, the legal status of persons or entities engaged in commerce, the recovery of debts, securities, means of enforcement, administration and court-ordered liquidation, arbitration, employment, accounting, transport and sales. This is not a closed list of subjects, given that the definition also covers any other matter that the Council of Ministers may unanimously decide to include within the field of business law, in accordance with the object and purpose of the Treaty.

SECTION 1: UNIFORM ACTS ON SPECIFIC SUBJECTS DEFINED IN THE TREATY

Since the entry into force of the Treaty, the seven Uniform Acts discussed in the preceding chapters have been adopted, covering all the specific topics listed in Article 2 except employment, transport and, to a certain extent, sales[1].

A draft Uniform Act on contracts for the carriage of goods by road is expected to be finalized in the near future. A draft Uniform Act on

---

[1] The Uniform Act on General Commercial Law contains certain provisions relating to sales, but these apply only to sales between persons or entities professionally engaged in commerce.

employment law is also in the process of being prepared, as is a draft on sales to consumers.

A. Draft Uniform Act on Contracts for the Carriage of Goods by Road

The draft Uniform Act on Contracts for the Carriage of Goods by Road is based in part upon the 1956 Geneva Convention to which almost all countries in Europe are parties[2]. At the time of writing, a preliminary draft is with the Member States, and it is anticipated that there will soon be an agreed draft and that the Uniform Act will be adopted in the course of 2002.

The provisions of the Uniform Act will be mandatory, and any contractual clause which purports to derogate from them will be null and void.

The Uniform Act will be applicable to contracts whereby a carrier undertakes as his principal obligation, against remuneration, to carry by vehicle and by road goods that are entrusted to him by another person. In this context, 'goods' are defined as being any movable goods that can be traded.

All such contracts will be subject to the Uniform Act when the place where the carrier takes over the goods and the place designated for delivery are located either on the territory of a Member State or on the territories of two different States where at least one of those States is a Member State. As a result, the Uniform Act will be applicable not only to contracts involving international carriage, like the Geneva Convention, but also to contracts to be performed within a single Member State.

Since Uniform Acts cannot have extraterritorial effect and therefore cannot be binding upon the authorities of a country which is not a Member State, this means that when a non-Member State is involved, the Uniform Act on Contracts for the Carriage of Goods by Road will be applicable only if it has been expressly chosen by the parties to govern their contract, or if the parties have chosen the law of one of the Member States as the applicable law, or if the applicable rules of conflict otherwise designate the law of a Member State.

The draft provides that the contract for carriage will be formed as soon as the parties have agreed upon the goods to be carried, the destination, and the price.

---

[2] Convention on the Contract for the International Carriage of Goods by Road (CMR), Geneva, 19 May 1956.

Various conditions are laid down for the bill of lading, which may be negotiable if the contract so provides. In accordance with modern business practices, the draft provides that if the bill of lading is not to be negotiable, it may be made in electronic format, with the carrier being obliged to provide the appropriate electronic signature.

The draft further lays down certain classic requirements for customs documents, packing, declarations and instructions to be given by the sender of the goods, performance of the contract, inspection of the goods, delivery, payment and liability. A special set of provisions deals with situations where several carriers transport the goods consecutively, using either the same type or different types of transport.

Finally, the draft contains a number of articles on rights of action and jurisdiction. It is specifically provided that the contract may contain an arbitration clause, and that if the arbitral tribunal is required to give its decision in law, it must apply the terms of the Uniform Act. The draft goes on to say that any such arbitration will be governed by the Uniform Act on Arbitration. This is a rather surprising provision, since it appears to oblige the parties to apply the Uniform Act on Arbitration as the procedural law even if the seat of arbitration is not in a Member State and even though parties to an arbitration agreement are in principle free to determine which law, if any, will be applicable to the procedure.

B. Draft Uniform Act on Employment Law

At the time of writing, it is hoped that there will be a preliminary draft of a Uniform Act on employment law by the end of August 2002.

There are fears, however, that the harmonization of law on this inherently sensitive subject will be a very complicated task, and that a Uniform Act may be difficult to enforce because of the national specificities in each Member State. Some Member States already have very advanced legislation on the subject, providing considerable protection for employees, but this is not the case in all the Member States. For this reason it is expected that the Uniform Act will try to strike a balance between the two. This will clearly be difficult, since some States will not want to take what appears to be a retrograde step, and others may consider that they cannot enforce the high levels of protection that are available in other States.

One way of resolving this problem, or at least of going some way towards its resolution, may be for the Uniform Act to lay down certain basic regulations, while leaving other aspects to collective bargaining agreements. As a result, certain fundamental principles, such as those already laid down by the International Labour Organization relating to equality of treatment, the employment of women, child labour, etc, could be included in the Uniform Act, while detailed provisions regulating relations between employers and employees would be excluded.

C. Draft Uniform Act on Sales to Consumers

A draft Uniform Act on Sales to Consumers is also in preparation. However, this has not reached a very advanced stage, and details are not yet available.

SECTION 2: SUBJECTS NOT SPECIFICALLY DEFINED IN THE TREATY

The specific subjects listed in Article 2 of the OHADA Treaty have been added to by a decision of the Council of Ministers of 23 March 2001, following a proposal by the Permanent Secretariat[3]. As a result, business law is now deemed also to comprise the law relating to banking, competition, intellectual property, co-operative and mutual societies, civil companies, contract and evidence.

As was already the case with the original list of subjects, it appears that some of these new subjects will go beyond the domain of what is traditionally considered as business law. This is not a criticism. On the contrary, the extension of the OHADA system should be viewed as a sign of its success and of the Member States' realization that if the law is made more modern and accessible, even if the subject concerned is only peripheral to business activity, this can only enhance the climate for investment.

Some of the new subjects, especially intellectual property and banking, are already regulated by other regional organizations of which OHADA Member States are also members. In these circumstances, care will have to be taken to ensure that any new legal framework created by OHADA does not conflict with regulations by which the Member States are already bound by virtue of their membership of such regional organizations, and that no confusion is created as to which system is applicable. In order to avoid such conflicts, special committees have been set up between OHADA and some regional organizations such as UEMOA and

---

[3] Decision No. 002/2001/CM.

CEMAC, and there are also informal contacts and consultative exchanges with other organizations.

As a result, when it is decided to undertake the preparation of a Uniform Act on a subject which is already regulated by a regional organization, the Permanent Secretariat, through its Director in charge of relations with institutions, will coordinate contacts between OHADA and the organization concerned. For example, the first draft for a Uniform Act on cooperative and mutual societies has been prepared by the West African Central Bank (BCEAO) and a non-governmental organization. It is anticipated that a Uniform Act on banking law could be drafted very quickly, with input from the BCEAO and the Central African Bank (BEAC). Similarly, when a Uniform Act on intellectual property is envisaged, this will be coordinated with OAPI.

Finally, certain subjects should perhaps be given consideration as future areas for harmonization in order to facilitate the development of infrastructure projects on the continent, in accordance with the aims of NEPAD. For example, it would certainly be helpful for international financial institutions and private investors if OHADA were to enact a legal framework for public/private partnerships and if a unified land tenure system could be created. Uniform Acts on these subjects are not yet envisaged by OHADA and might perhaps meet with some opposition based on national specificities; but given OHADA's success in overcoming or accommodating such national specificities in order to achieve its ambitions, there seems to be no reason why such harmonization should not be envisaged in the future.

12

The legal context beyond OHADA

As will have been understood from the preceding chapters, OHADA does not exist in isolation. On the contrary, there are numerous regional organizations in sub-Saharan Africa, some of which are complementary to OHADA, while others may give rise to conflicts of laws.

These regional organizations fall into two main categories: (i) economic organizations and (ii) specialized organizations dealing with specific subjects such as intellectual property or insurance law.

SECTION 1: REGIONAL ECONOMIC ORGANIZATIONS

The regional economic organizations are UEMOA, CEMAC and ECO-WAS. UEMOA and CEMAC together form the CFA Franc Zone, which in turn forms part of the overall Franc Zone. The CFA Franc Zone includes all the OHADA Member States, with the exception of the Comoros which form a separate sub-zone within the Franc Zone[1], and Guinea, which is not a member of any part of the Franc Zone. It will be convenient to deal briefly with the Franc Zone before turning to the organizations themselves.

---

[1] The Comoros has its own currency, the Comorian Franc. For the sake of simplicity, this chapter will refer only to the CFA Franc, but it should be borne in mind that the same principles apply to the Comorian Franc.

A. *The Franc Zone*

The Franc Zone is an economic and monetary area. In addition to France, its membership consists predominantly of former French colonies, although Equatorial Guinea and Guinea-Bissau are also members.

There is monetary co-operation between France and the members of the CFA Franc Zone and also among the members of the CFA Franc Zone themselves, based on four principles:

- fixed parity of the CFA Franc, initially with the French Franc and now with the Euro, determined in consultation with France[2];
- a common issuing bank for each of the sub-zones: the West African Central Bank (BCEAO), the Bank of the Central African States (BEAC), and the Central Bank of the Comoros;
- convertibility guaranteed by the French Treasury; and
- free transferability within the Franc Zone (including transfers to and from France), whether the transfer is an everyday transaction or a movement of capital.

The African banking authorities have not yet clearly indicated an opinion as to whether the rules of free transferability of funds will henceforth apply *de jure* to relations with the whole Euro Zone or whether they will continue to apply only with France.

The Franc Zone is divided into two principal sub-zones: UEMOA for West Africa and CEMAC for Central Africa.

B. *UEMOA*

The acronym UEMOA stands for *Union Economique et Monétaire Ouest Africaine* – West African Economic and Monetary Union. The Treaty creating this Union was signed on 11 January 1994 and was ratified in July 1994, replacing the former UMOA (West African Monetary Union), created in 1962, and the former CEAO (West African Economic Com-

---

[2] Pursuant to a decision of the European Council of Ministers dated 23 November 1998, upon the substitution of the Euro for the French Franc, France was authorized to continue its existing agreements concerning exchange rate matters with UEMOA, CEMAC and the Comoros. Prior to introduction of the Euro, the exchange rate was 1 FF = 100 FCFA. The exchange rate is now 1 Euro = 655.957 FCFA, reflecting the fixed conversion rate from the French Franc to the Euro.

munity), created in 1973[3]. The current members of UEMOA are Benin, Burkina Faso, Côte d'Ivoire, Guinea-Bissau, Mali, Niger, Senegal and Togo.

UEMOA is an organization which in many respects is reminiscent of the European Union, having far-reaching ambitions and a number of analogous institutions.

1. Institutions

UEMOA's institutions comprise governing bodies, regulatory bodies and autonomous financial institutions.

(a) Governing bodies

UEMOA has three governing bodies, the highest of which is the Conference of Heads of State and Government. This body lays down the broad lines of Union policy and may issue rules to govern the functioning of the Union. It meets at least once a year and decides upon any questions that have not been resolved unanimously by the Council of Ministers.

The Council of Ministers comes second in the hierarchy of governing bodies. It meets at least twice a year. It defines the monetary policy of the Union and may enact binding legislation. As in the European Union, the Council of Ministers issues regulations, directives, decisions, recommendations and opinions.

The Council of Ministers works in liaison with the Commission, the third and final governing body, which is the executive branch. The Commission lays down rules for the application of legislation issued by the Council of Ministers, and itself issues recommendations and opinions.

UEMOA legislation is applied in a similar way to European Union legislation. Regulations are directly applicable in the member States and override any conflicting national legislation. Directives are not directly applicable, but indicate certain results that must be achieved by the enactment of legislation in each member State. Decisions are mandatory, but apply only to the persons or entities specified in each decision.

---

[3] The dissolution of these two institutions was pronounced by a decision dated 14 March 1994.

(b) Regulatory bodies

UEMOA has a Court of Justice which ensures the uniform interpretation and application of its law and arbitrates when there are conflicts of interpretation between the member States.

A Court of Auditors controls the accounting of the Union's institutions.

Finally, there is an Inter-parliamentary Committee which plays a consultative role vis-à-vis the Commission. This Committee is regarded as an embryonic UEMOA Parliament.

(c) Autonomous financial institutions

There are two autonomous financial institutions: the West African Central Bank (*Banque Centrale des États de l'Afrique de l'Ouest – BCEAO*) based in Dakar (Senegal) which issues the currency for the UEMOA States; and the West African Development Bank (*Banque Ouest-Africaine de Développement – BOAD*) based in Lomé (Togo), whose purpose is to foster the balanced development of the member States and to promote their integration.

2. Functions

UEMOA's main objective is the creation of a common market based on the free circulation of goods, services and capital. It also co-ordinates national policies in certain sectors, such as energy or transport, and harmonizes its member States' legislation. An additional aim is the co-ordination of economic policy and performance by instituting procedures of multilateral surveillance.

According to UEMOA law, nationals of its member States enjoy freedom of establishment throughout the territory of the Union. Companies are considered as being nationals of a member State if they have been constituted in conformity with the law of the State in question.

Any restrictions on the free flow of capital within the Union are prohibited. With this in mind, in 1998 UEMOA issued a regulation governing the transferability of funds within the member States and with foreign countries both within and outside the Franc Zone[4]. According to this regulation, movements of funds of whatever type are unrestricted within UEMOA, whereas movements outside the Franc Zone are, in certain cases, subject to restrictions or authorizations.

---

[4] Council of Ministers Regulation No. R09, 20 December 1998, which entered into force on 1 February 1999.

As of 1 January 2000, UEMOA became a single customs territory. This has resulted in exemption from customs duties for industrial products, local products and handicraft originating in any of the member States, and the establishment of a common external tariff (*TEC*), consisting of both permanent and temporary duties and taxes, depending on the category of product imported.

UEMOA has recently adopted new legislation on competition and trade law, covering restrictive practices and anti-competitive practices, abuses of dominant position and public aid[5]. A draft unified investment code is also under way. However, at present the member States are still discussing the contents of this investment code, especially with regard to its fiscal provisions.

C. CEMAC

CEMAC (*Communauté économique et monétaire de l'Afrique Centrale* – Central African Economic and Monetary Community) was created in 1994 to replace the former UDEAC (*Union douanière des États d'Afrique Centrale* – Central African Customs Union) which was established in 1964. Its six members are Cameroon, the Central African Republic, Chad, Congo, Equatorial Guinea and Gabon. Like UEMOA, CEMAC has a number of permanent institutions and has adopted specific regulations in a number of areas, although the process of regional integration in CEMAC has proceeded at a slower pace than in UEMOA.

The CEMAC treaty establishes two Unions:

- UEAC (*Union Economique en Afrique Centrale* – Economic Union in Central Africa); and
- UMAC (*Union Monétaire en Afrique Centrale* – Monetary Union in Central Africa).

The supreme governing body of CEMAC is the Conference of Heads of State. Each of the Unions then has a Council of Ministers. A single Executive Secretariat serves both Unions and plays a pivotal role in ensuring the application of CEMAC legislation and in co-ordinating the work of all the CEMAC institutions. These institutions function in a similar manner to their counterparts in UEMOA, and the various types of legislation are again applied in the same way as UEMOA and European legislation.

---

[5] Regulations Nos. 02/2002/CM/UEMOA, 03/2002/CM/UEMOA and 04/2002/CM/UEMOA, respectively, all of 23 May 2002.

1. UEAC

The main objective of UEAC is the free circulation of goods, services and capital, and the co-ordination of national policies on matters such as the environment, transport, industry, communications and infrastructure. In order to encourage economic competitiveness and move towards a common market, UEAC has taken various measures, including the establishment of a customs union with free exchange within the Union and a common tariff on imports from outside. The customs regime consists of a common external tariff (*TEC*) and a generalized preferential tariff (*TPG*), ie a zero per cent rate applicable to exchanges within the Union.

In addition, an investment charter has been issued, defining the general investment framework and future measures to be enacted to improve the institutional, financial and tax environment[6]. At present, this consists of general commitments which will need to be complemented by other regulations. UEAC has also issued regulations concerning competition law, which deal with merger control, abuse of dominant position, anti-competitive practices and public aids[7].

UEAC has various specialized institutions including technical educational establishments and the Development Bank of the Central African States (*Banque de Développement des Etats de l'Afrique Centrale – BDEAC*), whose purpose is to encourage the economic and social development of the CEMAC member States, notably by financing multinational projects and projects for economic integration.

2. UMAC

The role of UMAC is to consolidate monetary co-operation among the CEMAC member States by instituting a single monetary and exchange policy and by overseeing its application by the member States. UMAC's policies are carried out by the Bank of the Central African States (*Banque des Etats de l'Afrique Centrale – BEAC*) which issues the CFA franc in the CEMAC area, and by the Central African Banking Commission (*Commission Bancaire de l'Afrique Centrale – COBAC*).

The rules relating to transferability of funds are similar to the UEMOA rules[8].

---

[6] Regulation No. 17/99/CEMAC-020-CM-O3 dated 17 December 1999.

[7] Regulations Nos. 1/99/UEAC-CM-639 dated 25 June 1999 and 4/99/UEAC-CM-639 dated 18 August 1999.

[8] A CEMAC Regulation dated 29 April 2000 has effected the harmonization of exchange controls in the CEMAC member States.

3. Regulatory bodies

CEMAC has two regulatory bodies, namely the Community Court of Justice and the Inter-parliamentary Commission. The judicial chamber of the Court of Justice ensures the implementation of Community legislation within the member States, arbitrates in conflicts between the Community and the agents of its institutions, and contributes to a uniform interpretation of the Treaty's scope of application. The Court of Justice also has an auditing chamber, which serves the same purpose as the Court of Auditors in UEMOA.

The role of the Inter-parliamentary Commission is to ensure that CEMAC's institutions are controlled democratically.

D. ECOWAS

ECOWAS is the Economic Community of West African States, which was founded in 1975. Its present members include nine OHADA Member States: Benin, Burkina Faso, Côte d'Ivoire, Guinea, Guinea-Bissau, Mali, Niger, Senegal and Togo. In addition, there are six non-OHADA members: Cape Verde, Gambia, Ghana, Liberia, Nigeria and Sierra Leone.

The purpose of ECOWAS is to promote economic integration in all fields of economic activity, not only in terms of economic policy but also through development projects, with the overall aim of establishing an Economic Union in West Africa.

ECOWAS has a number of institutions, as follows:

- the Authority of Heads of State and Government, which is responsible for the general direction and control of the Community. Its purpose is to determine the general policy and major guidelines of the Community, give directives, and harmonize and co-ordinate economic, scientific, technical, cultural and social policies. Its decisions are binding on the member States and the other ECOWAS institutions;
- the Council of Ministers, which is responsible for the functioning and development of the Community. It makes recommendations to the Authority, issues directives on matters concerning the co-ordination and harmonization of economic integration policies, and approves the work programmes and budgets of the Community and its institutions;
- the Community Parliament;
- the Economic and Social Council, which plays an advisory role;
- the Executive Secretariat, whose role is to ensure the smooth functioning of the Community;

- the Fund for Co-operation, Compensation and Development, one of the objectives of which is to guarantee foreign investment in the ECOWAS member States in respect of enterprises established in pursuance of the provisions of the Treaty on the harmonization of industrial policies;
- the Court of Justice, which is intended to be the principal legal organ of ECOWAS, but which is not yet functioning; and
- the Arbitration Tribunal, which is also not yet in operation.

The main fields of co-operation within ECOWAS are far-reaching and comprehensive. Technical commissions have been established in the following fields:

- food and agriculture;
- industry, science, technology and energy;
- environment and natural resources;
- transport, communications and tourism;
- trade, customs, taxation, statistics, money and payments;
- political, judicial and legal affairs, regional security and immigration;
- human resources, information, social and cultural affairs; and
- administration and finance

To date, ECOWAS has achieved a reduction of customs duties, the free movement of designated goods and of persons (regarding the right of residence and of establishment) and, to a certain extent, the harmonization of economic and fiscal policies, the facilitation and liberalization of payments and the standardization of transport legislation. However, a great deal still remains to be done as regards priority programmes in the other fields.

These priority programmes include trade liberalization, where it is intended to establish a customs union. This was supposed to have been done by 1 January 2000, but the deadline was not met. It is also intended to eliminate all customs duties (and not just to reduce them) and to establish a common external tariff.

Trade liberalization is itself just one aspect of the final objective of economic and monetary union which, rather optimistically, is supposed to be achieved by 2005. This should include the free movement of goods, persons, capital and services as well as total freedom of establishment and common economic and monetary policies.

Perhaps conscious that UEMOA is far in advance of ECOWAS in achieving economic and monetary union, non-UEMOA members of

ECOWAS have created their own monetary zone, with the intention of merging it with the UEMOA zone to give birth to a single ECOWAS monetary zone in 2004 which, in the long term, could merge with the CFA Franc Zone. However, it is believed that it is very unlikely that the goal of an ECOWAS monetary zone will be achieved in 2004.

Moreover, most member States are in arrears with their contributions to the ECOWAS budgets and funds, and have neither made sustained efforts nor committed the necessary resources towards the implementation of programmes designed to publicize the Community.

However, although the implementation of a number of ECOWAS projects has therefore not always been totally satisfactory, the importance of ECOWAS should not be underestimated. On the contrary, it is becoming more and more significant. For example, a recent development arising out of an ECOWAS initiative may be mentioned. In the 1980s ECOWAS and the governments of Benin, Ghana, Nigeria and Togo conceived the idea of regional pipeline systems to enhance regional economic growth and stability. This idea has now led to the initiation of the project for the West African Gas Pipeline, which is to run between Nigeria and Ghana, passing through Benin and Togo. It is hoped that construction of the pipeline will begin in 2003. A similar initiative which is underway relates to the creation of a West African Power Pool among the member States. This was mooted by ECOWAS in 2000 and, in April 2002 a steering committee laid down an organization chart for membership and management and decided to create an institutional regulatory entity for the implementation of the project.

A map of the UEMOA, CEMAC and ECOWAS countries is attached in Appendix C.

SECTION 2: SPECIALIZED ORGANIZATIONS

A. OAPI – Intellectual property

The African Intellectual Property Organization (*Organisation africaine de la propriété intellectuelle – OAPI*) was established by the Bangui Convention of 2 March 1977. At present, the following countries are members of OAPI: Benin, Burkina Faso, Cameroon, Central African Republic, Chad, Congo, Côte d'Ivoire, Equatorial Guinea, Gabon, Guinea, Guinea-Bissau, Mali, Mauritania, Niger, Senegal and Togo.

The Organization comprises three institutions:

- an Administrative Council which defines OAPI's policy and ensures the proper implementation of its law;
- a General Management which executes the decisions of the Administrative Council; and
- a Higher Committee of Appeal which examines appeals against refusals to register intellectual property rights.

OAPI's overall objective is to be closely involved in the technological development of its member States. In order to achieve this goal, OAPI seeks to:

- ensure the protection and the publication of intellectual property rights by a common registration for every member State; as a result, the filing of an application for registration within one of the OAPI member States or with OAPI itself is deemed to be a national filing in each member State and produces rights in each member State.
- make the legal framework attractive to private investment by creating conditions that are favourable to the effective application of the principles of intellectual property; and
- encourage creativity and the transfer of technology.

OAPI has drawn up legislation in ten fields of intellectual property, including patents, trademarks or trade names and industrial drawings or models.

The original Bangui Convention of 1977 was revised in February 1999, and the revised version entered into force in February 2002[9]. As a result, certain procedures which were rather cumbersome under the original Convention have been simplified. In particular, the registration of licence agreements, which originally required prior submission of the agreement to the national authorities for review, is now exempt from this requirement.

B. CIMA – Insurance

The Inter-African Conference on Insurance Markets (*Conférence Interafricaine des Marchés d'Assurances – CIMA*) was established by a treaty signed on 10 July 1992 by 14 States, all of which are members of OHADA. These are Benin, Burkina Faso, Cameroon, Central African Republic, Chad,

---

[9] Agreement of 24 February 1999 revising the Bangui Convention of 2 March 1977 on the creation of an African Intellectual Property Organization.

Comoros, Congo, Côte d'Ivoire, Equatorial Guinea, Gabon, Mali, Niger, Senegal and Togo.

CIMA entered into force in February 1995. Its main aim is to unify insurance law within its member States. To achieve this it has drawn up a Code which is applied throughout the member States without the need for national legislation to make it applicable. CIMA is however still of limited scope, applying only to land insurance and not to other types of insurance.

The CIMA Code deals with the general provisions of an insurance contract; mandatory insurance; rules governing insurance and capitalization companies; the accounting law applicable to such companies; and the rules applicable to general agents, brokers and other insurance and capitalization intermediaries.

The Code lays down the fundamental principle that where an individual or a corporate body resident in the territory of a member State enters into an insurance contract, the contract must be made in CFA Francs with an insurance company registered in a member State.

As regards insurance companies, any such company based in the territory of a CIMA member State must be constituted in accordance with the CIMA Code, and must obtain approval from the minister in charge of insurance matters in the State concerned in order to exercise its activity.

C. CIPRES – Social security

The Inter-African Conference on Social Welfare (*Conférence Interafricaine de la Prévoyance Sociale – CIPRES*) was established by a treaty signed on 21 September 1993 by the Franc Zone member States. The main objective of this organization is the harmonization of social legislation in the member States.

There are three institutions within CIPRES:

- a Council of Ministers which is to define the organization's policy, ensure the application of the convention by the member States and, if necessary, modify the scope of the convention;
- a Supervisory Commission whose purpose is to ensure the proper management of social security bodies; and
- a Regional Inspectorate which is to propose new rules for the harmonization of social legislation.

CIPRES entered into force on 10 October 1995. However, to date, the law has not been harmonized, and national laws continue to be applied. Future developments will need to be coordinated with the OHADA institutions, which are in the process of adopting a Uniform Act on Employment Law[10].

A chart showing the geographical scope of each of the regional organizations mentioned in this Chapter is attached in Appendix C.

---

[10] See Chapter 11.

Appendix A

Essential items to consider before investing in an OHADA Member State

1. CHOICE OF THE APPROPRIATE ENTITY AND MANAGEMENT STRUCTURE

It should not be automatically assumed that the establishment of a commercial company will be the appropriate vehicle for an investment in an OHADA Member State. In fact, the choice of vehicle will first depend on the type and expected volume and duration of activity. For instance, in certain cases, a branch office of a foreign company or of a company already registered in a Member State may be sufficient and more flexible. In other cases a GIE may be the ideal solution if the intention is to share certain facilities with other partners or to develop a common project without necessarily making profits.

If it is decided that a commercial company will be the appropriate entity to be created, the number of shareholders and their respective envisaged roles, along with the amount of capital to be invested and the question of whether the company will want to make public offerings, will all have an influence on the type of company to be established. As a general rule, it is usually considered that the SA is best suited to companies involved in major investments or when it is wished to organize management powers through a joint venture agreement or shareholders' agreement. Otherwise, for smaller investments, especially those where the investor has 100% control, an SARL may well be sufficient.

2. PROTECTION OF THE INVESTMENT AGAINST RISKS

The Member States are parties to numerous multilateral and bilateral treaties which will need to be carefully examined to determine whether they offer protection to an investor in the country concerned. For example, many bilateral investment treaties lay down conditions that must be complied with by the host State in the event of an expropriation, and contain the host State's advance consent to ICSID arbitration if disputes arise in connection with the investment.

In addition, foreign investments in many OHADA countries may be covered by the World Bank's Multilateral Investment Guarantee Agency (MIGA). At regional level, the African Export-Import Bank (Afreximbank) as well as the African Re-Insurance Corporation may be useful in providing some coverage of risks.

Finally, export credit agencies from the investor's home country and local African investment entities or agencies may also be consulted in advance to negotiate assistance and determine what guarantees or protections may be available.

3. EXCHANGE CONTROLS

The determination of the rules applicable to exchange controls will be of great importance in assessing what actions will be required of the investor in connection with the transfer of funds into and out of the country concerned. Such rules may be applicable when capital is transferred at the beginning or end of the investment, and they may also have an impact on transfers of funds relating to inter-company loans, the distribution of dividends, technical or management agreements, or other transfers.

In this regard UEMOA and CEMAC have adopted unified rules applying to exchange controls and common external tariffs in their respective regions. These rules should therefore be consulted with regard to exchanges involving either of these regions, which cover all the Member States with the exception of the Comoros and Guinea.

4. TAX STRUCTURE

In general, many areas of the tax legislation of the Member States are often similar to the corresponding French tax legislation. However, any new French tax legislation usually takes some time to be incorporated in the Member States' systems, and there may be local variations.

It should always be verified whether there is a tax treaty between the country of origin and the country of investment and, if there is, how it may best be used to minimize tax exposure. Additionally, when an investor is envisaging investments in several Member States, it is sometimes useful to examine whether tax schemes in relation to the investment as a whole may be set up to limit taxation or if specific holding regimes might be applicable which would result in tax savings. Furthermore, a number of tax incentives are applicable in many countries, for example for offshore companies or companies located in free zones.

When envisaging the purchase of an activity in a Member State, it is also advisable to make a comparison between the respective tax costs of purchasing a company's shares or purchasing its business (*fonds de commerce*).

A summary table of tax rates in OHADA Member States is contained in Appendix E.

5. INVESTMENT CODES AND INCENTIVES

Each Member State has enacted an investment code which includes a number of incentives for investors. These codes should be carefully examined before any investment is made, in order to determine whether any specific advantages might be granted to the investor's business.

For example, certain tax benefits will usually be accorded, depending upon the amount of the investment, the sector concerned, and the prospective number of employees. Investment codes also generally put in place a system of investment protection.

In some countries, such as Mali, the scope of application of the investment code is limited to commercial activities. Moreover, particular activities may be excluded from the benefit of the investment code, but may be dealt with elsewhere. For example, petroleum activities are often excluded, but these may be dealt with in specific petroleum legislation, which will itself often comprise the applicable investment framework.

Even if the investment code is not applicable to a particular invest-ment, but if the investment is perceived as important for the State concerned, it may be possible for the investor to enter into an incentive agreement with the State. In such an event incentives and guarantees similar to those contained in the investment code are usually provided in the form of a ministerial decree or an establishment agreement (*convention d'établissement*). Care needs to be taken in the negotiation and drafting of these documents if they are to have a substantive effect.

Attached in Appendix B is a list of investment codes currently in force in the Member States.

6. SPECIFIC LAWS

Depending upon the nature of the investment project, it will sometimes be necessary to take into account specific laws such as those applicable to public tenders, concessions or agreements for the delegation of public services; environmental regulations; insurance regulations; and any sector-specific legislation.

7. NECESSARY AUTHORIZATIONS

In some of the Member States, an authorization is needed in order to operate as a foreign shareholder of a foreign-owned company.

Moreover, in most Member States, the directors of a company will need to obtain a commercial identity card (*carte de commerçant*). This card is issued automatically, after registration of the company with the RCCM and once certain formalities have been accomplished.

Special authorizations may also be necessary to operate in a given sector, particularly in what have traditionally been considered as strategic sectors, such as petroleum or mineral products. Permits and/ or concessions or production sharing agreements, which will need to be negotiated separately, will include details of authorizations and condi-tions of operation.

8. EMPLOYMENT LAW OBLIGATIONS

Most of the Member States have enacted employment laws or codes which regulate employment conditions and social security matters. In addition, a collective bargaining agreement may be applicable to the particular activities envisaged by the investor. These should be reviewed to assess their consequences for the investment with regard to human resources.

When an investor enters into a partnership with a State-owned company or when it takes on employees of an existing company, specific obligations may be imposed on the investor with regard to employment. These should be assessed to determine what liabilities may result for the investor, in particular as regards employees' rights and pensions.

9. INTELLECTUAL PROPERTY RIGHTS

As mentioned in Chapter 12, all the Member States except the Comoros are members of OAPI. OAPI's rules should be taken into account when trademarks, patents, licences or other intellectual property rights need to be protected and/or used in connection with the investment project, and there may also be specific national rules covering intellectual property.

Appendix B

Investment codes in the OHADA Member States

- **Benin:** Law No. 90-002 of 9 May 1990 modified by a law of 24 December 1990
- **Burkina Faso:** Law No. 62/95 of 14 December 1995 modified by Law No. 15/97/AN of 17 April 1997
- **Cameroon:** Ordinance No. 90/007 of 8 November 1990 modified by Ordinances Nos. 94/001, 002 and 003 of 24 January 1994
- **Central African Republic:** Law No. 96 of 31 May 1996
- **Chad:** Ordinance No. 025/PR/87 of 8 December 1987 and Decree No. 446/PR/MCI/87 of 8 December 1987
- **Comoros:** Law No. 95-015/AF of 30 June 1995
- **Congo:** Law No. 008-92 of 10 April 1992
- **Côte d'Ivoire:** Law No. 95-620 of 3 August 1995
- **Equatorial Guinea:** Law No. 7/92
- **Gabon:** Law No. 15/98 of 23 July 1998
- **Guinea:** Ordinance of 3 January 1995
- **Guinea-Bissau:** Investment code of 1991 modified in 1996
- **Mali:** Law No. 91-048/AN-RM of 26 February 1991 and Decree No. 95-423/P-RM of 6 December 1995
- **Niger:** Ordinance No. 89-19 of 8 December 1999 modified by Ordinance No. 97-09 of 27 February 1997 and ratified by Law No. 97-019 of 20 June 1997
- **Senegal:** Law No. 87-25 of 18 July 1987 modified by Law No. 89-29 of 12 October 1989

- **Togo:** Law No. 89-22 of 31 October 1989 completed by Decrees of 20 April 1990 and 2 October 1990

As regards the CEMAC countries, Regulation No. 17/99/CEMAC-020-CM-03 of 17 December 1999 relating to the CEMAC Investment Charter is designed to create a general harmonized framework for investments those countries. The Member States of CEMAC are required to adapt their existing legislation to this Charter within five years of its signature.

Appendix C

MAP OF THE OHADA MEMBER STATES

OHADA MEMBER STATES
(as of July 2002)

Map Prepared by: International Mapping Associates.

MAP OF REGIONAL ECONOMIC ORGANIZATIONS

REGIONAL ECONOMIC ORGANIZATIONS
(as of July 2002)

Legend:
- UEMOA
- CEMAC
- ECOWAS

Map Prepared by: International Mapping Associates.

CHART OF REGIONAL ORGANIZATIONS

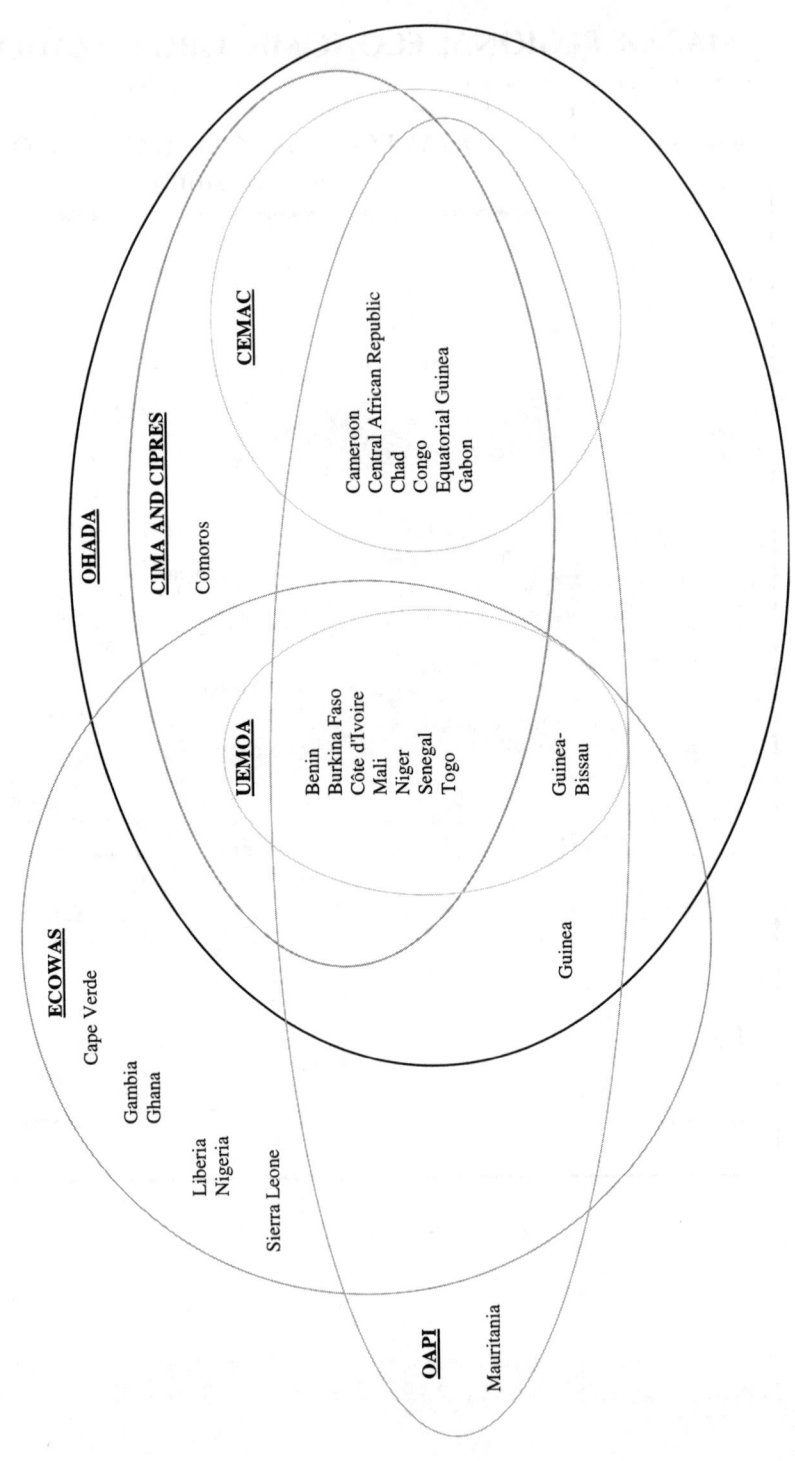

Appendix D

RCCM Forms

The standard forms for the various types of registration to be made with the RCCM in any of the Member States are reproduced on the following pages. These forms are as follows:

M0: To be used for the registration of a new company, a secondary establishment, or a branch of a foreign company. In addition to information identifying the company and details of its activity, the identity of any shareholders with unlimited liability, the members of the management and the statutory auditors must be provided.

M0 bis: To be used if there is not sufficient space on the M0 form for the information concerning shareholders and the management.

M2: To be used for modifications of the information provided in form M0 and any modifications in the company's status.

M2 bis: Like form M0 bis, to be used if there is not sufficient space on the M2 form.

M4: To be used to register the total cessation of activity of a corporate entity or the closure of a liquidation.

P0: To be used to register the opening or the taking-over of an individual business, or the opening of a secondary establishment.

P4: To be used to register a temporary or definitive cessation of activity of an individual business or the death of a person operating an individual business.

Mo
A.P. Porto Novo 23/24 juin 1999

DECLARATION ☐ de CONSTITUTION DE PERSONNE MORALE
ou ☐ d'OUVERTURE **d'un ETABLISSEMENT SECONDAIRE**
ou ☐ d'OUVERTURE d'une **SUCCURSALE** d'une personne morale ETRANGERE

RENSEIGNEMENTS RELATIFS A LA PERSONNE MORALE

1 DENOMINATION: _____
  NOM COMMERCIAL:_____ ENSEIGNE:_____, SIGLE: _____
2 ADRESSE DU SIEGE: _____
3 ADRESSE DE L'ETABLISSEMENT CREE: _____
  FORME JURIDIQUE:_____, N° R.C.C.M. du siège:_____
4 CAPITAL SOCIAL: _____ DONT NUMERAIRES: _____, DONT EN NATURE: _____
5 DUREE:_____

RENSEIGNEMENTS RELATIFS A L'ACTIVITE ET AUX ETABLISSEMENTS

6 **ACTIVITE:** ACTIVITE PRINCIPALE: (préciser) _____
7
8   Date de début: _____, Nbre de salariés prévus: _____

PRINCIPAL ETABLISSEMENT OU SUCCURSALE:
9   Adresse: _____

10 Origine: ☐ Création, ☐ Achat, ☐ Apport, ☐ Prise en location gérance, ☐ Autre
11 (préciser):_____
12 Précédent exploitant: Nom: _____, Prénoms: _____
13 Adresse: _____, N° RCCM: _____
    Loueur de fonds (nom/dénomination, adresse): _____

14 **ETABLISSEMENTS SECONDAIRES**: (autres que celui créé) ☐ Non , ☐ Oui (préciser):
   Adresse: _____
   Activité: _____

ASSOCIES TENUS INDEFINIMENT ET PERSONNELLEMENT (*)

15 (*) La totalité des renseignements relatifs à ces associés doit IMPERATIVEMENT figurer sur le formulaire complémentaires M.o Bis annexé.
   RESUME DES INFORMATIONS:

NOM	PRENOM	DATE LIEU DE NAISS.	ADRESSE

RENSEIGNEMENTS RELATIFS AUX DIRIGEANTS (*) (**)

16 (*) Concerne les Gérants, Administrateurs ou associés ayant le pouvoir d'engager la personne morale
   (**) Les renseignements ne pouvant figurer ci-dessous doivent IMPERATIVEMENT être reportés sur le formulaire M.o Bis annexé.

NOM	PRENOM	DATE LIEU DE NAISS.	ADRESSE	FONCTION(***)

(***) Preciser: Gérant, PDG, Administrateur, Associé

COMMISSAIRES AUX COMPTES

17

NOM	PRENOM	DATE LIEU DE NAISS.	ADRESSE	FONCTION
				TITULAIRE
				SUPPLEANT

LE SOUSSIGNE (préciser si mandataire) _____
demande à ce que la présente constitue ☐ **DEMANDE D'IMMATRICULATION AU R.C.C.M.**

Fait, à
Le
Signature :

18 **La conformité de la déclaration avec les pièces justificatives produites en application de l'Acte Uniforme sur le Droit commercial général a été vérifiée par le Greffier en Chef soussigné qui a procédé :**
   à l'inscription le _____, sous le NUMERO _____

MoBis
A.P. Porto Novo 23/24 juin 1999

**INTERCALAIRE COMPLEMENTAIRE
AU FORMULAIRE M0 (*)**

* Cette intercalaire doit **IMPERATIVEMENT** être annexée au formulaire M0 lorsque les rubriques 15 et 16 de ce formulaire n'ont pu être entièrement renseignées.

15 ASSOCIES TENUS INDEFINIMENT ET PERSONNELLEMENT

INSCRIRE CI-DESSOUS LES NOMS, PRENOMS, DOMICILE PERSONNEL, DATE ET LIEU DE NAISSANCE, NATIONALITE, DATE ET LIEU DU OU DES MARIAGES, REGIME MATRIMONIAL, CLAUSES RESTRICTIVES OPPOSABLES AUX TIERS, SEPARATIONS DE BIENS, DE <u>TOUS LES ASSOCIES</u> TENUS INDEFINIMENT ET PERSONNELLEMENT DES DETTES SOCIALES :

16 RENSEIGNEMENTS RELATIFS AUX DIRIGEANTS (*)

(*) Concerne les Gérant, administrateurs ou associés pouvant engager la personne morale.
INSCRIRE CI-DESSOUS LES NOMS, PRENOMS, DATE ET LIEU DE NAISSANCE, ADRESSE, QUALITE (Préciser : Gérant, PDG, PCA, administrateur ou associés) CONCERNES ET QUI N'ONT PU ETRE INSCRITS SUR LE FORMULAIRE M0 EN RUBRIQUE 14 .

La conformité de la déclaration avec les pièces justificatives produites en application de l'Acte Uniforme sur le Droit commercial général a été vérifiée par le Greffier en Chef soussigné qui a procédé à l'inscription le _____, sous le NUMERO

Fait, à
Le
Signature :

_____.
(reporter ici le numéro de formalité figurant sur le formulaire Mo)

M2 A.P. Porto Novo 23/24 juin 1999	**DECLARATION DE MODIFICATION** ☐ de la **PERSONNE MORALE** ☐ d'un **ETABLISSEMENT** ☐ Caractéristiques, ☐ Activités, ☐ Dirigeants, ☐ Transfert, ☐ Fermeture, ? Dissolution

MODIFICATIONS RELATIVES A LA PERSONNE MORALE

LA PERSONNE MORALE MODIFIE: N° RCCM de l'entreprise: _____

1 ☐ Son **SIEGE** : Nouveau siège : _____
Ancien siège : _____ RCCM : _____ Date : _____
2 ☐ Sa **FORME JURIDIQUE** : Nouvelle : _____, Ancienne : _____ Date : _____
3 ☐ Son **CAPITAL :** Nouvelle : _____, Ancienne : _____ Date : _____
4 ☐ Son **ACTIVITE:** ☐ Activités supprimées: _____
Date: _____ ☐ Activités ajoutées: _____
5 ☐ Son **NOM COMMERCIAL,** ☐ **ENSEIGNE ,** ☐ **SIGLE;**
Nouveau: _____, Ancien: _____, Date d'effet:
6 _____
7 ☐ **AUTRE**: (préciser) _____
☐ La personne est **DISSOUTE**: (Indiquer les coordonnées du liquidateur à la rubrique «dirigeants») Date:_____

MODIFICATIONS RELATIVES A L'ETABLISSEMENT

8 **NUMERO RCCM** actuel : _____
9 **ADRESSE** ou NOUVELLE ADRESSE : _____
Cet Etablissement est :
10 ☐ **TRANSFERE**, Ancienne adresse : _____ ,Date : _____
11 ☐ **VENDU**, Acquéreur : _____
RCCM de l'acquéreur : _____ ,Date : _____
12 ☐ **FERME**, Date : _____
13 ☐ **MODIFIE**, ☐ Activités supprimées : _____
☐ Activités ajoutées : _____
14 ☐ **AUTRE** : (préciser) _____

MODIFICATIONS RELATIVES AUX ASSOCIES (*)

15 (*) La totalité des modifications et informations relatives aux associés indéfiniment et personnellement responsables doit IMPERATIVEMENT figurer sur le formulaire complémentaires M.2 Bis annexé.
RESUME DES INFORMATIONS:
• Identité: _____ , ☐ Nouveau, ☐ Partant, ☐ Maintenu - modifié
Ancienne qualité: _____ , Nouvelle qualité: _____ , Date: _____
• Identité: _____ , ☐ Nouveau, ☐ Partant, ☐ Maintenu - modifié
Ancienne qualité: _____ , Nouvelle qualité: _____ , Date: _____
• Identité: _____ , ☐ Nouveau, ☐ Partant, ☐ Maintenu - modifié
Ancienne qualité: _____ , Nouvelle qualité: _____ , Date: _____

RENSEIGNEMENTS RELATIFS AUX DIRIGEANTS (*) (**)

16 (*) Concerne les Gérants, Administrateurs ou associés ayant le pouvoir d'engager la personne morale
(**) La totalité des modifications et informations relatives aux dirigeants doit IMPERATIVEMENT figurer sur le formulaire complémentaires M.2 Bis.
• Identité: _____ , ☐ Nouveau, ☐ Partant, ☐ Maintenu - modifié
Ancienne qualité: _____ , Nouvelle qualité: _____ , Date: _____
• Identité: _____ , ☐ Nouveau, ☐ Partant, ☐ Maintenu - modifié
Ancienne qualité: _____ , Nouvelle qualité: _____ , Date: _____
• Identité: _____ , ☐ Nouveau, ☐ Partant, ☐ Maintenu - modifié
Ancienne qualité: _____ , Nouvelle qualité: _____ , Date: _____

COMMISSAIRES AUX COMPTES (*)

17 (*) La totalité des modifications et informations relatives aux commissaires aux comptes doit IMPERATIVEMENT figurer sur le formulaire complémentaires M.2 Bis.
Changement de Commissaire aux Comptes: ☐ OUI, ☐ NON
Modification des informations sur les Commissaires aux Comptes : ☐ OUI, ☐ NON

LE SOUSSIGNE (préciser si mandataire) _____ demande à ce que la présente constitue ☐ **DEMANDE D'IMMATRICULATION AU R.C.C.M.** ☐ **DEMANDE DE RADIATION AU R.C.C.M.**	Fait, à Le Signature :

18 **La conformité de la déclaration avec les pièces justificatives produites en application de l'Acte Uniforme sur le Droit commercial général a été vérifiée par le Greffier en Chef soussigné qui a procédé :**
à l'inscription le _____ , sous le NUMERO _____

M2Bis

**INTERCALAIRE COMPLEMENTAIRE
AU FORMULAIRE M2 (*)**

A.P. Porto Novo 23/24 juin 1999

---

* Cette intercalaire doit IMPERATIVEMENT être renseignée et annexée au formulaire M2 lorsque des modifications sont intervenues au titre des rubriques 15, 16 et 17

15 MODIFICATIONS RELATIVES AUX ASSOCIES

INSCRIRE CI-DESSOUS LES INFORMATIONS OU MODIFICATIONS RELATIVES AUX NOM, PRENOM, DOMICILE PERSONNEL, DATE ET LIEU DE NAISSANCE, NATIONALITE, DATE ET LIEU DE MARIAGES, REGIME MATRIMONIAL, CLAUSES RESTRICTIVES OPPOSABLES AUX TIERS, SEPARATIONS DE BIENS DES ASSOCIES TENUS INDEFINIMENT ET PERSONNELLEMENT DES DETTES SOCIALES EN PRECISANT S'ILS SONT « NOUVEAU » ; « PARTANT » « MAINTENU MODIFIE ».

16 MODIFICATIONS RELATIVES AUX DIRIGEANTS

INSCRIRE CI-DESSOUS LES INFORMATIONS OU MODIFCATIONS RELATIVES AUX NOM, PRENOM, DATE ET LIEU DE NAISSANCE, ADRESSE, QUALITE (Gérant, PDG, PCA, administrateur ou associé) DES ASSOCIES POUVANT ENGAGER LA PERSONNE MORALE EN PRECISANT « NOUVEAU » « PARTANT » « MAINTENU-MODIFIE ».

17 MODIFICATIONS RELATIVES AUX COMMISSAIRES AUX COMPTES

INSCRIRE CI-DESSOUS LES INFORMATIONS OU MODIFCATIONS RELATIVES AUX NOM, PRENOM, DATE ET LIEU DE NAISSANCE, DOMICILE DES COMMISSAIRES AUX COMPTES TITULAIRES ET SUPPLEANT EN PRECISANT LES MODIFICATION INTERVENUE.

La conformité de la déclaration avec les pièces justificatives produites en application de l'Acte Uniforme sur le Droit commercial général a été vérifiée par le Greffier en Chef soussigné qui a procédé à l'inscription le _____, sous le NUMERO _____.

(reporter ici le numéro de formalité figurant sur le formulaire M2)

Fait, à
Le
Signature :

DECLARATION DE

☐ **CESSATION TOTALE D'ACTIVITE** ☐ **CLOTURE DE LA LIQUIDATION**

M4

A.P. Porto Novo 23/24 juin 1999

MODIFICATIONS RELATIVES A LA PERSONNE MORALE

1 | DENOMINATION : _____
NOM COMMERCIAL : _____, ENSEIGNE : _____, SIGLE : _____
2 | ADRESSE DU SIEGE : _____
3 | FORME JURIDIQUE : _____, N° R.C.C.M. du siège : _____
4 | CAPITAL SOCIAL : _____
5 | LIQUIDATEUR : _____

CESSATION D'ACTIVITE

6 | **A COMPTER DU :** _____

CONSEQUENCES SUR LE SIEGE :
7 | • Le siège est : ☐ Vendu, ☐ Apporté, ☐ Apport, ☐ Mis en location gérance; ☐ Disparaît
8 | • Identité du bénéficiaire : Nom - Prénom / Dénomination :

Adresse : _____, N° RCCM : _____

CONSEQUENCES SUR LES ETABLISSEMENTS :
A la suite de la cessation d'activité, préciser pour chaque établissement:
ETABLISSEMENT 1:
9 | • Adresse : _____, N° RCCM : _____
10 | • L'établissement est : ☐ Vendu, ☐ Apporté, ☐ Apport, ☐ Mis en location gérance; ☐ Disparaît
11 | • Identité du bénéficiaire: Nom - Prénom / Dénomination :

Adresse : _____, N° RCCM : _____
ETABLISSEMENT 2:
• Adresse : _____, N° RCCM : _____
• L'établissement est : ☐ Vendu, ☐ Apporté, ☐ Apport, ☐ Mis en location gérance; ☐ Disparaît
• Identité du bénéficiaire: Nom - Prénom / Dénomination :

Adresse : _____, N° RCCM : _____
ETABLISSEMENT 3:
• Adresse : _____, N° RCCM : _____
• L'établissement est : ☐ Vendu, ☐ Apporté, ☐ Apport, ☐ Mis en location gérance; ☐ Disparaît
• Identité du bénéficiaire: Nom - Prénom / Dénomination :

Adresse : _____, N° RCCM : _____

(*) S'il existe d'autres établissements, préciser les mêmes données sur une intercalaire et cocher cette case ?

12 | **FUSION - SCISSION :**
En cas de ☐ **FUSION** ou de ☐ **SCISSION**, préciser : La Date: _____
Le NOM, le SIEGE et le N° RCCM des personnes ayant participé à l'opération :
_____
_____
_____
_____

LIQUIDATION

13 | En cas de **CLOTURE DE LA LIQUIDATION**, indiquer la date : _____

ADRESSE PERMANENTE POUR LA CORRESPONDANCE

14 | PRECISER : _____
_____

LE SOUSSIGNE (préciser si mandataire) _____ | Fait, à
demande à ce que la présente constitue ☐ **DEMANDE MODIFICATIVE AU R.C.C.M.** | Le
☐ **DEMANDE DE RADIATION** | Signature :

18 | **La conformité de la déclaration avec les pièces justificatives produites en application de l'Acte Uniforme sur le Droit commercial général a été vérifiée par le Greffier en Chef soussigné qui a procédé :**
à l'inscription le _____, sous le NUMERO _____

P0

DECLARATION de ☐ **DEBUT** ou de ☐ **REPRISE D'ACTIVITE**
ou ☐ d'**OUVERTURE** d'un **ETABLISSEMENT SECONDAIRE**

A.P. Porto Novo 23/24 juin 1999

RENSEIGNEMENTS RELATIFS A L'EXPLOITANT

1 **NOM** : ☐M. ☐Mme ☐Melle _____ **Prenoms** :

2

DATE et LIEU de NAISSANCE : _____ **NATIONALITE** (*) : _____
3 (*) Pour les ETRANGERS, titre de séjour : _____ et date de validité : _____
4 **DOMICILE** (réel et postal) : _____
SITUATION MATRIMONIALE: ☐ Célibataire, ☐ Marié, ☐ Veuf, ☐ Divorcé
Conjoint(s) (*)

	Nom - Prénoms	Date et lieu de naissance	Régime matrimonial	Clauses restrictives
Conjoint 1				
Conjoint 2				
conjoint 3				

(*) Si toutes les informations ne peuvent figurer dans le tableau, une intercalaire doit être annexée et cette case ☐ cochée

RENSEIGNEMENTS RELATIFS A L'ENTREPRISE

5 **ENSEIGNE** : _____ **NOM COMMERCIAL** : _____
6 **ACTIVITE PRINCIPALE** (préciser) : _____
7
8 **Date de début** : **N°RCCM** _____ **Nbre de salariés prévus** : _____

PRINCIPAL ETABLISSEMENT OU SUCCURSALE:
9 • **Adresse** *(réelle et postale)* : _____
10 • **Origine**: ☐ Création, ☐ Achat, ☐ Apport, ☐ Prise en location gérance, ☐ Autre (préciser) :
11 _____
12 • **Précédent exploitant**: Nom : _____, Prénoms : _____
13 Adresse : _____, N° RCCM : _____
• **Loueur de fonds** *(nom/dénomination, adresse)* : _____
_____

14 **ETABLISSEMENT SECONDAIRE OUVERT**: ☐ Non ☐ Oui (préciser) :
Date de d'ouverture : _____
Adresse : _____
Activité: _____

Identité de l'exploitant précédent : _____, RCCM : _____

RENSEIGNEMENTS RELATIFS AUX ACTIVITES ANTERIEURES

15 **EXERCICE D'UNE PRÉCÉDENTE ACTIVITÉ COMMERCIALE**: ☐ NON, ☐ OUI, (préciser)
• Période: de (mois et année) _____, à _____, Précédent N° RCCM : _____
• Nature de l'activité : _____
• Principal établissement : _____
• Etablissements secondaires : _____, RCCM : _____

PERSONNES POUVANT ENGAGER L'ENTREPRISE

16 Outre l'Exploitant, les personnes suivantes ont le pouvoir d'engager l'entreprise :
• Nom : _____, Prénom : _____, Date-lieu de Naiss. : _____
Nationalité : _____, Domicile : _____

• Nom : _____, Prénom : _____, Date-lieu de Naiss. : _____
Nationalité : _____, Domicile : _____

LE SOUSSIGNE (préciser si mandataire) _____
demande à ce que la présente constitue ☐ **DEMANDE D'IMMATRICULATION AU R.C.C.M.**

Fait, à
Le
Signature :

La conformité de la déclaration avec les pièces justificatives produites en application de l'Acte Uniforme sur le Droit commercial général a été vérifiée par le Greffier en Chef soussigné qui a procédé :
à l'inscription le _____, sous le NUMERO _____

P4

DECLARATION DE
- **CESSATION TOTALE D'ACTIVITE ☐ TEMPORAIRE ou ☐ DEFINITIVE**
- **DECES DE L'EXPLOITANT ☐ AVEC ou ☐ SANS CONTINUATION**

A.P. Porto Novo 23/24 juin 1999

RENSEIGNEMENTS RELATIFS A L'EXPLOITANT

1 NOM : _____ PRENOMS : _____ NATIONALITE : _____
2 DATE et LIEU de NAISSANCE : _____ DOMICILE PERSONNEL : _____

3 SIEGE DE L'ENTREPRISE : _____ RCCM : _____

CESSATION TEMPORAIRE D'ACTIVITE

4 DATE : _____
CAUSE : ☐ Maladie ☐ Accident ☐ Sinistre ☐ Autre
_____

CESSATION DEFINITIVE D'ACTIVITE

5 DATE : _____
CAUSE : ☐ Vente ☐ Disparition ☐ Location Gérance ☐ Décès ☐ Autre _____

DECES DE L'EXPLOITANT

6 DATE : _____ Continuation par les héritiers : Oui Non
Si oui, préciser : Nom ou domiciliation, Adresse ou siège, date et lieu de naissance, nationalité des personnes ou héritiers
poursuivant l'exploitation et le mode d'exploitation (Direct, location gérance) :
_____
_____
_____
_____

CONSEQUENCES SUR LE SIEGE DE L'ENTREPRISE

7 A LA SUITE DE LA CESSATION D'ACTIVITÉ, LE SIÈGE :
☐ Disparait ☐ Est Vendu ☐ Est Mis en location gérance ☐ Autre
_____
IDENTITE DU BENEFICIAIRE (acquéreur ou gérant) : Nom ou dénomination, adresse ou siège : _____
RCCM : _____

CONSEQUENCES SUR LES ETABLISSEMENTS

8 A la suite de la cessation d'activité, indiquer l'adresse et le RCCM des établissements en précisant s'ils sont (pour chacun) cédés,
mis en location gérance, s'ils disparaissent et l'identité des bénéficiaires (acquéreurs ou gérant) :
_____
_____
_____
_____
_____
_____

ADRESSE PERMANENTE POUR LA CORRESPONDANCE

9 Préciser coordonnées du correspondant permanent : _____
_____

LE SOUSSIGNE (préciser si mandataire) _____
demande à ce que la présente constitue ☐ **DEMANDE MODIFICATIVE AU R.C.C.M.**
☐ **DEMANDE DE RADIATION**

Fait, à
Le
Signature :

10 **La conformité de la déclaration avec les pièces justificatives produites en application de l'Acte Uniforme sur le Droit
commercial général a été vérifiée par le Greffier en Chef soussigné qui a procédé :**
à l'inscription le _____ , sous le NUMERO _____

Appendix E

Tax rates

Member States	Corporate income tax	Sale of business (fonds de commerce)		Transfer tax — Sale of shares*	
		Basis	Rates	Basis	Rates
1 Benin	38%	Transaction: – Business – New inventory	12% 2%	Fixed duty	6,000 FCFA
2 Burkina Faso	35%	Transaction: – Business – New inventory	12% 2%	Transaction	3%
3 Cameroon	35% + Local Tax = 38.5%	Transaction: – Business – New inventory	15% 2%	Transaction Only for non-UDEAC shares	2%
4 Central African Republic	40%	Transaction: – Business – New inventory	15% 4%	Transaction	6%
5 Chad	45%	Transaction:	3%	Transaction	3%
6 Congo	39%	Transaction: – Business	10%	Transaction	5%

#	Country					
7	Côte d'Ivoire	35%	– New inventory / – Receivables	5% / 4%	Fixed duty	1,000 FCFA
			Transaction: / – Business / – New inventory	10% / fixed duty: 6,000 FCFA		
8	Gabon	35%	Transaction: / – Business	6% (+2% for Libreville and Port Gentil)	Transaction	3%
			– New inventory	2%		
9	Guinea	35%	Fixed duty	50,000 FCFA	SA shares: / Fixed duty	50,000 FCFA
					Other shares: / Transaction + / Fixed duty	2% / 50,000 FCFA
10	Mali	35%	Transaction: / – Business / – New inventory	20% / 5%	Fixed duty	6,000 FCFA
11	Niger	42.5%	Transaction: / – Business / – New inventory	10% / 3%	Transaction	5%
12	Senegal	35%	Transaction: / – Business / – New inventory	15% / 2%	Transaction	4%
13	Togo	37% for industries / 40% for other activities	Transaction	12%	Transaction	6,000 FCFA

* Shares of companies whose assets consist mainly of real estate may trigger duties for transfer of immovable property.

Shares issued against a contribution in kind may trigger higher duties, if sold within a certain period.

NB: the information contained in this table is merely indicative, and should not be regarded as offering a complete overview of each tax covered, which may be subject to frequent changes in the law or in its applicability. The tax rates mentioned apply only to current situations, and do not take into account exceptions or exemptions that may be applicable from time to time.

Appendix F

Useful addresses and websites

THE AUTHORS:

Eversheds Frere Cholmeley

42, avenue du Président Wilson
75116 Paris
France
Tel: +33 1 44 34 71 00
Fax: +33.1 44 34 71 11
www.eversheds.com
borismartor@eversheds.com
nanettepilkington@eversheds.com
davidsellers@eversheds.com
sebastienthouvenot@eversheds.com

African Development Bank

Headquarters
Rue Joseph Anoma
01 BP 1387
Abidjan 01
Côte d'Ivoire

Tel: +225 20 20 44 44
Fax: +225 20 20 49 59
www.afdb.org

University of Buea

Department of Law
Faculty of Social and Management Sciences
P.O. Box 63
Buea, South West Province
Cameroon
Tel: +237 32 21 34
Fax: +237 32 22 72

OHADA INSTITUTIONS:

Common Court of Justice and Arbitration

01 BP 8702
Abidjan 01
Côte d'Ivoire
Tel: +225 20 33 60 51/52
Fax: +225 20 33 60 53

ERSUMA

02 BP 353
Porto Novo
Benin
Tel: +229 22 58 04
Fax: +229 22 43 67

Permanent Secretariat

BP 10071
Yaoundé
Cameroon
Tel: +237 21 09 05
Fax: +237 21 67 45

WEBSITES PROVIDING GENERAL INFORMATION ON OHADA:

www.ohada.com
www.ohadalegis.com
www.jurisint.org/pub/ohada./ohada.html
www.juriscope.org/infos_ohada/
www.bj.refer.org/benin_ct/edu/ersuma/
www.refer.org/camer_ct/eco/ecohada/ohada.htm

OTHER USEFUL WEBSITES:

Afrexim Bank

www.afreximbank.com

Belgolaise Bank

www.belgolaise.com

BRVM

www.brvm.org

ECOWAS

www.ecowas.int

European Investment Bank

www.eib.org

Franc Zone

www.izf.net

ICSID

www.worldbank.org/icsid

International Business Law Journal

www.iblj.com

Lex africana

www.lexana.org

MIGA

www.miga.org

NEPAD

www.nepad.org

OAPI

www.oapi.wipo.net

UEMOA

www.uemoa.int

UNCITRAL

www.uncitral.org

UNIDROIT

www.unidroit.org

World Bank

www.worldbank.org

Glossary

Action en comblement du passif   Proceedings against members of the management of an insolvent debtor, whereby their liability is sought for all or some of the debts.

Actions   Shares in an SA.

Active partner   A shareholder in an SCS who has indefinite and joint and several liability for the company's debts.

Ad hoc **arbitration**   Arbitration conducted without the assistance of an arbitration centre.

Administrateur général   *See* Managing director.

Administration proceedings   Collective proceedings designed to permit the financial recovery of insolvent businesses and to clear their debts by means of a composition agreement with creditors.

Administrator   In preventive settlement proceedings, a court-appointed officer who monitors performance of a composition agreement. In administration proceedings, a court-appointed officer who represents the creditors and assists the debtor.

Ad nutum **revocation**   Revocation of the tenure of an office-holder, without the need to indicate any reasons or provide any compensation.

Amiable compositeur An arbitrator authorized to give an award in equity.

Apport en industrie *See* Contribution in services.

Apport en nature *See* In-kind contribution.

Apport en numéraire *See* Cash contribution.

Apport partiel d'actifs *See* Partial business transfer.

Arbitral award A final decision given by an arbitral tribunal.

Arbitration Means of achieving the settlement of a dispute by a private tribunal instead of a national court.

Associé commanditaire *See* Sleeping partner.

Associé commandité *See* Active partner.

Bail commercial *See* Commercial lease.

BCVM or *Bourse camerounaise des valeurs mobilières* Cameroon Stock Exchange.

Bordereau de nantissement *See* Pledge certificate.

Branch A business establishment which has some management autonomy but does not have a legal personality separate from that of the individual or company which owns it.

Broker A commercial intermediary who acts neither in his own name nor for his own account, but who arranges contacts between persons in order to facilitate or conclude commercial transactions.

BRVM or *Bourse régionale des valeurs mobilières* Regional Stock Exchange for the UEMOA region.

Bulletin de souscription *See* Subscription bulletin.

Bureau des hypothèques Land registry.

Business   Various tangible and intangible movable assets which as a whole allow a commercial operator to attract and retain its clientele, referred to in French as a *fonds de commerce*.

BVMAC or *Bourse des valeurs mobilières d'Afrique Centrale*   Central African Stock Exchange for the CEMAC region.

Cancellation   Cancellation of a contract is termination with retroactive effect where, to the extent possible, the parties are returned to the situation they were in before signature of the contract.

Cash contribution   Contribution made in cash to a company's capital in exchange for shares.

Caution   A guarantor under a surety-bond.

Cautionnement   *See* Surety-bond.

CCJA   The OHADA Common Court of Justice and Arbitration.

CEMAC* or *Communauté Economique et Monétaire d'Afrique Centrale   Central African Economic and Monetary Community.

Cessation des paiements   *See* Insolvency.

CFA franc or *FCFA*   Currency of the CFA Franc Zone comprising all the OHADA Member States except the Comoros (which have a similar currency, the Comorian franc) and Guinea. Since 1999, the parity of the CFA franc has been fixed at 1 Euro = 655.957 FCFA.

Chairman and general manager   The officer who, in an SA with a board of directors, exercises the functions of both chairman of the board and chief executive officer.

CIMA   Inter-African Conference for the Insurance Market.

CIPRES   Inter-African Conference for Social Welfare.

Collective proceedings   Various types of proceedings (preventive settlement, administration or liquidation) involving a debtor in financial difficulties and its creditors.

Commerçant   *See* Commercial operator.

Commercial agent   A commercial intermediary who has the standing power to enter into negotiations for, and possibly to conclude, contracts for sale, purchase, rental or services, in the name and on behalf of agricultural, industrial or commercial clients, and who is not bound by an employment contract with such clients.

Commercial lease   A lease between a lessor and a commercial operator for commercial premises.

Commercial operator   A person or company whose regular occupation is to carry out commercial transactions.

Commissaire à la fusion   *See* Merger appraiser.

Commissaire aux apports   *See* In-kind contributions appraiser.

Commissaire aux comptes   *See* Statutory auditor.

Commission agent   *See* Factor.

Commissionnaire   *See* Factor.

Commissionnaire ducroire   *See Del credere* agent.

Composition agreement   An agreement whereby special arrangements are made between a debtor and its creditors with regard to outstanding debts. In preventive settlement proceedings, the composition agreement is known as a *concordat préventif;* in administration proceedings, it is known as a *concordat de redressement.*

Concordat   *See* Composition agreement.

Condition precedent   A situation or event which must exist or occur before a contractual obligation enters into force.

Condition suspensive   *See* Condition precedent.

Conférence Interafricaine de la Prévoyance Sociale   *See* CIPRES.

Conférence Interafricaine des Marchés d'Assurances   *See CIMA.*

Contribution in services   Contribution to the capital of a company in the form of an undertaking to work for the company, given in exchange for shares.

Controller   A person appointed from among the creditors in collective proceedings to assist the supervising judge and to watch over the creditors' interests.

Cour Commune de Justice et d'Arbitrage   *See CCJA.*

Courtier   *See* Broker.

De facto **partnership**   A situation where two or more individuals or corporate bodies act as partners without having formed one of the companies provided for by the Uniform Act on Commercial Companies and Economic Interest Groups.

Del credere **agent**   A factor who guarantees the performance of his principal's obligations.

Directeur général   *See* General manager.

Dirigeants sociaux   Generic term used in the Uniform Acts to refer to various members of the management of a company including, in an SA, both members and non-members of the board of directors.

Droit de rétention   *See* Right of retention.

Ducroire   Additional commission payable to a *del credere* agent.

Early warning procedure   A procedure designed to alert the management of a company when it appears that the continuation of the company's activity is at risk.

École Régionale Supérieure de la Magistrature   *See* ERSUMA.

Economic Interest Group   A legal entity whose exclusive purpose is to facilitate or develop the economic activities of its members and to improve or increase the results of those activities.

ECOWAS   The Economic Community of West African States.

Enforceable right   Within the context of the Uniform Act on Simplified Recovery Proceedings and Enforcement Measures, either a court decision that has been declared enforceable; a foreign deed or court decision or an arbitral award that cannot be suspended and has been declared enforceable; official minutes of conciliation; a notarized deed that has been declared enforceable; or a decision having the same effect as a court decision.

ERSUMA   The OHADA Regional Training Centre for Legal Officers.

Exequatur   An enforcement order.

Ex parte **proceedings**   Court proceedings where the party against whom a ruling is sought is neither heard nor informed about the proceedings.

Factor   A commercial intermediary who acts in his own name but on behalf of a principal in matters of sale or purchase.

FCFA   *See* CFA franc.

Folle enchère   Proceedings whereby a new auction sale is organized following failure by a successful bidder at a previous auction to comply with obligations resulting from his bid.

Fonds de commerce   *See* Business.

Force majeure   An event which makes performance of a contract impossible and which is beyond the control of the parties, cannot be avoided, and was unforeseeable at the time of contracting.

Fusion   *See* Merger.

Gage   *See* Pledge.

Garant   A guarantor under a letter of guarantee.

General Manager   The chief executive officer in an SA.

Gérant   *See* Manager.

GIE **or** *Groupement d'Intérêt Economique*   *See* Economic Interest Group.

Hypothèque   *See* Mortgage.

ICC   The International Chamber of Commerce, whose International Court of Arbitration acts as an arbitration centre.

ICSID   The International Centre for Settlement of Investment Disputes, which provides facilities for the arbitration of international disputes between States and investors.

In-kind contribution   Contribution made to the capital of a company in the form of assets other than cash, in exchange for shares.

In-kind contributions appraiser   An auditor appointed to value in-kind contributions.

Insolvency   A situation where it is impossible for an individual or company to meet all its due liabilities with its available assets.

Institutional arbitration   Arbitration conducted under the auspices of an arbitration centre.

Interim measures   *See* Provisional or interim measures

Intuitu personae   When a contract is entered into *intuitu personae,* the personal qualities of one of the parties are considered as an essential condition of the contract.

Joint and several liability   A situation where several persons are jointly liable for the same debt, but where a creditor may seek payment of the whole amount from any one of such persons.

Journal officiel   *See* Legal journal.

Juge-commissaire   In preventive settlement proceedings, a judge appointed to supervise the proceedings following the adoption of a composition agreement. In administration and liquidation proceedings, a judge appointed to supervise the proceedings following the judgment ordering the debtor to be put into administration or liquidation.

Legal journal   An official journal in which legislation is published for public information or a newspaper which is empowered to publish legal notices.

Letter of guarantee (or counter-guarantee)   An agreement whereby, at the request or on the instructions of a principal (or guarantor), a guarantor (or counter-guarantor) undertakes to pay a fixed amount to a beneficiary (or guarantor), upon the latter's first call.

Liquidation proceedings (*Liquidation judiciaire*)   Collective proceedings for the purpose of realizing a debtor's assets in order to clear its liabilities.

Liquidator   In liquidation proceedings, a court-appointed officer who represents the debtor in administering or disposing of its assets, and who acts in the creditors' collective interest.

Locataire-gérant **and** *Location-gérance*   *See* Management lease.

Management lease   A contract whereby the owner of a business leases it to a manager (*locataire-gérant*) who manages it at his own risk.

Manager   The person responsible for the management of any type of company other than an SA.

Managing director   The officer who, in an SA with no board of directors, exercises the functions of both sole director and chief executive officer.

Masse (des créanciers)   The creditors of an insolvent debtor, who are constituted into a single body upon the delivery of a judgment putting the debtor into administration or liquidation.

Member States   The OHADA Member States are currently Benin, Burkina Faso, Cameroon, the Central African Republic, Chad, the Federal Islamic Republic of the Comoros, Congo, Côte d'Ivoire, Equatorial Guinea, Gabon, Guinea, Guinea-Bissau, Mali, Niger, Senegal and Togo.

Merger   A transaction whereby two companies join to form a single company either by the creation of a new company or by the absorption of one company by the other.

Merger appraiser   An auditor appointed to report upon the conditions of a merger project and in particular upon the exchange ratio for shares.

MIGA   The Multilateral Investment Guarantee Agency, part of the World Bank Group, which offers political risk insurance to investors and lenders.

Mortgage   A security on real property.

Nantissement   *See* Pledge without dispossession.

NEPAD   New Economic Partnership for Africa's Development.

Notary   A type of lawyer who is competent to authenticate deeds and other documents. In the English-speaking provinces of Cameroon, notaries' functions are exercised by solicitors.

OAPI or *Organisation Africaine de la Propriété Intellectuelle*   African Intellectual Property Organization.

Ordre public   *See* Public policy.

Partial business transfer   A transaction whereby a company contributes an autonomous division of its activity to another existing or newly created company.

Parts sociales   Shares in companies other than SAs.

Période suspecte   *See* Suspect period.

Pledge   A contract whereby a movable asset is handed over to a creditor or to an agreed third party as security for a debt.

Pledge certificate   A document issued by the RCCM, to be endorsed in favour of the beneficiary of a pledge over stock.

Pledge without dispossession   A pledge whereby certain assets may be offered as security for a debt without leaving the possession of the debtor.

Preferential right   A right which gives a creditor precedence over other categories of competing creditors.

Président-directeur général   *See* Chairman and general manager.

Preventive settlement   Collective proceedings designed to avoid insolvency or a cessation of activity, and to permit the clearing of debts by means of a composition agreement.

Privilège   *See* Preferential right.

Procédure collective   *See* Collective proceedings.

Procédure d'alerte   *See* Early warning procedure.

Provisional or interim measures   Provisional seizures of assets, pending a decision on the merits of a claim.

Public policy   Overriding considerations of morality or security which require that certain legislation cannot be derogated from by private agreement.

RCCM or *Registre du Commerce et du Crédit Mobilier*   A centralized system of commercial registries, with local and national registers and a regional register held by the CCJA.

Redressement judiciaire   *See* Administration proceedings.

Registre foncier   Land registry.

Règlement préventif   *See* Preventive settlement.

Résiliation   *See* Termination.

Res judicata   An issue is *res judicata* when it has been decided by a court and cannot be subject to any further court proceedings.

Résolution   *See* Cancellation.

Responsabilité solidaire   *See* Joint and several liability.

Right of retention   The right of any creditor who is legitimately in possession of an asset belonging to his debtor to retain that asset pending full payment of his due.

SA or *Société anonyme*   A type of joint-stock company with a minimum capital of 10 million FCFA, in which the liability of each shareholder for the debts of the company is limited to its contribution to the capital.

Saisie-appréhension   The seizure of tangible movable assets where the debtor has an obligation to deliver or return such assets to the seizing party.

Saisie-attribution (de créances)   The seizure and forced attribution to a creditor of debts owed to his own debtor by a third party.

Saisie immobilière   The seizure and sale of tangible immovable assets.

Saisie-revendication   The provisional seizure of tangible movable assets where the debtor has an obligation to deliver or return such assets to the seizing party.

Saisie-vente   The seizure and sale of tangible movable assets.

SARL or *Société à responsabilité limitée*   A type of private limited company in which the shareholders are liable for the company's debts up to the amount of their respective contributions to the capital.

Scission   *See* Spin-off.

SCS or *Société en commandite simple*   A company organized as a type of sleeping partnership in which active partners are indefinitely and jointly and severally liable for the company's debts, while sleeping partners are liable only up to the amount of their respective contributions to the capital.

Sleeping partner   A shareholder in an SCS who is liable for the company's debts only up to the amount of his contribution to the capital.

SNC or *Société en nom collectif* A company organized as a type of private partnership in which all the partners have commercial status and have unlimited liability for the company's debts.

Société anonyme *See SA.*

Société à responsabilité limitée *See SARL.*

Société de fait *See De facto* partnership.

Société en commandite simple *See SCS.*

Société en nom collectif *See SNC.*

Société en participation A type of joint venture which is not registered in the RCCM and has no corporate personality.

Spin-off A transaction whereby a company's assets and liabilities are shared out among several existing or newly created companies.

Statutory auditor An auditor appointed to verify and certify a company's annual accounts.

Subscription bulletin A document evidencing the subscription of cash contributions to the capital of a company.

Succursale *See* Branch.

Surety-bond A contract between a guarantor and a creditor whereby the guarantor stands surety for a debtor's obligation.

Suspect period Period between the date a debtor is determined to have become insolvent and the date of the judgement ordering it to be put into administration or liquidation. Transactions carried out by the debtor during this period are subject to challenge.

Syndic *See* Administrator, Liquidator.

SYSCOA or *Système Comptable Ouest Africain* The accounting system laid down by UEMOA.

Termination   Termination of a contract is effective only for the future and has no retroactive effect on relations between the parties.

Titre exécutoire   *See* Enforceable right.

The Treaty or the OHADA Treaty   The Treaty instituting the Organization for the Harmonization of Business Law in Africa, signed in Port Louis (Mauritius) on 17 October 1993.

UEMOA* or *Union Economique et Monétaire Ouest Africaine   West African Economic and Monetary Union.

Ultra vires   An act is *ultra vires* if it has been performed by a person lacking the necessary authority to perform the act.

UNDP   United Nations Development Programme.

Uniform Acts   OHADA legislation.

Bibliography

The OHADA Treaty, the Rules of Procedure of the CCJA and the first five Uniform Acts (on General Commercial Law; Commercial Companies and Economic Interest Groups; Securities; Simplified Recovery Procedures and Enforcement Measures; and Collective Proceedings for the Clearing of Debts, respectively) are collected and annotated in French in a single volume entitled *OHADA – Traité et Actes uniformes commentés et annotés*, published by Juriscope in 1999. An annotated collection of the CCJA's orders, advisory opinions and judgments (in French) up to March 2002 has been assembled on CD-ROM by Virgile Ngassam Njike, *Avocat au Barreau du Cameroun*.

In addition, OHADA has been widely written about in French. There is however very little material in English, with the exception of the articles published in the *Revue de droit des affaires internationales (International Business Law Journal)*, where a translation is provided alongside the original French text.

GENERAL

P.K. Agboyibor, "Récents développements du projet d'harmonisation du droit des affaires en Afrique (OHADA)", *Revue de droit des affaires internationales*, No. 3, 1996, p. 301.

P.K. Agboyibor, "OHADA: la Cour Commune de Justice et d'Arbitrage a rendu ses premiers arrêts le 11 octobre 2001", *Revue de droit des affaires internationales*, No. 8, 2001, p. 1015.

C. Aqueruburu, "L'État, justiciable de droit commun dans le Traité OHADA", *Penant*, 2000, p. 48.

G. Bamodu, "Transnational law, unification and harmonization of international commercial law in Africa", *Journal of African Law*, No. 38, 1994, p. 125.

M. Bolmin-Bouillet, G. Cordonnier and K. Medjad, "Harmonisation du droit des affaires dans la zone franc", *Journal du droit international*, No. 1, 1994, p. 375.

F. Ferrari, "The OHBLA draft Uniform Act on contracts for the carriage of goods by road", *Revue de droit des affaires internationales*, No. 7, 2001, p. 898.

O. Fille-Lambie, "Aspects juridiques des financements de projets appliqués aux grands services publics dans la zone OHADA", *Revue de droit des affaires internationales*, No. 8, 2001, p. 925.

T. Gervais de Lafond, "Le traité relatif à l'harmonisation du droit des affaires en Afrique", *Gazette du Palais*, 1995, 20–21 September 1996, p. 2.

J. Issa-Sayegh, "L'intégration juridique des Etats de la zone franc", *Penant*, Nos. 823 and 824, 1997, pp. 5 and 125.

J. Issa-Sayegh, "Présentation générale de l'Acte uniforme de l'OHADA sur les procédures simplifiées de recouvrement et les voies d'exécution, du droit des sûretés et des procédures collectives d'apurement du passif", *Penant*, No. 827, 1998, p. 204.

J. Issa-Sayegh, "Quelques aspects techniques de l'intégration juridique: l'exemple des Actes uniformes de l'OHADA", *Revue de droit uniforme*, 1999, p. 5.

J. Issa-Sayegh, "L'OHADA, instrument d'intégration juridique", *Revue de jurisprudence commerciale*, June 1999, p. 237.

G. Kenfack-Douajni, "Les conditions de la création dans l'espace OHADA d'un environnement juridique favorable au développement", *Revue juridique et politique*, January–March 1998.

M. Kirsch, "Historique de l'OHADA", *Penant*, No. 827, 1998, p. 129.

T. Lauriol, "Le droit OHADA passe à une vitesse supérieure", *Revue de droit des affaires internationales*, No. 5, 2001, p. 596.

T. Lauriol, "OHADA: l'intensification du processus d'harmonisation", *Revue de droit des affaires internationales*, No. 6, 2001, p. 752.

G.A. Likillimba, "Où en est-on avec le Traité relatif à l'harmonisation du droit des affaires?", *Dalloz Affaires*, No. 27, 1997, p. 844.

J. Lohoues-Oble, "L'apparition d'un droit international des affaires en Afrique", *Revue internationale de droit comparé*, 1999, p. 543.

K. Mbaye, "Avant-propos", *Penant*, No. 827, 1998, p. 125.

J. M'Bosso, "Le rôle des juridictions nationales et le droit harmonisé dans l'OHADA", *Revue de droit des affaires internationales*, No. 2, 2000, p. 216.

A. Polo, "L'OHADA : Histoire, objectifs, structure", *L'OHADA et les perspectives de l'arbitrage en Afrique*, Bruylant, Brussels, 2000.

P.G. Pougoué, *Présentation générale et procédure en OHADA*, Presses Universitaires d'Afrique, 1998.

J.P. Raynal, "Intégration et souveraineté: le problème de la constitutionnalité du Traité OHADA", *Penant*, 2000, p. 5.

A. Sall, "Jurisprudence du Conseil Constitutionnel du Sénégal du 16/12/1993, n° 3/C/93", *Penant*, No. 827, 1998, p. 225.

L. Savadogo, "Le traité relatif à l'harmonisation du droit des affaires en Afrique", *Annuaire français de droit international*, 1994, p. 823.

A. Seck (dir.), "Numéro spécial – Afrique et le droit, investir en Afrique -No. 5: OHADA", *Gazette du Palais*, Nos. 48 and 49, 17 and 18 February 1999.

D. Tapin, "Un nouveau droit des affaires en Afrique noire francophone", *Dalloz Affaires*, No. 107, 5 March 1995.

G. Taty, "Brèves réflexions à propos de l'entrée en vigueur d'une réglementation commune du droit des affaires des États membres de la zone franc", *Penant*, No. 830, 1999, p. 227.

P. Tiger, *Le droit des affaires en Afrique*, PUF, Collection Que sais-je?, 1999.

A. Zinzindohoué, "Les juges nationaux et la loi aux prises avec le droit harmonisé", *Revue de droit des affaires internationales*, No. 2, 2000, p. 227.

GENERAL COMMERCIAL LAW

A. Fénéon, "Le registre du commerce et du crédit mobilier", *Cahiers juridiques et fiscaux de l'exportation*, CFCE, No. 2, 1998, p. 281.

A. Fénéon, "Les intermédiaires du commerce", *Cahiers juridiques et fiscaux de l'exportation*, CFCE, No. 2, 1998, p. 293.

A. Fénéon and A. Delabrière, "Présentation générale de l'Acte Uniforme sur le droit commercial général", *Penant*, No. 827, 1998, p. 136.

A. Fénéon and R.J. Gomez, "Le droit de la vente commerciale", *Cahiers juridiques et fiscaux de l'exportation*, CFCE, No. 2, 1998, p. 271.

A. Fénéon and R.J. Gomez, *Droit commercial général, Commentaires de l'Acte uniforme*, EDICEF, Paris, 1999.

F. Ferrari, "International sales law in the light of the OHBLA Uniform Act relating to general commercial law and the Vienna sales convention", *Revue de droit des affaires internationales*, No. 5, 2001, p. 599.

J.R. Gomez, "Réflexions d'un commercialiste sur le projet d'harmonisation du droit des affaires dans la zone franc", *Penant*, 1994, p. 3.

J.R. Gomez, "Un nouveau droit de la vente commerciale en Afrique", *Penant*, No. 827, 1998, pp. 145-185.

J. Nguebou Toukam, *Le droit commercial général dans l'acte uniforme O.H.A.D.A*, Presses Universitaires d'Afrique, 1998.

E. Nsié, "La formation de la vente commerciale en Afrique", *Penant*, No. 829, 1999, p. 5.

COMMERCIAL COMPANIES AND GIES

P.K. Agboyibor, "Nouveau droit uniforme des sociétés", *Revue de droit des affaires internationales*, No. 6, 1998, p. 673.

P.K. Agboyibor, "OHADA – Droit des affaires en Afrique, Chronique sur l'Avis n°02/2000/EP du 26 avril 2000 de la Cour Commune de Justice et d'Arbitrage", *Revue de droit des affaires internationales*, No. 7, 2000, p. 914.

F. Anoukaha, *Le droit des sociétés commerciales et du groupement d'intérêt économique OHADA*, Presses Universitaires d'Afrique, 1998.

O. Boisseau Chartrain, "Quel avenir pour les succursales des sociétés étrangères dans l'OHADA?", *Revue de droit des affaires internationales*, No. 3, 2000, pp. 358–363.

Ernst & Young, *Droit des sociétés commerciales et du GIE – Commentaires*, EDICEF/EDITIONS FFA.

A. Fénéon, "La mise en harmonie des statuts des sociétés anonymes en Côte d'Ivoire", *Penant*, September 1999, p. 324.

Fidafrica-PricewaterhouseCoopers, *Mémento, droit des sociétés commerciales et du groupement d'intérêt économique*, 1998.

L. Homman-Ludiye and P. Djedje, "Le contrôle de la gestion des SA et des SARL", *Cahiers juridiques et fiscaux de l'exportation*, CFCE, No. 2, 1998, p. 317.

L. Homman-Ludiye and H. Epessé, "La société anonyme unipersonnelle et le groupement d'intérêt économique – Deux nouvelles formes originales", *Cahiers juridiques et fiscaux de l'exportation*, CFCE, No. 2, 1998, p. 303.

L. Homman-Ludiye and N. Gerault, "L'harmonisation du droit des affaires en Afrique – Présentation générale", *Cahiers juridiques et fiscaux de l'exportation*, CFCE, No. 2, 1998, p. 261.

L. Homman-Ludiye and J.E. Missainhoun, "La gestion des SA et des SARL", *Cahiers juridiques et fiscaux de l'exportation*, CFCE, No. 2, 1998, p. 309.

M. Lecerf, "La procédure d'alerte – Un nouveau moyen de prévention des difficultés de l'entreprise", *Cahiers juridiques et fiscaux de l'exportation*, CFCE, No. 2, 1998, p. 325.

M. Lecerf, "La nouvelle réglementation de la diminution des capitaux propres : de la perte des trois quarts du capital social à la perte de la moitié du capital", *Cahiers juridiques et fiscaux de l'exportation*, CFCE, No. 2, 1998, p. 333.

M. Lecerf, "Comment interpréter les dispositions transitoires de l'Acte uniforme relatif au droit des sociétés commerciales et du groupement d'intérêt économique", *Cahiers juridiques et fiscaux de l'exportation*, CFCE, 1998, No. 2, p. 343.

B. Martor and S. Thouvenot, "La fusion des sociétés issues du droit OHADA", *Revue de droit des affaires internationales*, No. 1, 2002, p. 47.

B. Martor and S. Thouvenot, "Les acteurs des marchés financiers et l'appel public à l'épargne dans la zone OHADA", *Revue de droit des affaires internationales*, No. 6, 2002.

D. Tapin, "Droit des sociétés commerciales et du GIE en Afrique", *Penant*, No. 827, 1998, p. 186.

COLLECTIVE PROCEEDINGS

S. Agbayissah, "OHADA: Aperçu général de l'acte uniforme sur les procédures collectives d'apurement du passif", *Cahiers juridiques et fiscaux de l'exportation*, CFCE, No. 1, 1999, p. 23.

K. Assogbavi, "Les procédures collectives d'apurement du passif dans l'espace OHADA", *Penant*, 2000, p. 55.

K.M. Brou, "La protection des vendeurs de biens avec clause de réserve de propriété dans les procédures collectives : l'apport du traité OHADA", *Revue de la recherche juridique – Droit prospectif*, 2001, p. 273.

P. Roussel-Galle, "OHADA et difficultés des entreprises", *Revue de jurisprudence commerciale*, Nos. 2 and 3, 2001, pp. 9 and 62.

F.M. Sawadogo, *Droit des entreprises en difficulté*, Bruylant, Brussels, 2002.

SECURITIES

F. Anoukaha, *Le droit des sûretés dans l'Acte Uniforme OHADA*, Presses Universitaires d'Afrique, 1998.

F. **Anoukaha, A. Cisse-Niang, M. Foli, J. Issa-Sayegh, I. Yankhoba Ndiaye and M. Samb,** *OHADA – Sûretés*, Bruylant, Brussels, 2002.

J. **Issa-Sayegh,** "Organisation des sûretés", *Cahiers juridiques et fiscaux de l'exportation*, CFCE, No. 2, 1998, p. 351.

T. **Lauriol,** "Aspects juridiques de l'apport de titres miniers en garantie dans les États parties de l'OHADA", *Revue de droit des affaires internationales*, No. 2, 2001, p. 175.

J.C. **Otoumou,** "La lettre de garantie OHADA", *Revue de droit des affaires internationales*, No. 4, 1999, p. 425.

SIMPLIFIED RECOVERY PROCEDURES AND ENFORCEMENT MEASURES

P.K. **Agboyibor,** "Chronique bibliographique et présentation de l'Acte Uniforme relatif aux procédures simplifiées de recouvrement et des voies d'exécution", *Revue de droit des affaires internationales*, No. 2, 1999, p. 228.

P.K. **Agboyibor,** Observations sur l'Avis Consultatif n° 001/99/JN du 7 juillet 1999 sur les articles 13, 14, 79 et 297 de l'Acte Uniforme portant organisation des procédures simplifiées de recouvrement et des voies d'exécution", *Revue de droit des affaires internationales*, No. 6, 1999, p. 677.

C. **Aqueruburu,** "La procédure d'injonction de payer dans l'Acte uniforme de l'OHADA", *Penant*, 1999, p. 287.

A.-M. H. **Assi-Esso and N. Diout,** *Recouvrement des créances*, Bruylant, Brussels, 2002.

K.M. **Brou,** "La procédure d'injonction de payer en droit ivoirien : l'apport du droit OHADA", *Revue de la recherche juridique – Droit prospectif*, 2001–2, p. 1143.

M. **Sawadogo,** "La procédure d'injonction de payer de l'OHADA à l'épreuve de la pratique", *Bulletin du CREDAU*, No. 1, p. 5.

G.G. **Wamba Makollo,** "La procédure simplifiée de recouvrement des créances civiles et commerciales: l'injonction de payer dans le traité OHADA", *Penant*, No. 830, 1999, p. 135.

ARBITRATION

P.K. **Agboyibor,** "Présentation du Règlement et de l'Acte uniforme relatif à l'arbitrage", *Revue de droit des affaires internationales*, No. 3, 1999, p. 340.

R. **Amoussou-Guenou**, *Le droit et la pratique de l'arbitrage commercial international en Afrique Subsaharienne*, thesis under the direction of P. Fouchard, Université Panthéon-Assas, Droit, Economie et Sciences sociales, 1995.

R. **Amoussou-Guenou**, "L'arbitrage dans le Traité relatif à l'harmonisation du droit des affaires", *Revue de droit des affaires internationales*, No. 3, 1996.

R. **Amoussou-Guenou**, "Les investissements étrangers en Afrique et l'arbitrage international", *Revue camerounaise de l'arbitrage*, No. 2, 1998, p. 7.

R. **Amoussou-Guenou**, "L'Acte Uniforme et son environnement juridique", *Revue camerounaise de l'arbitrage, Numéro spécial*, October 2001, p. 11.

J.P. **Ancel**, "Le contrôle de la sentence", *L'OHADA et les perspectives de l'arbitrage en Afrique*, Bruylant, Brussels, 2000, p. 189.

R. **Bourdin**, "Le Règlement d'arbitrage de la Cour commune de justice et d'arbitrage", *Revue camerounaise de droit*, No. 5, 1999, p. 10.

R. **Bourdin**, "A propos du Règlement de la Cour commune de justice et d'arbitrage", *L'OHADA et les perspectives de l'arbitrage en Afrique*, Bruylant, Brussels, 2000, p. 151.

K. **Diaby**, "L'entrée en vigueur du droit OHADA en Guinée", *Revue camerounaise de l'arbitrage, Numéro spécial*, October 2001, p. 18.

A. **Dieng**, "La pratique arbitrale et les institutions d'arbitrage en Afrique: le cas du Sénégal", *L'OHADA et les perspectives de l'arbitrage en Afrique*, Bruylant, Brussels, 2000, p. 163.

A. **Dieng**, "Le nouveau droit de l'arbitrage en Afrique", *Revue camerounaise de l'arbitrage, Numéro spécial*, October 2001, p. 20.

R. **Dossou**, "La pratique de l'arbitrage en Afrique", *L'OHADA et les perspectives de l'arbitrage en Afrique*, Bruylant, Brussels, 2000, p. 125.

A. **Fénéon**, *Le droit de l'arbitrage, Commentaire de l'Acte uniforme de l'OHADA*, EDICEF, 2000.

P. **Gélinas**, "L'Afrique et l'arbitrage de la CCI", *L'OHADA et les perspectives de l'arbitrage en Afrique*, Bruylant, Brussels, 2000, p. 167.

D. **Hascher**, "Les rapports entre le juge étatique et l'arbitre, *L'OHADA et les perspectives de l'arbitrage en Afrique*, Bruylant, Brussels, 2000, p. 209.

J. **Issa-Sayegh**, "Réflexions dubitatives sur le droit de l'arbitrage OHADA", *Revue camerounaise de l'arbitrage, Numéro spécial*, October 2001, p. 22.

J.M. **Jacquet**, "Le droit applicable au fond du litige dans l'arbitrage OHADA", *L'OHADA et les perspectives de l'arbitrage en Afrique*, Bruylant, Brussels, 2000, p. 101.

M. **Kamto**, "La participation des personnes morales africaines de droit public à l'arbitrage OHADA", *L'OHADA et les perspectives de l'arbitrage en Afrique*, Bruylant, Brussels, 2000, p. 89.

G. Kenfack-Douajni, "L'abandon de souveraineté dans le traité OHADA", *Penant*, No. 830, 1999, p. 125.

G. Kenfack-Douajni, "Le cadre juridique de l'arbitrage au Cameroun", *Revue camerounaise de l'arbitrage*, No. 4, 1999, p. 3.

G. Kenfack-Douajni, "L'arbitrage CCJA", *Revue camerounaise de l'arbitrage*, No. 6, 1999, p. 3.

G. Kenfack-Douajni, "La portée abrogatoire de l'Acte Uniforme relatif au droit de l'arbitrage", *Revue camerounaise de l'arbitrage, Numéro spécial*, October 2001, p. 28.

G. Kenfack-Douajni and C. Imhoos, "L'Acte Uniforme relatif au droit de l'arbitrage dans le cadre du traité OHADA", *Revue camerounaise de l'arbitrage*, 1999, No. 5, p. 3.

G. Kenfack-Douajni and C. Imhoos, "Le Règlement d'arbitrage de la Cour Commune de Justice et d'Arbitrage de l'OHADA", *Revue de droit des affaires internationales*, No. 7, 1999, p. 825.

T. Lauriol, "Le centre d'arbitrage O.H.A.D.A: formation et effets de la convention d'arbitrage", *Revue de droit des affaires internationales*, No. 8, 2000, p. 99.

T. Lauriol, "La langue de l'OHADA", *Revue camerounaise de l'arbitrage, Numéro spécial*, October 2001, p. 28.

P. Leboulanger, "L'arbitrage et l'harmonisation du droit des affaires en Afrique", *Revue de l'arbitrage*, 1999, p. 541.

P. Leboulanger, "Présentation générale des actes sur l'arbitrage", *L'OHADA et les perspectives de l'arbitrage en Afrique*, Bruylant, Brussels, 2000, p. 63.

A. Malle, "La coopération du juge lors de la procédure arbitrale", *L'OHADA et les perspectives de l'arbitrage en Afrique*, Bruylant, Brussels, 2000, p. 185.

J. M'Bosso, "Le fonctionnement du centre d'arbitrage et le déroulement de la procédure arbitrale", *Revue camerounaise de l'arbitrage, Numéro spécial*, October 2001, p. 42.

P. Meyer, "L'Acte Uniforme OHADA sur le droit de l'arbitrage", *Revue de droit des affaires internationales*, No. 6, 1999, p. 629.

P. Meyer, *OHADA –Droit de l'arbitrage*, Bruylant, Brussels, 2002.

P.G. Pougoué, "Le système d'arbitrage de la Cour commune de justice et d'arbitrage", *L'OHADA et les perspectives de l'arbitrage en Afrique*, Bruylant, Brussels, 2000, p. 129.

P.G. Pougoué, J.M. Tchakoua and A. Fénéon, *Droit de l'arbitrage dans l'espace OHADA*, Presses Universitaires d'Afrique, 2000.

R. Sorieul, "Convergences entre la CNUDCI et l'OHADA", *L'OHADA et les perspectives de l'arbitrage en Afrique*, Bruylant, Brussels, 2000, p. 43.

Index